Coaching Beyond the X's and O's: By the Experts

Edited by
Earl Browning

COACHES CHOICE™

ISBN: 1-58518-309-1

Library of Congress Catalog Number: 00-105368

Cover Design: Paul Lewis
Developmental Editor: Kim Heusel
Page Layout: Kim Heusel

Coaches Choice
P.O. Box 1828
Monterey, CA 93942
www.coacheschoiceweb.com

Table of Contents

Chapter 1

TURNING A PROGRAM AROUND

Frank Beamer
Virginia Tech University
1998

When I was at Murray State we set a record for staying in the top 20 for consecutive weeks. We won a lot at Murray State. When I went to Virginia Tech, I went into a program that was going to be penalized some scholarships and we had some setbacks. Soon we got the program almost turned around. My fourth year there we were 6-5. My fifth year we were 6-4-1 and won three out of our last four games. Those three games were against teams going to bowls. The one team that we didn't beat that year was Georgia Tech, who shared the National Championship with Colorado. We had that thing almost turned around. Then six years ago, we went 2-8-1. We were leading in seven of those games in the fourth quarter. We were down 3, 6, and 12 points to three more teams in the fourth quarter. That is 10 teams we had a legitimate chance of beating. The only team that beat us soundly that year was the University of Miami. The bottom line was, we won two games and tied one. Something just wasn't quite right.

After that year I went back and studied everything about our program. I visited with people, and I made some changes. I put what I did to turn our program around together in a lecture. These are things that we all have talked about a lot. We are not going to take long with any particular area, but these are some things I think are worthy of talking about. These are things we feel are good in our program. I will tell you the reasons why I think they are good and why we do things. This is how we turned our program around.

We have gone to five straight bowl games. It gets back to personnel, and we all know that, but we are one of 10 teams in the country that have done that. These are some of the reasons why we got it turned back around.

1

There is a real thin line from being 2-8-1, going to five straight bowl games, and almost having it turned around. It is those little things that make a difference that I am going to talk about. Some of these things were things we did before and some things were things we changed. I will explain them as we go. They are all things we believe in a lot at Virginia Tech.

I will start out by talking about dealing with punishment. We only have two types of punishments. I don't want it to be just a question of what type of punishment you are going to get. In other words, one coach is running steps, another coach is doing pushups or up-downs, or whatever. That is not the issue. The issue is to *do it right*. Do whatever we are saying and do it right and let's get on with it. It is not so much what the punishment is that I am stressing.

There are two things we do. We have what we call Reminders. These are for the minor things. The coach will work you up-down for 40 seconds, and then rest for 20 seconds, and when the coach feels you are reminded, that is it. So that is one way to handle punishment.

The other one is the Sunrise Service at 6 a.m. on Wednesday for more serious things. That is it. After that it gets into suspensions and things like that I would be involved with. We are not going to do a lot of different punishments. Again, the punishment is not the issue. If you screw up you are going to get punished. But the deal is this. We do not want them to worry about the punishment, but to worry about getting things done right. The punishment is not the issue.

Some of these things apply to high school and some do not. Even if some of them don't, I think the theories behind them apply.

Let me talk about study hall hours. We have our freshmen go, plus if you don't have a 2.0 GPA, you have to get 10 hours of study hall in per week. Again, if you don't do it right, you are going to have to come in and make it up on Sunday, plus you're going to be at that Sunrise Service on Wednesday morning. Get it done right! The bottom line is get things done right because you're going to have to do it one way or another.

We are presently involved in our winter program. This is how our program works. Number 1, it is at 6 o'clock in the morning. There is not a reason why they will not be there on time. With our schedule sometimes there is a class conflict during the season. But, you are going to be there at 6 o'clock in the morning. It's tough, and you are going through a tough experience together. Your toughness and togetherness come out and your leaders start to develop. Our coaches go in after each session and they vote to see if each person gave a winning performance for the session. If he did then he has a shirt he gets to wear the next time. The shirt states that he had a winning performance the last time. If he doesn't get it done the next time, he gives the shirt back. In other words there is an immediate reward. We get things done right and we get some togetherness going.

This is one that I go back and forth on a little, and all of us have discussed. When you are talking about a football team, this is one you should give a lot of thought to. Generally speaking there are three or four guys you want leading your football team. It may be more than three or four. The year after that 2-8-1 season, we had four captains. A couple of years ago when we went to the Sugar Bowl, this is what we did. In the spring we took a vote and we had nine or 10 players who got a lot of votes. That year we went back to the old ways. We said we would have game captains and then elect season captains after the season. But more times than not, you elect these guys in the winter, have your vote and make sure it turns out the way you want it. Have the guys you want leading your football team. Give them responsibility, let them take that football team over a little.

This is one of the reasons I think it helps to have three or four team captains. Because every season there is going to be a critical problem. Something is going to happen somewhere, some way. It is going to be a touchy issue. I'd rather go into a room and talk to three or four guys than I would to go into a room and talk to 15 guys. The reason is this: Sometimes people get braver when there are more people around them. Go through your captains to solve this problem and let them help you solve this problem. I think generally it's easier when you are working with a fewer number of people.

The next thing we did after that 2-8-1 year was this: We said; *if we say it, we mean it*. That is the one deal. I have never been big on rules. At one time we had some rules that I knew were going to be broken, but at the time I felt we needed to have the rule. Then I said no, that is not the way it's going to be. Let's treat these guys like men, let's treat them with respect. We only have rules that we can absolutely enforce.

I have chosen a couple here to discuss. First, is curfew. Before we had the curfew on Monday, Tuesday, and Wednesday at 11 o'clock. We had players come see us with all kinds of excuses. "I've got to work on an English paper with so and so Tuesday night. OK, tell me where you're going to be and write your number down." You know, it just got too hard to enforce. I went back and went the other way. I told them I expect them to get their rest. If you care enough about winning, you will get your rest during the week. But, on Thursday night there is no reason why you shouldn't be home at 11 o'clock. If we call, you'd better be coming to the phone. You'd better figure out how you are going to do your studying on Monday, Tuesday, and Wednesday. In other words, we want rules we can enforce. That is the deal. If you say it, follow up on it.

Drinking is always a big deal, even at the college level. If you are mature enough to drink you will have to decide that. You are responsible for your actions. On Thursday, if you think anything of this football team, you'd better not be out drinking. On Friday night we are traveling together and that is not an issue on that night. Again, the bottom line is to have rules you can enforce.

This kind of goes back to my days at the Citadel when I coached down there. At times some guys see how sloppy they can dress. It just drives me crazy. There is something about being sloppy and it's not in line with being disciplined. At the Citadel they wore those uniforms and it didn't make any difference if you were poor, or rich, or the color of your skin, you all dressed the same. It got back to the point where we said we are going to dress the same on trips. When we leave for a trip, we say this is a Virginia Tech football team and we're going to be the same. We're going to dress the same, and we are going to wear ties if we're on a plane. We have warm-ups and we are going to wear them. Everyone will be dressed the same way. We have one common purpose when we leave for that trip.

Even in practice it is the same way. Some of my coaches crack on me a little on this, but I'm the same way in practice. You watch these pro guys with their shirt tails out. Anytime you put the football uniform on I want you to be sharp. I want you to do things exactly right. It is not the same situation when you are dressed during the day. It's something different and it's something neat, and it it's something good. We don't have our shirt tails out in practice, and we don't look sloppy. We are going to have the best equipment that you can imagine. We only want the players to come out in maroon and orange and white colors. I do not want any of those other colors.

This next area gets to be an issue. All of us have people who come out, work their butts off and you want to reward them for it. But I'll tell you this, our dress squad for home is the same as it is for away games. The reason is this: I want everybody who is involved with a road trip to have a chance to get into that football game. And if they know that then I think they will be into the game. I think you can be as *one*. If I know that I have three or four guys over here who know they are not going to get into that football game, they will be jacking around. If they are jacking around then they are causing someone else to jack around. The travel squad is the same as it is for the home games. It gives the players a goal.

Sometimes things can be too easy for them. You may need to be a little harder to make the football team. The issue there is that when you're in battle everybody has the same purpose on his mind.

In the year when we went 2-8-1, a lot of guys were calling attention to themselves. I know the college rules have helped a little on this issue. I wish we would even enforce it more. However, I do believe this. I think there is something important about celebrating together. I hate to see all of the things we see athletes do right now. They don't respect other people in bars at night. You read things about athletes who are not showing respect to some other groups of people. Sometimes it starts on the football field. As I watch pro football on Sunday, I've never seen so many people disrespect other people. To me this is not what we are all about.

To me that was an issue. We said "You didn't score that touchdown by yourself, you better go find those guys who blocked for you." That became a real issue when we tried to go from 2-8-1 to five straight bowl games.

We watch video from Saturday's game on Monday morning. The reason I like it in college is because it gets them out of bed and you have a chance to get them to class. The other thing I like about it is that it gets the past game over with. We have a team meeting, give out the final awards from Saturday's game and now get started on the next one. We're not spending a lot of time Monday afternoon watching film from last week.

A lot of receivers get to the end of practice and they have a pulled hamstring. You get a group of guys who aren't finishing practice. That is not good for any group, because you have somebody who is busting his butt. Those lineman have been working their butts off all practice, and you have this group of guys with their hamstring problems over here. We just said if you don't finish practice for whatever reason, then you're going to be in that training room at 7 o'clock the next morning. It kind of keeps everybody in that same boat.

Anybody who knows Virginia Tech knows this. We have always been tough. It's a tough part of the country. When we started losing at Tech, we got where we weren't tough. We got to where we were not able to finish tough. That totally went against everything I believed in. We were tougher after the play than we were during the play. It seemed like we had a lot of fights during practice.

I will never forget when I was playing for Coach Jerry Claiborne at Virginia Tech. We had a spring scrimmage one Saturday and we were awful. Monday we went out there and had the best session you have ever seen. This was back in the days when a lot of things went on that do not go on today. But we would run a play and then a fight would break out. We would fight for about five minutes. We would run another play and another fight would break out. I will never forget Coach Claiborne calling us up after practice and saying, "This is one of the greatest practices I have ever seen." I know what he was trying to do. He wanted to get some emotion going.

But it was different in our case when we were 2-8-1 that year. We were doing it the opposite way. We had kids who just weren't disciplined. You have to be able to control yourself. Football is a tough game. Penalties during the game are a big issue. They were costing us during games. We just weren't very disciplined. We said this: Prove your toughness on the field. If you fight in practice, you will have reminders after practice. Be able to control yourself. This is the message, help each other get better. If you are a defensive lineman, you better hope like heck that offensive lineman is going to be good on Saturday. Help him get better, make him work. Work together to get better. Don't be fighting with each other during practice because you think one guy took a cheap shot at you. We're not going to do the cheap-shot stuff. Work together, that became an issue with us.

I used to do this for every yard of penalties. If you got a penalty you ran a hundred yards on Monday. However, it seemed like we still kept having penalties. This is one of the best things I have ever done. We started taking every penalty and showing them on video during that Monday meeting. Then you can go back and show them. "It wasn't very smart for you to clip that guy, right? Do you understand? You are hurting your football team by not being more disciplined. If you can't block him in the front, don't block him." Then I got a chart on our penalties. I wanted to know how we compared with other teams in the Big East. Penalties are gifts. They are just helping that other team beat you. Cut those down. Since then I think that has helped our situation.

Here is a word or two about goal charts. We used to have all these goals up on the board. The first thing you need to do is narrow them down. What is really important to you? What do you think it takes to win? Don't get to many goals. You can go over these goals in front of the team after each game. These are goals because they help us win.

We have summer goals. Our strength coach and our position coaches sit down with them and go over the goals. But we're going to set those goals before they leave for the summer. That is the one time we can get ahead. Most of you do basically the same thing during the year with your players in lifting weights. The summer is the time if you are dedicated and it's important to you to win, then you can get ahead. You can get a jump and outwork your opponents during the summer.

We set team goals to achieve what we are trying to do. When the players come back from the summer break we test them on those goals. They are telling me if they want to be a part of a successful program and if they want to win. They tell me how important is it to them. They may have been second team when they left and they want to be first team. If they outwork that guy during the summer they may be first team when they get back in the fall.

After a win our captains are going to select the outstanding offensive and defensive player and special teams players for that game. We give those awards outright there in the locker room. The reason it is good is because it gets some unselfish actions going in front of the group. A number of times the players have given an award to a coach. It is an unselfish and emotional time and some good things happen to bring football teams closer together by having the awards in the dressing room right after the game.

Then after we have seen the film we as coaches give some awards. This is a good thing and this might be the best thing as far as I'm concerned that we do.

I went to see Bobby Ross. Spike Dykes was talking about Bill Arnsparger and the defense. Bobby Ross had just taken over as the head coach of that San Diego team. They won about three or four games the year before. Then all of the sudden they make the playoffs the next year. I went out there and I said coach, "Tell me how you turned it around." I talked to him about everything. I did not care what it was; I discussed it and talked about my thoughts on that 2-8-1 season. He said this, and it made so much sense. Again, it gets back to video. Bobby Ross said, "After each game, and I didn't care if we won it, or lost it, I took positive plays and put them on the video. Those are the plays that the team saw the night before a ballgame. I now call it our 'Friday Night Video.'" It makes sense. Guys start seeing positive things and they start thinking positively. If you do it one time, why can't you do it all of the time? If you make that block one time, why couldn't you do it all the time? Positive thoughts! For us, every play I use in that Friday night video is a very good play, I promise you. You get offensive linemen running around racking people up. You point them out and put your spotlight on them. Run that tape back and forth. You can talk about an offensive linemen who doesn't get praised very much. You can talk about some good things on the field right there. It is good when players see their fellow players do things well. It is something about confidence.

This session turned into a togetherness time. Our Friday night video now is funny. We may put something that happened in practice that they have not seen, or something a coach has done. We will slip that in there. I believe our players look forward to the Friday Night Video during the week. With the video the way it is now, you can put it together. To me this is good because it works on the mind. I'll tell you this: I believe a lot of football is in the mind.

Another thing we started doing is let players decide our award winners. The hammer awards we talk about, the big hits, offense and defense. This is another thing we do on Monday. We'll have about three nominees for each award. The kids have some fun with this.

What I want to get across really, is that toughness is a part of our football program. It's important enough that we're going to come in here and grade it, but toughness is a part of our football program.

Special Teams are important. I have called offensive plays, I've called defensive plays, and now I work with special teams. As a head coach, if you were going to coach one area and you have capable assistants in other areas, that is were you should put an emphasis. Special teams are always important and add up as big-yardage plays. You're talking about a lot of yardage, and you are talking about momentum. When the head coach gets involved with the special teams, it adds value to it. I head up about three of our special teams. Everything we do offensively or defensively we'll do with our special teams. We have the meetings, the goals, the awards, a player of the year. I believe this. It is the quickest way to win the football game.

I know everybody says this, but I don't think it happens very often. Recognize players with nice pictures on the wall. If you want that guy to play well, then it should be first class when he sees his picture on the wall. It has all kinds of carryover value.

This is something I think all coaches should do with their football teams during the season. This happened to me after an important game. I had a player, and he was a pretty good kid. He was a defensive player. He made some strong statements right after a game. It had a chance to really wear our team out. You talk about separating and dividing the team. I think it is important to take care of this problem before it becomes a problem. We go over what to say, what not to say before and after a game. We have our list that we talk about at one of our first meetings at preseason.

Then after a tough game, I make it a point the last thing I talk to that football team about is what I better not see in the paper. I tell them what the feeling among this football team needs to be. I want to leave them when the press starts coming into the room. My last thing with them is what I want said to them. I think this is important. If kids are talking and they are out of control it can hurt. It is an emotional time. This is one of those critical situations I was talking about earlier.

Another thing I started with Mike Gottfried relates to the kicking game. When Mike was working for me at Murray State we started this. The Saturday before our first ballgame we cover every unusual situation that can come up in a game. Back then it was about 33 things we had in our script.

Everything I say here you probably talk about sometime with your football team. But what I try to do is physically put them through those 33 situations. Because sometimes when you are talking they get lost. I don't want to just say it, I want to actually, physically do it. For example, we score. We intercept a pass and we score. We make it a point right there. "Don't dare leave that field until you know if we are going to go for one or two points." We do not want to call a time-out because we have half of our team out of the game and we are trying to go for two points. Be disciplined at that point.

We might not have known the other team is going to huddle up on the hash mark on the PAT. But it doesn't matter because we're going to cover that situation. If you have a bad snap with the punter, work on it. With the team on the 1-yard line, we actually snap it back there and it'll be bad. If it looks as if you are going to get it blocked, then I'd rather you just throw it through the end zone and take the safety, rather than give them the ball right there, or give them points. Physically cover it.

Pride! Pride is our punt team. At the end of the practice we work on all punt situations.

Field goal. You're kicking a field goal with third down, there are eight seconds or more on the clock. If you get some kind of bad snap you can kick it on the fourth down.

You are on defense and you are defending against a long fourth-down pass with three minutes left in the game. Don't overcoach this, but in reality, you want to do what? Knock it down if you can. Then take the ball back over where it was on fourth down. Physically go through that.

We've added a lot more situations since my days with Coach Gottfried. We add a few every year. These are unusual situations that come up. We go over all of the teams on these unusual situations.

This came up against West Virginia. The quarterback threw the ball and it was batted back. He caught the ball and ended up trying to throw it again, and that is a penalty. So we go through that one. We tell them to just bat the ball down if it's coming back to you as a quarterback. If you are back 5 or 6 yards deep, you're probably going to get tackled before you get back to the line of scrimmage. We cover all of those unusual situations. This particular year we ended up with 75 particular plays.

Let me move on to some other areas. What always bothered me is when we come out at the start of practice to flex and some guys are still coming out after we have started. We tell them to get things done right on time. They have to be efficient on Saturday. Now we have a two-minute warning before we start practice. We blow a horn two-minutes before our flex. You better be ready to go when it's flex time or we will see you after practice for reminders.

We have a central meeting on the field. My meetings never go very long. I try and keep it to things that they need to know. I get them down on one knee and make sure their eyes are on me. If somebody is looking around and not paying attention I send them over to a shed next to our field. I do that because they aren't listening. After doing it a couple of times, everybody's listening. I don't keep them there very long. We take care of what they need to know as a team, because they've had their individual meetings, and get on with it.

We start our Monday practice with what we call converge. These are plays that usually turn out big one way or another, either for you or against you. They're just normal plays, but they are plays I love. I like screens, draws, delays, reverses, and halfback passes. We work the fundamentals of these against each other. This is how we start our Monday practice, and it does not matter if we won or lost the week before. We go against each other and it goes pretty fast. We're working on fundamentals against plays we need to see. We run our screens, and to me, a screen is a screen. I don't care. The principles of these things are all the same. But we are working on these plays against each other to start out practice on Monday.

Some of you don't have numbers, but it always bothers me going against the scout team during the year. In other words, you are running against that other team and trying to get them to run that other team's plays. It seems like we're just practicing bad habits. After a while those offensive linemen are knocking those defensive linemen about 20 yards off the ball and that is not the way it happens in a ballgame. What we started doing is one of the best things we do. We will go 10 minutes versus the scout team. We'll work motion we might see or some unusual stuff that is different from the team we're getting ready to play.

Then we go 10 minutes against each other, our first versus first and second versus second. To me, an isolation is an isolation. I don't care if it's a fullback and a tailback, sweeps are sweeps. If you've got blocking rules, I don't care where you line up, you've got rules to block. What happens in this period is this: We don't chop in this drill and we don't lay people on the ground. But when ones are going against ones you get "game tempo." Better people work better against better people. Other than this last year, we got better as a football team as the season went along. This has been true the last five years, other than last year as we kind of stumbled home. One of the reasons is the fact that we go against each other so much, ones versus ones. I think you've got a chance to get better. In practice, if you're going against a guy and beating him to death every day, you're going to have a hard time getting better.

At one time after the season started we would never tackle full speed. If they're going to get hurt, they might as well get hurt in the game. We got to be a soft football team. So on Tuesday every week, we are going to line up and go seven-on-seven. We call it the Middle Drill. We run isolations, sweeps, and kickouts. I mean, it's coming right up the middle. "Hi Diddle We Are Coming Up The Middle." It's a good period. I am worried just like anybody else that we are going to get some guys hurt. I don't know if you get better, but I do know this, our kids feel tougher.

It is the same thing with your perimeter, secondary, backs, and wide receivers. From a wide receiver's standpoint, if you have guys who will block downfield, you've got a chance to get some long plays. And from a defensive secondary standpoint, you can give up a lot of long plays if you do not work on it. It can be poor angles on the football, poor concept of when you need to be under control, or when you don't need to be under control.

I think you need to go out there one time during the week, and those wide receivers are blocking, they're chopping, and they're doing it full speed. Your backs are coming and your defensive secondary guys get angle on them. Make the tackle for a 10-yard gain, snap the ball, and lets go again. Don't let that 10-yard gain turn into 75-yard gain and a touchdown.

We have special teams practice on Wednesday. We have a five-minute specialty period. In other words, punters punt, snappers snap, holders hold. We don't do this so much for our starters, but for our backups. You know, if you are not careful, you'll get down to a game on Saturday and you have a guy in the game snapping, and he didn't get any work on it during the week. That guy can lose the game for you. We try to do it for the backups.

One way I like to do conditioning a lot of times is to take our punt return team and work them. You have to get two perfect punt returns before you quit. This way you can get your running in. We go against the scout teams. I always make sure they get off that field first. If you are not careful, players will not want to be on the special teams because they have to do things extra. While the rest of the team is over working on conditioning, we're going make sure you these guys get two punt returns perfect, then they are going out of the gate first. It's a reward to be on the special teams. That is a way of handling conditioning.

This is something a lot of people take for granted. There are some valuable things you can do while the team is working on conditioning. You can accomplish two things with this. A lot of times we take our receivers and quarterbacks and throw deep balls during conditioning. There is an art to throwing deep balls. If you have a guy who can throw deep you have a heck of a lot better chance to win a game on Saturday. I think you should practice throwing it a lot and get used to that receiver's speed. I don't think you will be very good at it if you don't practice it a lot. It's a hard thing to practice sometimes because there is so much running involved.

I like our offense, for their conditioning, to do the scramble drill. If you are organized and you have a quarterback who is going to do a lot of moving around, he can break a tackle and get himself out of trouble.

I would be very organized in what is going to happen when he starts scrambling. Your deep receivers are coming back to him, and your shallow receivers are going deep. What are you going to do with your crossing guys? That is a great time. I always like bootlegs, and counter passes, because you get defenses out of whack. If your quarterback is scrambling, you've probably got that defense out of whack. It is good to get some running in on drills like these.

I always like to get my kicker kicking field goals as much as he can when the full team is around him. I don't want to rush people full speed. Now, I don't want to have to do this rush. I want a good rush. So what we do is to rush three people. You do not know which three are coming. You don't know if it's three off the guard-tackle area, or if it's three off the corner, or three from the weak side. We have three people coming full speed.

This is something we do every Wednesday. I think things need to be up tempo, fast. You're not standing around and coaches are not talking slow. But this is one time where people kind of stand around. What we get out of it is good. We have a kicking period that takes about 10 or 11 minutes on Wednesday. Everybody comes to one field. Our pride team is our punt team and they have priorities. Pride and joy is our punt and block team. Pride has their first-team group, then we fill in with pride and joy. Then we have a rush against each other. It gets back to good people working against good people. We kick the ball and go cover. It is two-hand touch to the return guy. Then we go field goals, field-goal rush with three guys rushing. If the team we're going to play uses the same punt formation we do, we usually go pride versus pride and joy the whole time. Again, I like good people working against good people.

Then we go to our onside prevent team. We work with our hands team. We get them out there and work. We practice this two times per week. There is an art as to when to go for that football and how to position yourself for the ball. When it comes down to nitty-gritty time, I want that onside prevent team to be pretty good. We work on all phases of the kicking game in the rest of the drill. We do pride versus scouts, field goal versus scouts, and punt safe.

At the end of the practice we are going to give the offensive linemen some kind of sprints if the kicker doesn't make it, and reward them if he does make it. Those offensive linemen grab him and hug him if he does make one.

Thursday at the end of practice, we're going to have our kicker run out there and kick a couple during that time. We try to get him to kick as many times as we can with people around him.

We work on our two-minute offense and defense. You are talking about winning and losing. When you are in two minutes, it's nitty-gritty time. How much time do you actually practice it? In preseason in our scrimmages, it's one of our key issues. We're going to go over it every Thursday. The principles of the two-minute drill, both offense and defense are covered each week. We cover all situations. To me it's winning and losing.

At Friday's practice we cover the unusual situations that come up in kicking. To me these are things that just come up. We cover all these things on Friday, and we do it every week.

If we fumble or throw an interception, we're going to take that group and run or do push-ups or something. We do this anytime in practice. The bottom line is this: You are going to have a tough time winning football games if you keep giving the other team those gifts. I think there is something about always concentrating and always having focus. If you fumble and you stop the play and run the play again, then there is no consequence for that. It may disrupt practice, but I think it's worth it.

We have never done this defensively. But I was thinking about this as I was preparing this lecture. We dropped about 10 interceptions this past year. If we drop an interception in practice, that whole defense should have to go over there and do up-downs for a few minutes so that guy will concentrate the next time. If a guy jumps offside, the whole defense needs to do up-downs. So we're going to start doing that with our defense, too.

I don't like guys working their butts off and other guys standing around hurt all of the time. If you are hurt you must do exercises that you can do during certain periods of practice. You're not just going to be hurt and stand around.

I'm such a kicking guy that I used to put kicking at the top of the practice schedule. I would say let's get our kicking in first and then work on the rest of practice. It turned out the same every week. But that wasn't being fair to my offensive and defensive coordinator. Now our practice follows the same sequence each week. I think it's important, I think the kids get in a habit of practicing that way. The only way that changes, as the season goes on, is that I will cut the times back. I like to change it up a little bit. I think it's important that everybody knows exactly what he is doing. Our kicking is all planned out now; we know exactly how much time we're going to spend on each part of the kicking game.

I believe in taking personal interest in coaches and players when it comes to critical situations. I keep saying this. This is so important, and all of us do it to a certain extent. I can tell you, we probably cannot do this enough. When it comes to a critical time, which I say there will always be at least one, knowing that you care is super important, however you want to do it. I do know this: when that problem comes up, and if there is care and a good relationship, we have a chance at getting that problem solved. If you haven't developed the right relationships, and the players are just numbers out there, when that problem comes up, it can go south on you in a hurry. This is a key deal for down the road.

Be enthusiastic and assistant coaches and players will respond in the same fashion. I feel that better learning takes place in an up-tempo and alert fashion. You'll never convince me otherwise. I think things need to bounce around. We do not want to be standing around for very long. It shows how you are coaching and teaching. The players know whether you feel strongly about it or not.

When things go badly, go back to fundamentals. What you start doing if you're not careful, is start figuring out other ways to do things. What happens is that they all work on the blackboard. The problem is that you cannot get the guys to do it well enough in the game. When things aren't going well, you don't have as good of a chance of getting them to do something different or new as you did if things were going well. They're down a little bit during practice and I know you have to fire them up and all that stuff. To me it's execution. If things go badly go back to fundamentals and don't add new plays. If anything, take some out. That is your only chance of winning.

I will never embarrass another coach on the field. As a coach, you do not embarrass a player. I think you can do some damage if you do that. When it gets down to that critical time, it will turn on you. If it is a lack of effort, that is another deal. But otherwise you should not embarrass a player. You must be loyal to coaches and players. They must be loyal to you and to each other. Eliminate anyone who is not loyal.

Be productive in your work. Have preference and do not stay late after practice. Keep your staff fresh. When things get going bad, cut back on meetings and get your rest. Don't start going against yourself. Don't just sit around and watch the film. Have a purpose in what you are doing. Have a purpose when you turn that video on, or go on home.

I encourage new ideas. I don't think you need to stay the same. I don't want to do things just to be doing them. I like it when coaches can convince me this is a better way of doing things. I think all of us need to do that.

Less is *better* than *more*. Don't teach too much. When I was at Murray State we had nine or 10 different fronts. Now we play two fronts. We play an even and an odd front. We cover the center and then we don't cover the center. We can adjust to every formation thrown up there.

The more responsibility you can give them, the better off you are. It gets back to the people you have on your staff. My offensive coordinator is in charge of the offense, my defensive coordinator is in charge of the defense. I'm not going to get involved unless it's something we need to talk about. They handle those guys. I think it's important to be that way myself.

Assistant coaches' opinions are requested in every major decision in the program. Again, this is something I believe. It's our football team, not mine. I don't always take their opinions or advice, but they have a chance to give me theirs. To me, that is important.

I don't think these principles are going to change for a while. We may adjust them a bit, but I think these principles are going to stay with us for a while.

Chapter 2

MOTIVATION
AND ORGANIZATION

Bobby Bowden
Florida State University
1996

I want to talk about some of the things I believe in, and I hope I might say something that you can pick up and use in your program. Once you are a head coach you do not get involved in the X's and O's as much as you used to. I do not feel I should get up here and tell you about our plays. Our assistant coaches are experts on that, not me. The only thing I can give you is something I used to get from people like Duffy Daugherty and Bud Wilkinson and people such as those two when I started out coaching. They had years and years of experience that I could draw from. I can give you 42 years of coaching experience, and I can tell you some of the things I have learned from coaching those 42 years.

I will talk to you as if you were just starting out in coaching. One thing that you must have between a head coach and a player is honesty. It is very important to have trust in each other. If your players do not trust what you are telling them you will have a hard time being successful. I tell our players I will never lie to them. "I do not want you to lie to me. I will trust you." People may wonder why I have let players get by with certain things and have been a little more forgiving than some coaches. The reason for that is because I trust the players. I tell the players what they can and cannot do. I tell them that I will not sneak around to see if they are abiding by the rules. "As long as I can trust you, I will believe you." I think this is important. That is hard to find these days, isn't it? Trust and loyalty? Is that what we are seeing in professional sports? It seems to me that the trust factor is missing in pro sports. It may be that colleges are getting to the tip end of how far you can trust people. I think it is vital in our profession.

When I prepare a team for a season I will look at the schedule and try to figure out the teams that we must beat to be successful. If we play some teams that we are going to be heavy favorites over, I do not worry about those teams. There are not many upsets in football. There are some upsets—about two teams each Saturday. Usually, the best teams win. Usually, the teams with the best players win. Occasionally that will not happen. The thing that we are searching for as coaches is this: "What is going to be the winning edge when the two teams are equal?" If a team is rated 15 points better than us, it will usually win. If we are rated 14 points better than a team, we will usually win. Now, we have two teams that are equal. That is where you and I can become a factor. A slight edge from the coach could change the outcome of the game. That is what I am looking for.

There are a couple of intangibles that are very important. There are a couple of things that we can ingrain in our players that are very important. The first intangible is persistence. *Persistence*! We can't emphasize that word enough. We must be persistent in what we are doing. I go back to an old quote from Calvin Coolidge when he talks about persistence. Listen to this: "Nothing in the world can take the place of persistence." Did you hear that? Talent won't. We can see this every Saturday, but more so on Sundays with the pros. The best talent does not always win, nor do the most talented players give their best all of the time. Talent by itself is not the answer. Nothing is more common than an unsuccessful man with talent. A genius will not take the place of persistence. Unrewarded genius is almost a proverb. Education will not take the place of persistence. The world is full of educated derelicts. The world is full of educated derelicts, and this is true. Persistence alone is important. That is what we are looking for in those ballplayers. If I can get my players more persistent than you can get your players, then I do not care what your talent level is or isn't. In the long run, the persistence will probably win out.

There is a story that comes with this line of thought that I really like. This man and his wife had retired. They had a nice big back yard and every morning they would sit in the kitchen and look out the picture window to the backyard. It was all fenced in. It was a moderate neighborhood. On the other side of the back fence was an alley. The retired couple would sit in the kitchen and drink coffee each morning.

They had two good-looking dogs. They were full-grown retrievers. They were not vicious dogs, but they were not sweetie pies.

The couple were sitting in the kitchen having their coffee one morning, and they looked out back and saw a small bulldog about eight inches tall and about 18 inches long coming down the alley. The bulldog got to the back of the fence and saw those two labs. He started scratching and digging, trying to get inside the fence to those labs. Those two labs were attacking the fence barking at the bulldog. The bulldog was trying to get inside the fence. Finally the bulldog went to the corner of the fence and started digging a hole under the fence. He dug a hole deep enough so he could crawl under the fence. Those two labs went after the bulldog immediately. The bulldog fought the labs, but they just about killed him. Finally the bulldog turned and ran for the fence and ran down the alley. The couple sat in the kitchen and watched in amazement. They thought they would have to take the bulldog to the vet, but somehow he managed to get under the fence and out of the yard.

The next morning the couple was sitting in the kitchen drinking their coffee. They were shocked. Here came the bulldog up the alley. He came up to the corner and crawled under the fence and went after those two labs again. Those labs beat the bulldog up again. Finally, he went back under the fence and down the alley.

The next morning the bulldog came back again. Same results. Morning after morning it continued. Finally the man had to take a trip out of town for a week. He got back from the trip and asked his wife what had happened to the bulldog. The lady told him what happened. The bulldog would come back day after day. He would come inside the yard and walk around and those labs would come up next to the house so the bulldog could have his way.

Now, that is persistence. That bulldog did not have the talent or maturity or the numbers that the labs had. Those labs would whip his tail, but he finally won out. He did not win because of talent. He won because of persistence. He would not quit. Now, if we can get that into our players, we would not lose a game. But now it is so easy to quit. I tell my players this over and over: "There is only one thing easy about football and that is to *quit*." I tell them if they want the easy way out, just quit. There is nothing easy about football. Persistence is the key.

The second intangible is enthusiasm. That means a lot to me. *Enthusiasm*! I can go watch your football team on Friday night as a neutral party and pick out the team that has the most enthusiasm. You see one team that is full of pep and energy, and the other team is just going through the motions. You must get your team to play with enthusiasm each week. People talk about giving pep talks before each game. "What did you tell them that made them play so good?" The fact is you can't tell them much that will make them play good. You might fire them up one time. I usually try to save my "Fire-Ups" to about two a year. That is about all I can get out of them. The key is to get kids to fire up on their own. Good players want to play every Saturday. But, again, be enthusiastic. Enthusiasm is contagious. I have to continue to remind my coaches at Florida State to be enthusiastic when they are coaching. I want the kids to become enthusiastic. When they become enthusiastic and excited, they perform better. I continue to talk about it all of the time with our staff.

In thinking about enthusiasm, with me it is like this. I am a religious person. I am a good guy, and I have my faith and beliefs. I remember something Woody Hayes said about 30 years ago. He talked about the word *enthusiasm*. He put it up on the board for everyone. Enthusiasm comes from the Greek word *en theos*, means *full of spirit*. We all have kids with big structures that can run. I want those players full of spirit and full of enthusiasm. It is the spirit that makes you go. We all are looking for that button to press that will turn the kids loose. That is the key. The other part of the Greek word *en theos* was God. God in you. Full of God. If you want to give a simple talk to your kids, this isn't a bad line of thought. If we have persistence and enthusiasm, we will be good.

A lot of times my assistant coaches have a hard time the morning before the afternoon game, and I was the same when I was an assistant. They all hang around the office walking back and forth with nervous energy. They are a wreck. "I am so scared. I hope I have prepared them for the game today. I hope they do good." You see them sitting around all morning. I walk in and ask them what is the matter. "I hope we are ready for the game," they say. I say, "Coach, there is nothing you can do now. You have to do it Monday, Tuesday, Wednesday, and Thursday. If you have not done it through the week there is nothing you can put in today that will make a difference." Then I go on to tell them this: "Coach, there is one thing you can do; you can be enthusiastic." Be enthusiastic on the sideline because it is contagious. I will tell them if you are not enthusiastic at least act like you are. Fake it if you have to, but show some enthusiasm. Hopefully the players will catch on and play better. Those are two intangibles that I think are very important.

I want to tell you a story. This story goes back to about 1956. I went to a clinic at Florida State. At the time I was a small-college coach. Ray Eliot of Illinois gave a lecture at the FSU clinic. I copied his outline. He told several stories that day that I could relate to, and I am sure you could relate to them today. My story goes like this. It is a true story.

In 1982 we were playing the University of Miami in Miami. They had beaten us the two previous years. We really needed to beat them that year. The game came down to a fourth and 1 yard to go on the goal line. Miami had a quarterback by the name of Jim Kelly. They had a big tailback by the name of Rush. He was about 6'3" and 220 pounds. That was big for a tailback back then. They had a great football team. We were ahead by four points, and they had to have that touchdown to beat us. It was fourth and 1 to go. It is the *longest* three feet in the world if you have the ball. But, if you are on defense it is the *shortest* three feet in the world. The game has come down to this one play. Howard Schnellenberger was the coach at Miami at the time. When it came down to 1 yard you knew what Miami was going to run. They would take all of their receivers out of the game and put three tight ends in. Their fullback was 6'3" and 235 pounds. Jim Kelly is a big quarterback. They got into a tight wing formation out of the I set. We knew they would hand the ball to Rush on the dive on one side or the other. We just did not know which side they were going to run. We knew the big fullback would lead the play and the line would swarm at us and the tailback would be coming over the top.

The series had started out with a first and goal at the 3-yard line. Then it was second down at the 2½; then third and 1½. And now the game was riding on this fourth-and-1 play. I had a small linebacker on my team by the name of Tommy Young from Lake City. He was a fullback before we made a linebacker out of him because he could run. He weighed 180, but he was tough and aggressive. He was enthusiastic. He was all heart. We were getting lined up on defense and Miami was going back to the huddle to get the play, which the players already knew. Our linebacker, Tommy Young, started yelling at Jim Kelly. "Kelly, run Rush at me. *RUN RUSH AT ME!*" I yelled at Kelly, "Don't listen to Young." Tommy Young wanted Kelly to run the play at him.

Sure enough here came the dive play from Miami. Rush got the ball deep and propelled up over that big line and fullback. Tommy Young had read the play and propelled up over the defensive line. There it was. Two missiles coming at each other. My man got his helmet under the offensive man's helmet. Young hit Rush and turned him over on his back. He stuffed the play right back where it started from. We won the ballgame. Now, that is such a great example of *enthusiasm*. Enthusiasm makes our muscles so much bigger and so much taller. Enthusiasm makes us faster than we are. That is why it is so important.

I heard Ray Eliot tell that type of story about one of his players at that FSU clinic. It left an impression on me, and I hope it will leave you with the same feeling.

Next I want to talk about *The Six Commandments*. I started coaching in 1953. I was an assistant coach at a small college in Alabama. Then I went to Georgia as a junior college head coach. I went to Florida State as an assistant before taking the head coaching job at West Virginia University. Then I returned to Florida State as head coach. So 41 years have gone by.

When I came up in coaching there was General Bob Neyland, Bobby Dodd, Wally Butts, and Bear Bryant was just beginning to come on. Bud Wilkinson was flourishing out at Oklahoma. Of course Woody Hayes was big at Ohio State. Bo Schembechler was just getting started at Michigan. Duffy Daugherty was influential at Michigan State. All of the coaches had commandments or laws which they would talk about at clinics. So I have my commandments. Now, I do not stack up with those coaches; I stack up with Joe Blow! Everyone knows who Joe Blow is. The reason these are important to me is this: These are things I have mentioned to my football team every week the night before a game. On the night before we play I always have a meeting with the players. This is my last time to try to get my points across. It is my last chance to give the players something that I hope will give them the winning edge. I want to give them something that will allow them to go out and play their best the next day. When I make my talk to them I always cover these six points. I will cover them in different ways when I talk to them. That is how important I think these points are. How long have I done this? I have done this for the last 21 years. I call these the Keys to Victory. "Men, if we can do these six things we are going to win."

Keep this in mind, and I do not know if this will ever change. When you are coaching, "Don't Beat Yourself." If I could give you any advice it would be this. "Don't Beat Yourself." If I could give myself some advice it would be, "Hey, Bowden, Don't Beat Yourself." I have lost more games for us just because I have been stubborn and plain dumb. I should have listened to those coaches who said not to do this and not to do that. Don't Beat Yourself. You do not win games. You lose them. I must keep from losing. That is something we can coach. I can't coach a play so it will go for a touchdown every time. It just does not work that way. But there are some things I can coach. I think these six commandments can be coached.

■ *Have no breakdowns in the kicking game.*

If I want to win the game, I must not have any breakdowns in the kicking game. I go back to last year against Virginia. That was the only game we lost. We had a punt blocked that set up a touchdown. We got beat by three.

We do not have a kicking coach at FSU. We give each assistant a phase of the kicking game. He teaches his phase of the kicking game. We divide up the kicking game to all the coaches. When we get to the kicking game they take their phase of the game but they can get any of the other coaches to be a part of that phase. You do not need all of the coaches working on the kicking game because they just get in each other's way. Each of our coaches can have any player he wants on his phase of the kicking game. We give them the preference of players. One reason we do that is to emphasize to our players the importance of the kicking game. We try to sell our players on the kicking game.

■ *Have no missed assignments.*

We must not have missed assignments. I do not know about you, but down through the years, we have lost more games on missed assignments than anything. We do not lose many games on a bad kick, or by someone using a poor technique on a play. We lose more games on missed assignments. You have to get enough reps so the kids will not miss assignments. You can get a lot out of walk-throughs. You can't solve it all on the blackboard. The kids have to go through the plays. If you feel you can't take the chance of getting players hurt, and you do not want to scrimmage, line them up and walk through the plays. I know that takes time, but you must knock out the missed assignments.

When we practice 11-on-11, good-vs.-good, we have three speeds that we use. Of course, one speed is Live. "Go Get It." We do not do that a lot, but sometimes we will go down on the goal line and go live. The next speed we have is our Thud. It is full speed except the defense cannot wrap their arms up on the play. If you can knock the offense down with your body, that is fine. You cannot grab the man and throw him on the ground. The defense cannot leave their feet on Thud. The line is full-speed contact. When the ball carrier comes through the line they try to hit him with a hat and their shoulders. You are not likely to get anyone hurt at this speed. The defense cannot use their hands and arms and they cannot leave their feet. That is Thud. When we are going to Thud, the offense cannot block below the waist. That is where injuries occur on defense. The offense cannot leave their feet, either. If you can get the players to get the speed of Thud, you can accomplish more than you can going against dummies.

Let me give you a key in your use of the Thud speed. When you are drilling Thud, tell the players blocking and tackling to try to step on the man's toes before making their hit. If you don't do this you will get into a bad habit. They will overextend. You must emphasize for them to step on the man's toes before he makes the tackle or block. If you can step on the toes, you have the man. Once he leaves his feet he is overextended and can't change directions.

The third speed we go at is called Whiz. We are going full speed but there will be no tackling at all. We are not going to hit the backs. Instead of making the tackle we tell the defensive man to run full speed by the ball carrier. If it is full speed we try to make the tackle. If it is Thud, we try to butt the man without using the hands and arms. If it is Whiz, we just peel off behind the man and do not make contact. By doing this we can work good against good and work full speed and cut down on the injuries.

■ *You must play great goal-line offense and defense*.

We are going to do a lot of scrimmaging on the goal line. Injuries are not as apt to occur down on the goal line. We take the football and put it on the 1-yard line. "Okay, offense, it is fourth and 1. Get it in the end zone." Then we look at the defense and say, "Okay, defense, don't let them in there." We do not worry about the pass. Go get them. That gets some good hitting going on. Because they are all so close together you do not get as many injuries. We are going to make that fourth and 1. Next we put the ball on the 3-yard line. Now we say it is third and goal. Now it is run or pass. We scrimmage that situation over and over. We must play great goal-line defense.

Let me mention one additional point about the goal line. Do you practice your passing attack on the 3-yard line going in? I have a hard time getting my assistants to do this. If you do not practice your passing game down deep going in, it will be difficult to run it in a game. I have been guilty of this before. You go out and practice the passing game on the 40-yard line and then down on the 3-yard line it is a different pass route. Down on the goal line they do not have those deep one-thirds. You should have a separate passing attack down on the goal line. You must go down on the goal line and practice the passing game. Somewhere along the line you will have to have a fourth-and-3 touchdown to win the game.

■ *Have no foolish penalties.*

You are going to get penalties when you play football. There is no doubt about it. You can't say you must shut down all of your penalties. Some teams are not bad at this. If you shut down all of your penalties, you may not be aggressive enough to win. If you never get penalties, check your won-lost record. You may not be winning enough. If you are not winning, you may want to get a few more penalties. Hit until the echo of the whistle, not just the whistle. You may pick up a penalty every now and then, but you will tackle better. You do not want penalties. It is the foolish penalties that hurt you. It is hitting the man in the back when you had no reason to hit him in the back. You must eliminate the foolish penalties.

I blame my assistant coaches for penalties. I think all of the head coaches blame assistants for penalties. "Can't you teach that man to line up onside?" You can't stop all penalties, but you must knock out the foolish penalties. Discipline plays a big part in eliminating penalties. It seems we never have enough coaches. We always seem to need another coach. The NCAA will let us have nine assistants. That is all we can have. We get officials around town to be officials for our practices. These officials are from the high school officials associations or some college conferences. We have four to five officials each practice. I tell our coaches to use the officials to help them coach. I want them to tell our coaches if they see our players committing a penalty. A lot of referees want the experience working our practices. No foolish penalties.

■ *No long touchdowns.*

You may not be able to prevent short touchdowns. You can probably prevent the long run. You may not be physically able to stop some teams. Some teams are just physically overpowering. But stop the long touchdowns. That is the one that gets you beat. How do you stop the long touchdown? "We do not have the speed that we need at a certain position." Have you ever thought of backing that man up? Back him up a little. They may catch a pass in front of you, but back him up. If the assistant coach tells you his safety runs a 5.4 40, "Well, coach, you will just have to back him up some more."

I can remember my old high school coach telling me what to do if I could not find the ball. "If you can't find the ball, just back up." That was the first thing I learned in football. If you are playing defensive back, and you can't find the ball, just back up.

■ *Hold fumbles and interceptions to a minimum.*

I do not yell a lot at my quarterbacks about interceptions. We really hammer players about fumbles. If a player fumbles in practice he has to recover 25 fumbles after practice. If you fumble in practice one of our coaches will write it down. After practice he will call those players up and have them run the fumble recovery drill. That may sound harsh, but we want to eliminate fumbles. We are not that hard on interceptions. Interceptions are a lot harder to control. If you hammer a quarterback too much about interceptions he will do like some of my quarterbacks have done and will quit throwing the ball. He will be so sure he is going to throw an interception, he will not even throw the ball. You must be careful about how much you get on the quarterback.

Florida State was about fourth in the nation on the turnover ratio last year. We caused more fumbles and interceptions than we had. That is always a good sign. If there is anything you would want to lead your conference in, it is the turnover margin. I want to cause the opponents to fumble more than we fumble. I like to have more interceptions than they get. We have been good at this.

Each year we start out with "This is how to hold a football." This is the basic way we start out. We tell them fingers over the end of the ball. The other end is in the crevice of the arm. Elbow into the body. No daylight between the ball and your body. NO DAYLIGHT— remember that. If you have daylight the ball can be knocked out of the man's arm. We go back to the basics, and this is the way you hold it.

Then we practice recovering fumbles. A lot of times when we go out in shorts the first week in August this is what I tell my assistants. Make sure you tell them how to hold a football and how to cover a fumble. I want them to get those two things out of the way early. When we have a scrimmage and we have a ball on the ground I do not want someone on the ground who does not know how to recover the ball. If they get on the ball wrong, it hurts, right? If they dive on top of the ball and someone hits on top of them, it hurts.

We want to teach them to dive beside the ball and to wrap it up. We teach them how to cradle the fumble. You can hold the ball wrong and get hurt. We show them how to carry the ball and how to recover the ball and how to wrap it up.

The last thing I want to mention is the team slogan we have in our team room. Our kids see this every day. We stay on them about this all of the time. You may want to use it in your dressing room.

FLORIDA STATE UNIVERSITY

DO IT RIGHT

DO IT HARD

OR

DO IT AGAIN

This is our motto. If we go out and practice and run a play and someone messes it up, we do it again. If we run the play and some-one drops the pass, we do it again. If we run the play and someone jumps offside, we do it again. They are going to run the play until they do it right. They are going to do it right and they are going to do it hard. If one man loafs on the play then we do it again. DO IT RIGHT—DO IT HARD—OR—DO IT AGAIN. We try to get this across to them in practice, and we hope it carries over to the games.

Chapter 3

PHILOSOPHY
OF OFFENSIVE FOOTBALL

Terry Bowden
Auburn University
1995

I was a student of the game of football when I first started and I am a student of the game now. I was always a better student of the game than I was a player. I loved to play football. Not only is my job football, my hobby is football. It is important that coaches remain students of the game. I know it is important to continue to learn about the game each year. I was fortunate to go on the Nike Tour this year. It was the first time that I had a chance to go. Nike takes the coaches on a tour to Mexico, and other places. You talk about the kid in the candy store; I was sitting around with Joe Paterno, LaVell Edwards, my dad, Steve Spurrier, and other great coaches. I did a lot of listening. The point I am trying to make is that we can always learn football. We need to learn more football or we become stale. Nothing remains the same. If you are not going forward, you are going backwards. You are very seldom standing still.

I do not know if I am a better clinician now that I am the head coach at Auburn. The first 10 years as a head coach I coached at small colleges. I was at Salem College for three years and we had 1000 students. I coached almost the entire offense; ever single position. At Samford we were in Division III for one year, and Division I for five years. I have coached the line, the quarterbacks, wide receivers, running backs, and everything else. Then I was a much better X's and O's person. Now, when I talk at a clinic I do not give out a lot of details. My brother Tommy, is the offensive coordinator and he can do a better job of that. Coach Fisher would do a better job with the defense. I do try to tell you some of the things I am doing. As a young coach I always try to analyze what I am doing, and what I might do better, and what I can find to be important for the reasons for our success. I have a good base or foundation from which to speak. I have been running the same things and have had the same offensive philosophy since I have been coaching at all levels. At times as young coaches we may think the coaches at the next level know a lot more than we do and that they run a lot more than we do. Well, we are running the same offense that we ran at Samford and Salem College. We ran the same offense and went undefeated in the SEC. I feel the same situation is true in high school. There are certain principles that are true at all levels. As a head coach or as a coordinator, we need to remember these facts.

I have always felt the most innovative coaches in America are high school coaches. We are too uptight in college. We get in games and think our job is on the line and we do not do anything innovative. We look at a lot of films of high school games and see a lot of good things in those films.

I am going to talk about a few things on offense that I believe in. I will talk about what I believe in philosophically. Let me say this to begin with. I have been taught this and you should never forget this. I have been taught to be a positive football coach. The greatest thing you can do as a coach is to have a positive attitude and to accentuate the positive, as opposed to being a coach that is negative. I know at times we get caught up in poor mouthing our team and that we are no good. When you do that all you are doing is degrading your athletes. We can recruit. After we recruit that is all that we have. You must make the players that you have, believe they can win. Very seldom are you going to have athletes that are better than someone else has.

I would say this, it is so important to accentuate the positive. Develop a positive attitude to your players so that they can be successful. I have never had a better example of this than this year when we came to Gainsville to play the University of Florida. We were very fortunate to beat Florida in Gainsville. However, if our players had read the newspaper, we would not have had a chance. We were a 17-point underdog. We were playing the number 1 team in the nation. Coach Spurrier had not lost a game to an SEC team in Gainsville. We had won 17 straight games and another win would break our record for an Auburn team. The game was on national TV. We would have to win a scoring contest.

The biggest thing I had to do that week was to get to the newspapers to tell our players that I felt we could win that game. I went over all of the positive aspects that we had going for us. I had to get our players to believe we could win the game. If your players do not believe they can win, it will be tough to win. They will rise to your level of expectations. Coaching did not win that game; the players won that game because they believed they could win. You must always give your players the feeling that they can win.

I can go from Samford to Auburn and be successful. If I had listened to all the Auburn alumni, or believed all that I read in the newspaper, there was no way I could have been successful at Auburn. They were all convinced you could not go from a small school to an SEC school and be successful. You have to be a positive coach. I do not like negative coaches. You could not coach for me if you were not a positive coach. All I want to hear is how we are going to win. I want the assistant coaches to tell the players how they are going to make them winners.

I usually give a talk on attitude from a leadership standpoint. As a football coach, you must believe in yourself and that you have as much knowledge and ability as anyone else has. Then you have to get the players to believe in themselves. That is where it all starts.

Before I talk about our offensive philosophy and what I think is important to win, I want to tell you I am a Bowden. As a Bowden we talk offensive football all of the time. I run the style of program that my dad runs. As the head coach I call the offense. I am the offensive coordinator, and head coach, and I call the plays. I hire a defensive coordinator and he calls the defense. That has always been my philosophy and that is the way my father does it. I can't be in both offensive and defensive meetings so I hire the defensive coordinator. He is going to be given the credit or he is going to take the blame. It gets you a good coordinator this way. That is the way it works for me, but not all coaches do it that way.

As much as I am going to talk on offense I want you to know that offense does not win championships. Offense is not your answer to winning football games. Defense is going to win for you. That is the key to big games and the championships. Offense is a key, and it is a big part of a program, but defense wins it all. We will have two or three big games a year. Florida State will have two or three big games a year. Florida will have two or three big games a year and those games will be won with defense. The big games are generally low-scoring games.

Look at the last four national champions in college. Three of the four have led the nation in scoring defense. In 1991 Miami won it all and led the nation with nine points per game scoring defense. In 1992 Alabama won it and only gave up nine points per game. In 1993 Florida State won the championship giving up nine points per game. This year Nebraska won the championship and was second in scoring defense. Miami won the scoring defense giving up nine points per game. Nebraska was second with 10 points per game. Alabama averaged 26 points per game on offense when it won it in 1992. Florida State averaged 43 points per game in 1993. Nebraska was around 30 points this year on offense. The essential is defense. I am not going to talk about defense, but if you are going to take over a program and you want to give yourself a chance to win, make sure the defense dilemma is solved first.

As an offensive coach, I tell my defensive staff I want to be in the top five in scoring defense. I think I can average 32 points per game in a bad year. I think we know enough on offense to do that. I tell our defense we are not going to win the big games unless we are in the top five in scoring defense. To do that I tell our defense two things. The first is they have to have a great rush defense. That comes out to less than 3 yards per rush in college. The second aspect of the defense is giving up the big play. Great rush defenses do not give up the big play. You will never get beat if you do not give up the big play.

Florida played great defense this year, statistically. It had a great rush defense. It was in the top five. It did not give up the big play, even though it gave up a lot of in-between yardage. Alabama has been the most difficult defense to play against year in and year out. Bill Oliver, the defensive coordinator at Alabama, is a great challenge to me as a coach. He has never had a 300-yard passing game against him in the last 60 games and his team is always in the top five in scoring defense.

If you can develop a great rush defense and prevent the big play you will have a great scoring defense. A great rush defense should also give you a good pass rush. The best rush teams are playing eight or nine people close to the line of scrimmage. This is what we are seeing on offense. We played against two real tough teams last year. One was against was Ole Miss and Joe Lee Dunn, who is now at Georgia. If you look at their defense you will see nine people close to the line of scrimmage. He will play man coverage a lot of the time. He likes to blitz. If you will watch when they run the blitz, you will see they play a soft man or zone coverage behind the blitz. He has taken average football teams and done great things with them defensively. He knows he can play the run tough with nine men up close to the line, and that will force them into passing situations. But he does not play the secondary tight; he plays loose. That scares you. One year against Auburn, before I got there, he played with only two down linemen.

Alabama plays a little more Three Deep in the secondary. I think things are getting back to more Three Deep. Everything is four level, with four backs deep. It use to be quarter, quarter, half. Now, it is quarter, quarter, quarter, quarter in the secondary. However, I am seeing more of the Three-Deep concept now. The thing I am trying to tell you is this. Be great on the defensive side of the ball and the offense will be fun.

My dad and my brothers have continual discussions on what is the most important offense to be successful. As coaches we need to decide some definite things about offense. Just as I said scoring defense is an essential thing in winning a championship, I do not think scoring offense is always the most important thing in winning. I have always used Florida State as an example to explain what I mean. Also, I have used Florida to explain this because it scores so many points per game. Florida State will line up as 20-point favorites for eight games per year; probably. It will be 18- to 20-point favorites in most of its games. I do not care what offense Florida State lines up in, it is going to win by a whole bunch. The whole premise, or the big question is this: What offense should Florida State run for those other three games. Don't put your offense in for Podunk University. Put your offense in to beat Miami. If you are a throw-it-every-down coach and you average 50 points per game, and then all of a sudden you play against a great team that has equal athletes. The last thing you want to be doing is to be throwing the ball on your 5-yard line. What do you end up doing in that situation? You end up in the running game. That may not be your best offense. In the big games you end up *not* doing the things you do best. I am not saying this is the total answer, but this is what has taught me to debate this subject. Is it best to go out and use an offense where I can score the most points against a team I am going to beat anyway, or is it best to develop a balanced offense that gives you enough time to practice both phases of the game? Can you run both the passing game and running game in the big games? In big games turnovers will probably be the deciding factor.

In looking at the best teams in terms of winning the best teams are teams that run a balanced offensive attack. The teams that are run-oriented are usually not in the hunt for the national championship. An example would be the Air Force Academy and Vanderbilt. They ran the ball well, but did not have strong passing games. Passing-only teams are the same. An example would be Las Vegas and New Mexico. Take the top 10 teams in the country and you will see them at the top of total offense. Florida and Nebraska were exceptions this year. Florida had more passing and Nebraska had more running, but they both had outstanding defenses.

If you have an outstanding defense you can have some tendencies, and it will not make that much difference. The point I am trying to get to is this: If I want to have the best offense for winning a championship, and not the best offense for Terry Bowden to be the Coach of the Year, or to winning the scoring title, but for Terry Bowden, the head coach. The best offense for me is a balanced offense. We do not have to score 40 points a game. At my level it looks as if 31 to 32 points per game is what we need to achieve. If you are looking at your offense and you are going to make some adjustments, balance is the key. If you want to get to the championship level, with people with similar talent, this is where balance will help you. If you are a lot better than your opponent, you can run it or pass it every down. In high school I imagine the it should be a little more run than passing. However, in the big games you must have the ability to do both.

In talking about a balanced offense I was taught by my father to "Keep It Simple." It is the old *KISS* Principle. *Keep It Simple Stupid*. I recommend to you to keep it simple. Don't try to do too much. If balance is what you want, the key is combining *execution* with *unpredictability*. You must be able to combine the two. You must be able to execute and not make mistakes, but you also want to be unpredictable. If you only ran one play you probably would execute that one play perfectly, but you would be very predictable. If you ran 100 plays you may not be very predictable, but you probably could not execute very well. Our whole dilemma in getting the right offense is to find a way that we will be unpredictable, but one that we can also execute. My theory has always been to keep it simple. Again, when I say my theory, it is what my father taught me over the years. My father does go back five decades in coaching. He was a head coach in 1955, and a lot of football has been learned and forgotten since that time.

Let me give you a simple explanation of being able to execute and still be unpredictable. If I could only have five plays in my offense and we had two runs and three passes, it would mean you could execute any of those five plays on first down and 10, and any of the five plays on fourth down and inches to go, you would be pretty unpredictable. In a nutshell, that is the theory of my offense and that is the theory of my father's offense.

I was with my father during the Nike trip. He was telling me he did not need more plays. He said, "All we have to do is run the plays faster." He was talking about the no-huddle attack. Could you imagine running these five plays I referred to earlier from the no-huddle? Now, the defense cannot get ready for all of these plays. This takes the coaching out of the game. I keep thinking of ways I can get Coach Bill Oliver out of the game. I do not know if I can line up and beat him all of the time. He is that good. But, if I can get in the no-huddle and run those five plays, I could run them fast or I could run them slow. That would take the coach out of the game. Now, the offense is more unpredictable to the players.

As coaches, we want to add more and more on offense. We hear something nice about a coach and we want to add one of his plays. We watch games on TV and see good plays and we want to add them to our offense. My dad wants to run the same plays but to run them faster. I like this no-huddle concept. We will probably get to it someday. It does give you the ability to keep it simple, but it also makes it more unpredictable for the defense. I think there is some merit to this concept. It takes a commitment by a coach. That is a good example of not trying to do more; just do better.

Again the theory is to keep it simple on offense, and make sure you can execute what you run. The worst thing you can have happen in a critical situation is not being able to execute the play. The defense does not stop you; you stop yourself because of a lack of execution. We all have been through that situation.

Let me give you some examples of keeping your offense simple. Our offense at Auburn is no more complicated than it was at Samford. It is a little more complicated than what we ran at Salem College. We are getting better at it, and we are adding a little each year. It stays fairly simple. We do not use many formations offensively. I am not saying this is the only way to winning. It fits with what we believe at Auburn. As a coach that has to teach and assistants that have to teach, it gives you a lot more time than an offense that has a lot of formations and a lot of plays. At least you can sleep at night knowing the players will know where to line up. Some teams can't tell until halftime if the players will line up in the right splits on offense.

We have three basic formations at Auburn. We use no motion. I always qualify that by letting Georgia and Florida know that I may change that theory some day. Basically we run three formations. We run the I Formation, Split Backs With the Gun; we move the quarterback back and split the backs but do not move anyone else, and we use a One-Back Set with four wideouts. We substitute personnel when we go to the One-Back Set. We take the fullback out and put a wideout in, and we take the tight end out and put another wideout in. We run the same Shotgun Split. Those are our basic formations. If we ran Motion we would have to work on the snap count forever. That is a pain. You have to work on it and work on it. Then that guy gets hurt and you do not have a man that can run the motion the same as the first man. We try to stay with formations that are very basic.

The year we went undefeated we only had two formations. We ran the I and the Split Backs. We did not have the Four Wideout Set. We added one formation and we won nine, lost one, and tied one this year. The point I am trying to make is to keep it simple. Who do you think has the most uncomplicated offense in the SEC? FLORIDA! They just threaten you with simple things on offense every play. They have athletes that can execute on every play. It scares you to death because they are good at it. They are not afraid to try anything on any down. If you look at what they do you will see it is not complicated at all. We study them. It is not complicated. Other teams do a lot more complicated things on offense.

I worked the SEC championship between Alabama and Florida on TV. I thought I caught this in the paper the next day about one of the TD's Florida scored. They had a first down on the 1-yard line. The quarterback threw the slant pass and they scored. The next day the quarterback said, "We had a Quarterback Sneak called and I saw the defense was in a Pinch, so I checked off to the Slant Pass." I could not do that if I were the coach. I could not give my quarterback the audible on the 1-yard line. I would have run the sneak and taken the no-gain play and run the Toss Sweep on second down. That is part of our philosophy.

We believe in keeping it simple so we do not have any audibles. It takes a lot of work to run audibles. We do have some sight adjustments. These things could be a clinic talk. You could talk all day about these ideas. Both wide receivers and the quarterback will read the defense. If they see something different they may change their assignment. They may change their pattern, but no one else needs to know what they are doing. The rest of the team goes ahead and does what it is supposed to do. On running plays we do not change much at all. The most we would do would be to call two plays in the huddle and pick one of them to run at the line of scrimmage. We give them two choices. We would call a 46 or 46 Sweep *at the line*. We call it an "Either-Or" call. We do not do a lot mainly because we want to execute. We want our players very sure who to block and how to block. We can be successful doing this.

I am not just blowing smoke. You may not believe me if I was still at Salem College or Samford. But I am at Auburn and we have beaten some good teams with this philosophy. We have averaged 32.1 and 32.6 points per game the last two years. We need to get up to the 37-point range to be in the top five in the country. We have accomplished a lot with this philosophy. We only have one snap count. We do not have audibles and we do not have motion. We do not change the snap count because it messes us up more than the defense. Question: Do you run Check-With-Me plays? No! We do not do run Check-With-Me plays. Every now and then we run the Either-Or play. Again, we do a lot of sight adjustments.

A lot of coaches ask me how I can tell all of our opponents that we only have one snap count. We tell them we want them to know this and we want them to know what the snap count is. It is a simple DOWN - SET - HIKE. We do not change it. However, about every fourth play we call a FREEZE play. We come up to the line and do not have a play called. We go Down - Set - Hike; but we do not move. If the defense starts crowding us I will call the Freeze until we get them back off the ball. When they get a couple of penalties they back up and stop trying to beat us on the snap count. In high school all you have to do is to get them to break the line of scrimmage and it is a penalty. In college we snap the ball when they jump over the line of scrimmage. By doing this we do not jump offside. We do have some tricks we use with our snap count. About the third game of the year we may go one time on Down.

I found out there are certain things you do not want to have happen on national TV. You do not want a lot of illegal procedure calls, you do not want to have 12 men on the field, and you do not want to have a kick blocked. Those are coaching mistakes, and it makes you look bad. I am kidding just a little, but it seams that way. Perception is very important. A well-tuned machine doesn't jump offside. To mess up down inside the 5-yard line just kills me. If you are ever going to change the snap count it should be on first down. I do the tricky counts on first down.

We run a few plays and a few formations. We go on the same snap count. We do not have any audibles. We like to run the ball. We do not run it as well as we would like to. We averaged 199.6 yards per run in 1994. In 1993 we averaged 210 yards per carry. We run about eight running plays. We run six plays out of the I Formation and two plays from Split Backs. You have to run the Trap and the Draw. We call the Screen a running play. We think of the Screen as a counter to the passing game. It hurts teams that like to rush the passer. The Screen and Draw and Trap are all running plays to us. My dad always told me if I ever wanted to add a play to our offense not to do it unless you take one play out of the offense. You can't extend practice time. So, if we are going to add a play we have to take one out. Most of the time we can't find one that we want to take out. You can't rep the plays the same amount of time if you keep adding plays. With only six plays we can change the blocking schemes around. We can block the Sweep a lot of fun ways. We can give the Sprint Draw a different look by changing our blocking scheme.

I am not so concerned on the passing game about the number of pass plays you have as I am the number of pass protections you have. My favorite position to coach is the offensive line. We all know the more protections you have the more problems you have. Do you use a Man Protection, a Zone Protection, or a Hinge Protection? Do you do a Fan Out and a Double Read on both sides? Do you have a Bootleg or Waggle Protection? If you have all of those you have a lot of problems. You can do a lot of different pass routes off the same protection. That is not a real coaching problem. A receiver can run six different cuts, and you can run each of those six cuts off Play Action and Straight Dropback action. It is not a lot of teaching to involve this. I want to be very simple in the protection. We have about two or three protections.

We have gone to the Shotgun Formation with the Split Backs. I was not big on the Shotgun Formation at one time. Now I am sold on the Shotgun in passing situations. You can miss a lot of things and the quarterback can still get rid of the ball and not have to take a sack. We threw the ball 51 times against Florida and did not have a sack. We had less than one sack a game. If you don't pick them up, the quarterback has to heave it out of bounds. But that is better at times than taking a sack. We have found it is a big play.

I have always been a real detail coach for doing self-scouting analysis. When I was a grad student at Florida State I was in law school. I spent a lot of time in the classroom. I was my dad's graduate assistant for self-scouting. I would study all of our tendencies and all of the opponent's tendencies. After two games we would have Two-Game Tendencies. Then It would be Three-Game Tendencies. What do they do on first-and-10, second-and-7, and so on. For four years I was the main self-scout. By Tuesday I could give dad a self-scout. This is what your tendencies are. Now, I get a self-scout because I call the plays. If you call the plays you are going to have some tendencies.

I found out something about tendencies. They are not bad to have; they are good if you can win. Then you create tendencies. "Auburn may win, but they run the same play on first-and-10." Then it is, "They run the same play on second and third every time." By the seventh game you have created some unbelievable tendencies. Then, in the next game, you go out and make sure you do not run your tendencies. That is when we run our Split Backs. That is when we throw to the tight end like we did against Florida. We had not thrown to the tight end but three times all year. In that game we hit the tight end for seven passes and 123 yards. Tendencies are not bad to have IF YOU KNOW THEM. If you do have tendencies it is because you are successful.

It is like saying, "We are going to run the Toss Sweep, and you know we are going to run the Toss Sweep. Now, let's see if you can stop it." That has basically been our theory. Then when we know we are overdoing it, that is when I am going to hit you with a reverse, or the Fullback Belly Cutback, or the Halfback Pass. We could run our Quarterback Naked. In this philosophy you are going to have tendencies. Because of this you need to have counter plays that offset the other plays.

In our offense we run the Toss Sweep so we have to run the Fullback Belly. If we don't, the linebackers will move laterally too fast. We have to run the Reverse or Naked as we call it. This is to keep the safety from supporting too fast to one side. You have to run counters to your regular plays. If you run the Sprint Draw you run the Sprint Draw Passing Attack. If you run the Counter, you run the Bootleg off the Counter. Each play has a good counter play or a companion or complementary play off it. It allows you to stay simple but also to be unpredictable.

I am trying to give you some ideas offensively. I am sure most of you have faced the same problems that I have faced in my career. It is a matter of dealing with the time you can spend with a certain number of people in football and you are trying to get better at what you are doing. We want to be better coaches and we study and study. We work more and more. Someone asked me how it felt to be one of the youngest head coaches in the country. My dad told me it was not important to be the youngest coach in America; it is more important to be the oldest head coach in America. I think he was right. I have a long way to go. The older I get the more I see that the game gets very simple. We like to say that you win with blocking and tackling. You win with fundamentals. This is true. Now, it might be the fundamentals of a Vertical Passing Game as opposed to the fundamentals of an Isolation Play in the 1960s. It is still the fundamentals. It is very simple.

We do not start spring practice until April 1. We like to study our offense from last year. What do we need to improve? Are we developing tendencies? Is it a matter of personnel? This past year we lost about 30 yards per game out of our fullback. We lost two fullbacks the year before. This year we had two young fullbacks. We may not have to change things, just recognize that we may be less talented in that area. We are not going to jump the boat because of this fact. I try to recruit toward the scheme we run. I am reluctant to change my scheme. I can recruit and you can't. I do not like to coach things I do not know. Coach things you know and can teach.

Hopefully, I have covered some things that will help you become successful on offense. You win with defense. Don't give up the big play. Offensively, the teams that win the most are balanced offenses that run and pass the ball well. Those two things are essential.

Chapter 4

TEAM LEADERSHIP

Mack Brown
University of North Carolina
1993

As coaches, we must remember that things are changing in our profession. Many things in coaching are different. We have had experiences over the rebuilding process for the last five years that I would like to share with you.

I was an assistant coach in Oklahoma in 1984. Gary Gibbs was the defensive coordinator, and I was the offensive coordinator when we played Washington for the national championship. We got beat in the Orange Bowl.

The next year I went to Tulane, a small private school in New Orleans. We had 49 players on scholarship. Out of this 49, 41 were on academic probation. We also had to play six bowl teams during the next year, and we had to open up in the Super Dome with Florida State. So we went from Oklahoma, where we thought we could coach, to New Orleans, where nobody looked like a football player.

Later we did end up winning at Tulane. We go to a bowl, and we play Washington. We get beat in the Independence Bowl. Then I became the head coach at North Carolina, where we had back-to-back 1–10 seasons, 20 losses in two years. That is not very much fun. You're driving your daughters to school, and they are listening to their radio stations, and these Mack Brown–Carolina football jokes are coming over the radio. That's really impressive to your daughters—be proud of your dad. "Hey, if you have a child that has been abused, let him live with Mack Brown. He'd never beat anybody." Is that good? Again, it is funnier now than it was in '88.

The other comment on radio went like this. It was related with Dick Crum, who was the poor coach before me. They said, "What do Dick

Crum, Mack Brown, and Dean Smith, our basketball coach, have in common? None of them has ever coached football at North Carolina." This one really got to me. "If Mack Brown bought 7–11s, what would he name them? 0–11s!" Of course, we were excited.

When I coached at Oklahoma, we won the Big Eight championship. We played Washington in that bowl game, so I've got that championship ring that I wear, because until this year I couldn't get another bowl ring. One day, I'm running late for a foundation meeting. That's the fund-raising arm at North Carolina. And with a 2–20 record, you never want to be late to a board meeting when they may vote on something important to your program. You need to be there, and you need to have your kids there. They need to be in torn jeans, and all this kind of stuff.

I'm driving in Chapel Hill. It is a small community, and I'm driving out to this board meeting. I'm not sure what's going to happen after two years. I'm not real popular, as you all can imagine. I'm just about out of gas, and I was nervous about being late. I was not sure if I might get fired or not. I have my Oklahoma championship ring on, so I could try to remind them that I did win a game at some point in my career. I stopped at this little gas station outside of Chapel Hill. A guy comes out, and I say, "Can you fill it up? I'm in a big hurry. I'm late for a meeting, and I need to go." He said, "Sure. Hey, buddy, I like your ring. Let me see that thing." So I took the ring off, and I said, "Yeah, look at that." He said, "Yeah, that's a championship ring. That's nice, isn't it?" and I said, "Yeah, it is really nice. You know what we need at North Carolina? We need one of these rings for football at the University of North Carolina." He said, "Yeah, but as long as that damn Mack Brown is our football coach, we are never going to get one, I can tell you that." I didn't pay for the gas, and I haven't been back.

It is amazing what happens to all of us in this business. It is the greatest business in the world. There are more people that are hitting on football right now than ever before in its history. I've been doing this for 20 years, and the college game is better than it has ever been. The players get treated better; more players are graduating; the TV ratings are better; our Mississippi State Peach Bowl Game had the sixth-best viewing audience in ESPN history. People are more excited about football than ever before. But there is more visibility, there are more problems in society than ever before, there is more frustration with our economic situation, so they beat up you guys, and they beat up me because football is such an aggressive sport and it costs a lot of money. And now we are looking at gender equity and opportunities for women, which is great—but let's not take money out of football to try to help. Let's build and progress and grow in football to try to help the other sports. We're not talking about taking opportunities away from young people.

We are in a time when leadership is more important than ever before. And that is why I'm excited to be here. I look at the high school football in a state and base that on what I see in the colleges. You guys have always played great college football in this state, at many different levels. That is a credit to you, because if the football is not good at the lower levels, the players will not improve and play better as they go on. Notre Dame is one of the few schools in America that travels all over the country to get its players. If you will look, most of the other schools win with home-grown players in an area where they can recruit them. And Michigan is one of those. So when I was asked to speak, I was excited, because I have not been in Michigan very often. It's exciting for me to be here. You can tell by the attendance this time of the year that you do care about your football. So hopefully we can share in some things that will be really good.

As you look in the '90s, what are we involved with? We're involved with three or four or five teams this year that had meetings and decided not to practice. Two or three of those teams had a vote that they didn't think the coach was doing a good job. In fact, one of my friends coached at one of those schools. They were 0-5, and he called me and said, "You know, the players voted to fire me." I said, "You know what you ought to do? You have not lost a game. Vote to fire them. They're 0–5."

We are living in a time when young people are speaking out. That's the trend. That's not going to change. I went to school at Florida State in the late '60s and early '70s. I had the long hair. There was a walkout or a protest about something every week on campus. So we're back in the '70s. We're back in the '60s. It's the same thing. It's just different kids, and we're a little bit older. Lots of guys are wearing earrings now. If you wore an earring in Cookeville, Tennessee, when I was in high school or college, you would be shot, but now our guys are wearing earrings. They've talked to me about it; we've talked to them about it. We've shared it, and I'll talk to you a little bit about what we did there.

It is amazing. We are having a discussion right now about dress, within our program and away from our program, about curfew. We allowed our seniors to set the curfew in the Peach Bowl. Is that scary to take 120 young guys to Atlanta, and tell your players to handle it? And you know what? Not one guy was late for curfew. Not one person was late for a meeting or missed a meeting, because they each had the peer pressure within the group. If I had said, "You have to be in at 1:00 because Mississippi State's in at 1:30," it would have been a problem. But our players set the curfew. They felt that leadership and chemistry within. Now, if they had said 4:00, we would have been aware of that, and we would not have let them set it because it wouldn't have been good leadership to start with. The reason we won nine games this year and finished in the top 20 is the chemistry and the leadership of our program, because our players were just as good last year, and we won seven. That was the difference in this football team.

I saw a few quotes, and I wrote them down. "Leadership is poise under pressure." You ask your guys to win games. When do they need to win? When it's tight in the fourth quarter. Critical situations are the red zone. Critical situations are when you're sitting there, and it's third-and-4, third-and-3, third-and-2, fourth-and-1. No different for you. We're in crisis control. John F. Kennedy said, "Leadership is poise under pressure."

Look at another guy who has been pretty good to our game. It's not so much leading as having people accept you. You have to win the hearts of the people through your own personality and style—Vince Lombardi. Again, you cannot take what I say today and take it back to your school and use it. You have to let this be incorporated into your personality, because you are already dealing with your guys. I've coached for Barry Switzer; Donnie Duncan, who is the athletic director now at Oklahoma; Jerry Stovall, who is the athletic director at Louisiana Tech—who was a great pro player and head coach at LSU. I coached for Paul Deitzel, who is tremendous; Richard Williamson, who was a Tampa Bay head coach and who is now with the Cincinnati Bengals. One thing unique about all these guys is they all were very good football coaches, but they all had different leadership and management styles. Bobby Collins is included in that group.

"Leadership is the ability to get a person to do what you want him to do, when you want it done, in a way you want it done, because he wants to do it." Think about that. Our players wanted to win this year. That quote was from Dwight D. Eisenhower.

These ideas are not new. They have been around for a long time. So let's talk a little bit about leadership here, where it's going, and what it means.

I talked to Steve Sloan one time. He was a great player and a great coach. I asked him if I could coach for him at Vanderbilt as a graduate assistant. He said, "If you coach, you should coach for one reason, because it's really hard. You should coach because you can't live without it, and you should coach because you care about young people. You want to mold young people's lives." And it's harder to be young right now than ever before. We're talking about their lives educationally, their lives as far as the motivation to achieve and set goals, and as far as handling life's challenges in the midst of AIDS, drugs, pressure, stealing, financial problems. We have a higher divorce rate than at any time in our history, so the family structure is not as good at home. There is more talk about dysfunctional families than ever before. What does that mean? It means we are having more trouble with leadership at home. So as we talk about these things, they relate to the drugs and the alcohol and the AIDS and their problems. You have to spend more time with these people than ever before. So let's look at where the leadership comes in.

The first thing we feel is important, as far as leadership, is, "Observe people that you admire." Look at successful people, because there are some guys on your team that score touchdowns. They are productive. There are some guys that make tackles. And we've all said the guy that makes the tackle may not be the best guy. You're always trying to get this one guy on your team out of the lineup because he doesn't have enough ability, but he makes all the plays. Why? We don't know. So let's find out who's producing, whether it's on your staff or on your team, and let's look at those people and find out why they are producing.

One time when we were struggling at Tulane, I asked Pat Dye, "Coach, what about the really good player who can run and make all the test scores, and he jumps higher than anybody, and he's fast?" He said, "How long do you stay with a guy like that if he is not producing? You play the producers. You said he's a really good player. Well, he's not a good player. He's a good athlete. And he's got to have an obsession to be a good player."

Look at people who are winning. Look at people who are producing good young people. Look at people that have won for many years, and figure out why. Then you have to emulate the good and eliminate the bad. There are some coaches right now that are doing some great things, winning, and helping their players, but their image is not very good. Barry Switzer was one of those. Coach Switzer's image was not good, and he is a great guy. He was super to me, and he did a tremendous job helping young people in Oklahoma. He spent hours talking to them and helping them. Now, I didn't know that before I spent a year at Oklahoma. Barry's personality is very different from mine, and I'm not going to take all the things that Barry did every day and try to use them in my life, but there are a lot of good things I learned from him.

The other thing we found in that leadership role is that when we have our young freshmen coming in, we try to get them around players who are successful. It would be the same in your school, because we found that if a young guy gets with a guy who is going to class, talks positively about the coaches, and is working harder in that weight room than anybody else, he's going to make that young guy who looks up to him see the success he has accomplished because of that, and the young guy will do the same thing. You can just see it. If a young guy comes in and starts drifting a little bit, with a guy who doesn't work as hard, he really heads in that same direction. So let's find out who's doing it right, and let's make sure we talk to them about why and take the good that they're doing.

The second one is really big. It's something that we look at that we can talk about, and it really relates to the first one, and this is communication. What type of leader are you? How can you find out? Al Capone was a leader, but he's not the type of leader you want running your country or running your football program. You want positive leaders. So how do you find them?

You need to communicate with these guys. Seek feedback from those who were talking about leading. There is one thing I really believe in the '90s. You better become a good listener. We had some players come to me this summer and say, "Coach, we want to visit with you. We've got some real problems on this football team." I said, "Okay." We needed some aggressive leaders, because we had not been very good. We went from 1–10, 1–10, 6–4–1, 7–4, and we had to get over that 7–4 and get some confidence to get over the hump, so we needed some aggressive guys to take the leadership role. As I said, Al Capone was a good leader in a lot of people's eyes, but that is not what you want. So when you get these aggressive guys with the ability to lead, you better communicate with them, and you better channel them. That meeting I had with the players this summer—they had some critical problems in their minds. "Coach, we would like to be able to wear earrings up on campus. We know you'd rather not have us wear them when we come into this building, or on the practice field, or when we travel. But you say you'd like for us to be like the other students and have that freedom. Coach, our other students can wear earrings, so why can't we wear them?" Critical problem. So we discussed it. You know what came out of it? "Men, you are right. When you're out of this building, understand that in football you always represent the University of North Carolina. But when you're up on campus, you can have your own views. You can dress as you want, and you can handle yourself in the manner you need to. But the minute you rejoin this football team, there are some commitments. You lose some of that individualism, and you have to come back." So we ask our guys not to wear their earrings on TV, in a picture, on the trips. We ask them this for this reason. "If that banker is going to hire you, he's probably not going to hire you with an earring. It doesn't matter to me whether you wear it or not. It's not an issue to me. Not at all. I didn't wear them. Things have changed in the last 20 years. But there will be things that will limit your options when you get out of here as far as your opportunity to get a job, and you're going to ask me to help you get a job." You know what some of them told me? "That's fine, but coach, we'll take it out before we go interview. We wouldn't be that dumb." Isn't that amazing? They've thought about this. They're not going to wear that earring their whole lives. But it's a trend. I saw my pictures at Florida State. I had hair down to my shoulders. I didn't think it was bad then. I thought it was cool.

The other thing they said was, "Coach, on the training table sometimes the lettuce is wilted." I said, "Boy, that's bad." I sat there for an hour and a half, and I talked to kids. Yes, I'm talking about kids. I had some parents who used to get on me because we called them "kids" or "young people." They are kids. The ones you get are younger than the ones we're involved with. They're 17, 18, 19, 20, and 21 years old. I get confused, and I'm not sure what to do sometimes when I'm 41. And I go back, and I see how sensitive these guys are. We give them a T-shirt to go to the Peach Bowl, and it's like they've won a national championship, because they've accomplished something. They feel better about themselves.

We are working with insecurity. Listen to those you are leading. Find out what they think is right. Find out what their problems are. My kids had a list of 10 problems. Those were two of the most important problems to them. One thing they said was, "We wish you wouldn't tell us who to hang around with." There was one guy in our program that I wasn't sure was a good influence, and I said, "Men, be careful with this guy. Just be careful with him." They said, "Coach, we appreciate you being interested in us, but you don't need to be telling us who we can hang around with now. You don't need to be telling us that." And you know what? I said, "I wasn't telling you. I was suggesting that you be careful, because we care about you and we love you. That's what we were doing." And you know what they said? "Well, we didn't mind it, then. That's fine, if you care about us. We just didn't want you to tell us what to do."

There is a fine line of communication between forcing and telling and asking and caring and loving. As a head coach, how many times in your staff meetings have your assistant coaches said, "Boy, our players are sensitive. You can't get on them at all. You can't talk to them about anything they're doing. Isn't it amazing that they're so sensitive?" But you let me bring in one of the assistants and say, "You know, we had this 4.8 strong safety covering this 4.5 wide receiver and they scored three times. It was the same defense, and as head coach, I just kind of wondered, were we trying to let them score three times? Or was it a personnel mistake? We're probably not going to consider doing that again, are we?" I had one coach pout for about three months, and I didn't even know it, because as a head coach I questioned why one man ran by another one. Why did we have a slow one trying to cover a fast one? We jumped all over that slow one, and he had no chance. If he had a gun, he probably couldn't have gotten close enough to shoot the guy; that's how bad the mismatch was.

But we're all sensitive, too. I've quit reading the paper. And one thing, when you lose 20 games at North Carolina and you've sold out for 16 straight years, there is some criticism. So what you do is learn that in your job and in my job, if you are going to handle all of those positive articles they write and all those nice things they say, and that ego grows, then you better be ready to handle all the criticism that you will get, because if you take the positive, then you must take the negatives.

We're sitting in the dressing room at halftime of the Mississippi State game in the Peach Bowl. We've got 31,000 fans who bought tickets to go to Atlanta. There were 70,000 people in the Georgia Dome. It was the biggest crowd they've ever had, we're down 14–0, and we're lucky. Two passes were called back. We should have been down 28–0. We haven't done anything right. I know we have good kids, I know they wanted to play, and we had great preparation. I just can't figure out what's wrong. So we got in at halftime, and the first thing I did was to get on the coaches pretty good. I said, "We're not doing anything right. We're yelling at them on the sideline; we're frustrated; things aren't going good."

But I remembered, when I coached for Coach Switzer at Oklahoma and we played Kansas, Kansas had the worst team in the country. We were number 2 in the country. Danny Bradley, our quarterback, got hurt. Our second quarterback was ruled ineligible. And a guy that you probably have not heard a lot about until this year, Troy Aikman, was a pretty good player. He was a red-shirt freshman for us at Oklahoma. In fact, Coach Switzer said, "I told Troy that if he'd come to Oklahoma, he'd have a chance to win the Heisman. I just didn't tell him it would be after he transferred to UCLA." That's positive. Troy Aikman talks to me on Thursday before the game, because he hasn't played at all and he hasn't practiced much. "Coach, the only thing I'm worried about is throwing an interception to lose the game at Kansas." I said, "Troy, Kansas isn't very good. If you throw an interception that loses the game, then we've played very poorly. So don't worry about that. You go and have a good time." We're down 10–7 at halftime. The reason they have seven of their 10 is that Troy threw an interception that they ran back for a touchdown, and I didn't handle the situation very well.

I walked in at halftime, I jumped on the offensive players, and I probably jumped on Troy—I don't remember, because I was frustrated because we were in trouble. It was a rainy day, and we were flat, and I told that group that was struggling with a freshman quarterback—and a freshman quarterback that should not have been in the game—that they were doing bad. I told them they would probably get beat unless they picked it up. I convinced them at halftime that they were going to get beat. We went back out the second half, and we lost 23–11. Now, I tried to communicate to them to pick it up. I was trying to tell them this: "You all need to help your freshman quarterback." What I told them was, "You're going to get beat because of the way you are playing." And they believed me. I convinced them.

We got on the plane; we're going home. Coach Switzer comes over to me, and he doesn't say to me, "That's the dumbest thing I've ever heard." He doesn't say, "You lost the game." It still had not hit me what I did. I thought the players screwed up; they were flat. Coach Switzer came over and sat next to me and said, "You know, when you've got the best players, you usually win, don't you?" I said, "Yeah, coach, that's what hurts us so bad about today. Because we had better players than Kansas, and we got beat." He said, "Yeah, but you know what? The longer that game goes, if you can remain positive and cool with your team, the better chance you have to win, because one of those really good players is going to win the game.

Our guys always think they can win here, and Kansas wasn't sure. So if you just hang in there, don't you think, and be positive—still coach, but be positive—you have a better chance to win, don't you?" What he told me was, "You messed up." But at a time when I was really down and sensitive, he communicated to me a whole lot better than I did to that team.

We were playing Kansas State two weeks later. We were ahead 13–7 at halftime, and they were awful. We were walking into the dressing room. Barry grabbed me by the arm and said, "Hey, we are in great shape, aren't we? We're in great shape. Because you know what? The emotions are gone in the first half, and we've got the best players. We're going to go in there and get after this bunch in a positive way, and we are going to kill Kansas State, aren't we?" He just chewed me out again and reminded me that I messed up at Kansas. Now, you talk about being positive at halftime. I said, "Boy, are we doing great." We beat them 31–7.

In the Peach Bowl against Mississippi State at halftime, it hits me. I'm getting on the coaches; I'm frustrated; it's embarrassing; I know what this could mean to our program. After talking to the coaches, I got frustrated, and I finally said, "Let's go talk to the players. Let's be positive." So we walked back in with the players again, and we said, "Look, we've got a good football team. You've played well all year, and we know you're trying hard out there, but you're not playing very well. What you need to do is have some fun, relax, and go have some fun. You have every football fan in America watching this ballgame, and you haven't been very fair to them or to yourselves because you haven't shown them how much fun you have, how much love there is on this team, and how much caring there is in this room. You came down here to have a good time. This is an extra game. This is a reward. This is a fun game. Don't forget that it's a game. If we get beat, we can still go home. But you know what I believe? You all have not even started yet. We're going to take the ball and get some points early, we're going to get it back to 14–7, and all of a sudden they're going to be in trouble. You have 31,000 frustrated fans that are so excited, and we haven't done anything. We can get them excited very quickly, and this thing is going to turn around."

We went back out on the field for the second half, and we took the first drive. We hit a post route, we scored, and it was 14–7. We had a group of walk-ons on our sidelines, and they got these towels behind the bench and started waving the towels. That Georgia Dome got so loud that nobody could hear. We dominated the second half. We blocked two punts and moved the ball when we had it. I've never seen momentum change like that in a ballgame. And that's what we're talking about: communication. What I learned at Oklahoma, I put in the pot at North Carolina.

The second thing is, don't speak as an authority until you've researched the subject. As a young head coach, I know I was awful. If somebody asked me a question, I wanted to give an answer. If you give people the wrong answer, if you don't tell people the truth, or if you lie to them, you don't have another chance. It shows a whole lot more confidence to say, "I'm not sure." Let's think about that. You can still share and listen and be in a position to make those decisions, but don't make a decision until you've researched it.

I'm going to tell you something I've learned about our staff, too. If I say, "Men, what do you think about the earring issue?" the ones that pop their hands up really quickly are trying to impress you, but not the ones that say, "Coach, I've thought about it a lot, but I'm not sure yet. Let's look at the up sides and the sides of concern here, and see where we're going." A lot of times, that first decision may be what you come back to, but you're not pressed to make a quick decision in most cases, so make sure you know what you're talking about.

Show respect to subordinates. Listen to kids. Listen to your athletic director. Listen to your principal. Your principal may not have a clue. He may not have any idea what you are trying to accomplish. You better educate him. Everybody has a boss. It is easy to sit around and say you have a bad principal, but he's still the best one you have, because he's the only one you have. It is like that ugly baby. If it's yours, it's yours, so you better love it and hug it and care about it, because you're not going to give it away.

As long as you are working for that guy, you better work for him. I write a full report to our athletic director every spring on everything about our program. I spend a lot of time with him. If I know we're probably going to get beat on Saturday, I make him come over and watch a film of why the odds are against us. He'll sit there and watch Florida State and say, "Oh, I don't know. They don't look that good to me." But you know what? It's better that he was over there looking at it, because he did see them and it didn't shock him when we went in there, because they all think they're going to win. Principals are fans. Your boss is a fan, and all fans think they are going to win. That's why they call them "fanatics." So try to educate those people as you go. Talk to them. Be trustworthy, be fair, be factual, but always tell the truth.

We had a lot of criticism with our team early, because some people said, when we were 1–10, that we told our players some negative things. If a young guy comes in and asks me, "Coach, am I going to play Saturday?" Do you think about it and say, "Well, there's a good chance you are. You're doing so much better, and things are really good"? A lot of times the young assistant coaches always want the guys to like them, but when it gets in the heat of the game, you're not going to put him in if he's not any good. You're better off saying, "Probably not. You need to prepare for it, but here are the things you need to improve on before you can put yourself in a position to be successful on Saturday, because we can't let you play until you start doing better in practice." You know what? Young people appreciate that more than anything else in the world, because they really know it. It all goes back to the communication level. Make sure he understands that you love him, you want him to stay on the team, you do care about him, you don't think he's not going to ever play, but, "Right now you have some things you have to improve on if I'm going to put you out there with my check in your mouth." Basically, that is what we're doing with them, so make sure they understand that as you go along.

Show genuine concern, and show them you really care. Charlie McClendon was at one of our meetings last month. He had coached at LSU and won 70 percent of his games, and he got fired. This is something that can happen in our business. I asked Coach Mac, "If you had it to do over again, what would you do differently?" I like to ask winning coaches, "Why did you win?"

One time Darryl Royal came down to Tulane to look at our program and our practice field. I asked him, "Coach Royal, how did you overcome some of your losing teams?" He said, "I don't know. I never had one." Well, that really helped me.

Talk to your players about something other than football, especially your dominant players. How many times do you bring a guy in and say, "Don, how are you doing?" He says, "Well, coach, on the sweep . . . " and you say, "No, no, no. How are you doing? How is home? How is your mom? How are your mom and dad doing? I know they just got divorced. Are you doing okay with that? That's a real tough thing. If you ever need to just come in and sit and talk, let's do. Now, I saw that you made a B the other day on your English exam." You'll be amazed, because in many cases young guys worry about being used.

They don't think you care, and you're not talking to that young guy and trying to set him up. You do care. In many cases, we don't take time to show how much we care. If you didn't care, you wouldn't be in here, so we have to understand that we do care as much as we do.

Be positive. Don't talk about the negatives when you're sitting in there with him in that meeting. Be positive with him at that time about his life, about his goals. "Where do you want to go to school? You're a sophomore. Have you thought about college?" Something that worries me when I go into a high school is a young guy who is a great player, but his grades are so bad or he hasn't even taken the proper subjects to get into college. I know that somebody could have looked at that a little more closely, possibly, and helped that young guy, so make sure that you go back and study the person, not just the football player. The older I get and the longer I stay in this business, I believe that you have to have talent or you cannot win, but there is a lot more to it than just talent. There is that chemistry that we all talk about. All of those older guys tell me, "You know, my most-talented team was not my best team," or, "I don't know what happened to that team in '64. We had some really good players, but they just didn't play well together, and that really bothers me. I don't know why." That great chemistry we had at North Carolina last year, I don't have any idea if we'll have it next year, because you start over when that group leaves. All of them have their own personality and their own identity.

Lou Holtz has always been positive about this. In my life, I think more than ever before, I'm at a 41-year-old time when retirement starts being more important to me than ever before.

As we look at it, you have to have personal goals. A lot of people say you need a goal every morning. What am I going to get accomplished today? Boy, that's hard to do. I've never been able to do that. I think I work hard enough to get a lot of things done during the day. But at night before I go to bed, if I could make myself a goal of what I want to get accomplished for the next morning, I'd probably be a lot better off. At least I would know I had accomplished something.

You know, sometimes you'll work so hard during the day, and at the end of the day you'll say, "Golly, I'm not sure I got anything done. I know I worked hard, but I'm not sure I got anything done." In coaching, I think one of the negative things for us is that a lot of times we'll sit there and try to prove that we are outworking the other guy. It doesn't matter whether you outwork him. You better outproduce him. How many times did a coach say, "Man, I stayed over there until 12:00 every night this week." Well, how much of that did you waste in stories? How much did you waste arguing over something about a play that you probably weren't going to run but twice anyway and getting mad because you were exhausted and it was after 10:30? How much of it did you spend griping about what your wife said to you that afternoon? And how much of it did you get done in football? We could probably do a better job with a lot of those things than we do.

As we look at it, set short-term personal goals and long-term personal goals. Get a direction in your life. If you're a young assistant coach, what do you want to do this for? Do you want to be an assistant coach for the rest of your life? Can you handle that? Do you want to be a head coach? If you do, what type goals do you need to set for yourself to be a head coach? Do you need to move around? Do you need to stay? Do you need to go to a college and study? Do you need to go to Brother Rice High School and find out why they've won so many games? Call the coach and say, "Could I just stand around for a couple of days? Could I just watch and listen?" If you work hard, you can get done what you need to get done. To be successful, you need to go beyond that. As a young assistant coach, I made myself pay my own way to three different spring practices every year so I could go to practice.

I love to come and talk to you all. I'll get a lot out of this. I'm getting on a plane in a few minutes to speak to another group tonight, and I'm going out tonight with a guy that owns 17 Olds dealerships. The reason I'm going out with him is because he is a good friend and because he is really successful. I'm going to learn something at dinner tonight about the way this guy motivates and the way this guy organizes. It's easy when you're 1–10 to get to 7–4. It's a little harder to get to 9–3. Now we have to beat Southern Cal in the opening game, and we've got to beat Florida State in Chapel Hill in our fourth game. We still must maintain the other games we are winning.

So what do I need to do to set my goals for next year? Our team sets its own goals. We ask the players to do it. We ask them to figure out how good they can be. It's amazing what they'll tell you. This last year, this is what they said: "Coach, we'd like to have a winning season. Coach, we'd like to go to a bowl." They didn't say anything about winning the bowl. They'd just like to go, and that would be fine. So after the season, we had to reset the goals. We ended up in the top 20 at the end of the season, and we got a bowl bid. Well, now let's reset those goals for 1993. We have not won nine games for 10 years. We would like to win nine games instead of eight. Nine and three is a whole lot better than eight and four. To do that, we have to win the bowl game. It was nice to get here, but we have to reset those goals. The polls really aren't important, because they write down the polls at the end of the bowls, so we want to make sure we're in the top 20 at the end of it. Now they're talking about conference championship; now they're talking about top 10; now they're talking about the Orange Bowl, the Sugar Bowl, the Cotton Bowl, and the other bowls. I don't know whether they're capable or not, but as long as they don't know, they've got a chance, because funny things happen in this business. Fresno State beats SC. You don't expect that to happen. Things happen every week in college football because young guys think it can happen, and they set those goals to try to get them done.

Sit down with your players and ask them to do short-term and long-term goals as you go. It is important to me, and I have not done a very good job of it. I've been a lot more goal oriented with my job than I have with my personal life. I could do a better job with my money. I do not even have a budget at my house. It is amazing to me. I sat down last week with a financial advisor, and I started looking at the money I spend per month. It is amazing. You have to have some goals, and unity toward those goals.

Here's something we got last year from Grant Teaff. We took a piece of oak, and we cut it into 150 strips. We walked into our football team during two-a-days and handed those strips of oak out to every player. We said, "Men, stand up. Hold those pieces of oak above your heads. See how flimsy they are? See how thin they are? Now, break them." They looked at me like I was crazy, then they snapped them and broke them. I said, "Now, I want you to throw them up against the wall." They had a great time. They threw them all over the place. I said, "Those were individual strips of oak that come together to make a log. Right now, as we start two-a-days, we've got a lot of individuals who would like to be a team. Let's work at the end of two-a-days to make sure that we take all those strips and put them back together, glue them together, and bring them into unity." We did that. We put the strips together and painted it blue. We kept that blue log in our dressing room, and they had to touch it before they walked out on the field every day. This was a part of their commitment to the group and the goals that they set, because setting these goals is easy. Doing them is hard.

Constantly work on ideas to evaluate and improve. There is a difference between being critical and evaluating. After recruiting every year, I ask our coaches to write down anything they would have done differently in their area. I ask them to write down every player that signed a scholarship out of their area: if we were interested in him, he came to our campus to visit, and we offered him a scholarship, why he didn't come. If we didn't offer him a scholarship, why didn't we, and what would we have done differently, especially for the ones who we offered but did not come? You know, 75 percent of the staff's reaction was, "He's being negative. He's trying to be critical of us this year in recruiting." I had to go back to communicate and lead and say, "Men, some of you may think this is a critical evaluation of you. It is not. What we're trying to do is evaluate and improve." I think the hardest thing I have ever had to do was try to evaluate myself as a football coach and as a person. There is a fine line between self-confidence and ego, respect and fear, and when we're talking about leadership and discipline. There is a fine line in the old adage, "If you have too little discipline, then you have too much morale, and if you have too much discipline, you have poor morale." There is a fine line of balance between discipline and morale.

You want your team to feel as if it is making progress and for the players to feel good about their goals and their objectives, but you also want them to have fun at the same time. They won't have fun unless they accomplish something.

You may think that I let my players and coaches have too much input. Well, I'm not smart enough to do all of this myself. I want some input. They pay me to make the final decisions, and I'm the guy that gets fired. I'm the first one they come to. If a player gets in trouble, they call me; they don't call the assistants. If a mother is really mad because her kid didn't play, it'll get back to me before it's over. So I make all those final decisions, but I'd like to have some help. We don't spend a lot of time just sitting around wasting time. We usually spend about 15 minutes in our staff meetings. When I worked for Barry Switzer, we only had two staff meetings a year. I asked him one day why we didn't meet more as a staff, and he said, "That's what I hired you for. You're supposed to coach the offense. Gary's supposed to coach the defense. Why do I need to meet with you all?" And he said, "I don't like problems; I like solutions. So if there's a problem, you all handle it, tell me how you did it, I'm going to tell you that you did a good job, and then we'll move on. That way, I can keep paying you." Coach Switzer had an amazing way of being tough.

Exercise great time management. How much time do you waste every day at school? At home? Yesterday we were sitting at a staff meeting, and our guys were talking about the NBA all-star basketball game. I don't have enough time to sit there and talk about that. Get in, be organized, get your job done, and get out. Don't waste other people's time. When you're in a staff meeting, make sure the people who need to be there are there. Don't make the defense sit there and listen to you talk offense, unless there is a purpose for that. Don't waste your time, and don't waste anyone else's. That sends a negative message, and if you're not careful with leadership, there can be some mixed messages in there. You say one thing but you do another.

It is difficult to turn a program around. You can take some shortcuts and get there. It would have been easy for me to cheat as a head football coach and turn the thing around more quickly than we did, but I don't know how you coach a player that you buy. When I ask him to do this or this, he tells me he has the NCAA's number. He will tell me, "I don't want to do this or this." When that happens, then I'm not coaching that team any more. I've lost them. And if that's the price of success, I'll go do something else. So if you're cutting corners, I'd advise you to quit. In 1993, somebody is going to find out. Also, if you're going to be successful, is success getting there by cheating? No! It's a shortcut. Success is doing things right, winning, overcoming, achieving, and goal-setting, so you really are not successful if you cheat to get there. You know what's so frustrating about it? You've got some guys in your league that are probably cutting corners and winning. But I tell you, they don't sleep as well at night. In the long run, they are not going to be successful, because they probably have more problems with it than you can imagine.

I don't know how many of you remember Vince Dooley's last game, when he coached in the Gator Bowl against Michigan State a few years ago. They interviewed him at halftime. They asked him what was the one thing he would tell a young football coach nowadays about success. His answer really stuck in my mind. He said, "You're going to have a crisis every day. And the guys that can take those crises and turn them into positive things are the leaders for tomorrow." When you get a crisis, turn it into a positive.

For example, the meeting we had this summer with our players—the list of 10 problems—I think turned out to be one of the reasons that we won 10 games this past season. I really questioned whether I wanted to meet with some of those kids or not, but they were good kids, and when they asked if they could visit with me, I had a decision to make. Was I going to be a weak guy and let some group of kids come in and tell me how to run this football team, or was I going to be tough and say, "Forget it. I'm running this football team. You all stay out of here." I decided to listen. That was the best thing I could have done. What they thought was a crisis turned out to be positive, because I said, "Men, you're right. We can do all of those. None of those are problems."

We let our players have a dance after the spring game. One young guy said, "Coach, I came in one day to see you about some extra tickets to our dance." We let them have four tickets for their buddies and for their dates, and they go crazy over it. They love it, and they control it. We haven't had a problem in five years. He said, "I was really bothered because they told me you weren't in, and I wanted to talk to you about getting one more ticket for a friend. As I was walking out, I saw you leaving the building and getting in your car." Well, I didn't remember it. I said, "Look, if I'm going to come to this meeting and sit here and talk to you about problems, I'm sure going to talk to you about whether I can give you an extra dance ticket or not. But what probably happened was that I went downstairs to get dressed, because I speak a lot, and they probably told you I wasn't in because I wasn't. I was downstairs getting dressed, ready to leave. You saw me leave." Men, that's how sensitive it is. This young guy thought I was hiding from him over something like a dance ticket, which is ridiculous. So we go back and communicate.

Another thing I challenge you to do is be very aware of your image. This is a time when people are very negative about football. Some people would like to see the football coach get in trouble.

Also, I challenge you to be positive. Be positive with your young people, be positive with your staff, be a positive influence in your school. I know you don't like faculty meetings. Go shock them. Give them some input! If the coaches sit up front in the faculty meeting, they'll think you're wanting something. Be a positive influence in your school, and you'll be amazed at what might happen. Some teachers might even think that football is okay! A little sugar and a little honey will get you a whole lot further than trying to be rude and tough.

We were standing out in the middle of the field, when Georgia Tech had not won any games and we had not won any games. Bobby Ross ended up winning the national championship at Georgia Tech later. Now he's the head coach of the San Diego Chargers. I'm standing there, and it's the first year neither of us had won a ballgame. Bobby coached a football team that had the longest losing streak in ACC football history: 16 games. He is a great person and a great football coach. I asked Bobby, "How are you so positive? When do you give in? When do you quit? How do you keep your head up?" He says, "It's really simple with me, Mack. It's hard, but your players are involved in losing all the time. At home, their parents are probably griping. They go to class, and the students either don't care because they're losing or are making fun of them. The fans who they are around quit coming to the games, and the ones that come boo them and are critical. The media articles are always bad when you're losing, so the assistant coaches and the players and the fans and the students and the media look to me to see whether I think things are headed in the right direction or not. So I'm the barometer that people are looking at to see if this thing is making progress, or is it about over? If I'm not positive, the assistant coaches try to get jobs, they leave, and they're down. The players give up and quit, so I've got to be positive." And men, that is leadership.

Chapter 5

COACHES' RIGHTS AND RESPONSIBILITIES

Candace Calhoun
Attorney at Law
1996

There was a time when coaches gave little thought to the risk of lawsuits brought on by others. That has changed. Any person who coaches, whether at the little league, high school, college, or professional level, must contemplate the potential for lawsuits. To protect themselves, it is mandatory that coaches become familiar with the answers to questions, including the following:

- How far can coaches go when disciplining athletes?
- Can a coach be held personally liable if he suspects an athlete is using drugs and/or alcohol and does nothing about it?
- What is a coach's legal responsibility if a player becomes injured?

In a recent New Jersey case, for example, a jury rendered a $6.5-million verdict against the head high school football coach (40 percent negligent, $2.6 million) and his assistant interior line coach (60 percent negligent, $3.9 million) for failing to provide sufficient training, conditioning, equipment, and supervision to one of their athletes.

ELEMENTS NECESSARY TO WIN A LAWSUIT:

Whether a coach fulfilled the duty to use reasonable care in protecting the athlete

A coach has a duty to:

- Warn
- Instruct

- Properly supervise
- Hire and train competent coaches and staff
- Provide adequate and safe equipment
- Reasonably match participants

A coach has a duty of care to warn an athlete in regards to particular hazards of the sport, instruct the athlete in regards to proper tackling techniques, etc., properly supervise the player during practice and actual games, hire and train competent coaches and staff, provide adequate and safe equipment, and reasonably match participants. If a coach does not fulfill any of the above required duties, he will have been deemed to have "breached" his duty.

If a coach breaches his duty, the coach will be perceived by a jury as being negligent. The question then is whether the breach of a duty (negligence) on the part of the coach is the proximate cause of the injury. The issue of causation is a fact question which is decided by a jury on a case-by-case basis. In order for a player to win a lawsuit, the player must suffer some damages. In the sports field, damages are usually easy to prove as most players are injured quite frequently when engaging in sports activities.

The duties of a coach is the issue that gets you into a lawsuit. You have a duty to warn, particularly in the use of a football helmet, of the possibility of head injuries. You have a duty to teach proper tackling techniques. There are cases now where the head football coach may be held liable for the actions of assistants and student teachers. There is a trend today to require coaches to have certification before they can coach. As of this time eight states require some type of certification. This means they have to take certain courses including legal liability.

The question is asked about certification. Is a physical education instructor who is a coach more certified than a nonphysical education coach?

The answer is that it would depend on the sport involved. Most sports do not have the danger that you have in football. In a lot of states, if you have a teaching certificate you are qualified to be a coach. If the state does not have a certification, then all the person needs is the teaching certificate.

What are the things you can do to prevent a lawsuit? You can meet with your assistant coaches and players and go over some of the liability issues. If you or any of your assistants have any questions about any tackling procedure, you should review them. In one case a coach went over the risk involved in playing football and in tackling. He asked the players if they had any questions about tackling and if they had any questions about the dangers of a football helmet. On the other hand, if a coach talks too much about this the kids are not going to come out for football.

There is nothing wrong with giving out a written document that says this is what we are going to discuss in the meeting regarding tackling techniques. You can have the assistants and players sign their copy and turn one back in to the head coach. When you get to court the best thing you can have is documentation. You always have the "We said, he said." If you have something in writing that they understood the information, then that will be strong in court.

A suit should show four elements before it goes to court. You must show the 1) duty, 2) breach of duty, 3) causation, and 4) damages. If a player comes up and tells you he has a finger hurt but you cannot find the injury, you do not have a lawsuit. He must show damages. You have to show all of the elements above. That player would have to show injury and present testimony that he saw a doctor and that he has damages to have a lawsuit.

Liability in actual cases has been imposed when a coach:

1) Plays an injured player.
2) Fails to direct the movement of an injured player properly.
3) Fails to acquire proper medical attention for heat stroke.
4) Fails to instruct adequately on safe techniques for participation.
5) Fails to provide proper equipment.
6) Fails to warn the player of the danger inherent in the use of a football helmet.

There are a lot of cases to talk about in the area of equipment. If you have old equipment and cannot afford new equipment and do not have a big budget, it is your responsibility to bring it to the attention of the principal. Put it in writing that you do not have updated equipment and need to replace it. That helps you as far as liability because you have it on record that you brought this information to the attention of the authorities.

The other thing relates to the sales reps. If you buy equipment that is not up to standards, you are liable. When those sales reps come in I would ask them what the difference in the equipment is, because they are the experts in their equipment. Compare other brands and ask questions about safety of their equipment compared with competing brands. Keep documentation regarding their equipment.

PRACTICAL TIPS TO AVOID COSTLY LAWSUITS

Every athlete must be prepared before he enters the playing field. It is the responsibility of the coach to make sure the athletes under his charge are ready and prepared to participate.

Instruct athletes in a competent and thorough manner regarding safety procedures and methods to minimize injuries.

■ Provide safe and effective protective equipment as well as proper maintenance of equipment. Here are some things a coach can do:

- —Have equipment brochures and equipment specifications available to show a conscious effort to choose the best available equipment.

- —Read, understand, and file the fitting and maintenance instructions.

- —Follow manufacturer's recommended instructions for periodic instructions and maintenance.

- —Document the inspection, maintenance, and proper repair of equipment. (For example, there must be a maintenance history for each helmet.)

- —Check the equipment before the contest and develop an expertise in the sales so the equipment available is state-of-the-art.

■ Do not force an athlete to participate when that athlete has already sustained an injury. There is a risk that further participation will only aggravate the original injury.

■ Provide medical assistance when and if it is necessary.

■ Provide proper instruction and explain to the athlete how to play the game.

■ Show due concern the athlete is in proper physical condition.

■ Warn the football player of the danger inherent in the use of the football helmet. Specifically warn the student about the potential danger of using one's head as a battering ram in football. A student should also be warned that using the head in this way could cause permanent paralysis. To be on the safe side, the coach should reinforce this warning orally, if possible, prior to each game or practice.

- Correct an athlete's faulty maneuver during plays.
- Reasonably match participants.
- Constantly and consistently supervise players.
- Establish proper post-injury procedures.

RECENT TRENDS

There has been a recent movement to demand a basic minimum in education and experience before one could become certified as a coach. Also, coaches would be obliged to take a certain amount of continuing education to maintain certification. Recent trends include the following:

- Approximately half of the physical education departments in colleges provide professional training in coaching.
- A minor in coaching includes the following courses: medical aspects of coaching, problems with coaching, theory and techniques of coaching, physical conditioning, first aid, legal aspects of coaching, and kinesiological and physiological foundations.
- At least eight states have minimum requirements for coaches in addition to teacher certification. This trend seems certain to continue.
- Movement to require a minimum of three-to-five years of experience in coaching as a prerequisite to a head coaching position.

A possibility exists that coaches will be responsible for the actions of their assistants, whether paid or voluntary, whether student or nonstudent, and whether or not they were student teaching.

In professional sports, a participant can now sue another participant. For example, the reckless intentional striking of an opposing player during a professional football game may be cause for a lawsuit. (Players assume risk of unintentional injuries but will not assume risk of injuries that are intentionally inflicted or result from a disregard to safety.)

Athletes are starting to sue coaches for invasion of privacy and intentional infliction of emotional distress.

DRUG TESTING OF HIGH SCHOOL ATHLETES

Recent trends have developed in drug testing of high school athletes.

A high school consent program of drug testing of prospective athletes is legal (participation in high school athletics is a privilege rather than a right).

NCAA-college level—consent to drug testing is a prerequisite to eligibility.

If a coach suspects drug and/or alcohol use on the part of an athlete, the negligence standard applies.

Depending on how affluent the school district is, there is a trend to have random drug testing of high school athletes. There is a case in New Jersey where a student challenged this testing. He said it was an invasion of his privacy. The student said he did not use drugs; and therefore, it was an invasion of his privacy. The first thing the court said was this: Playing football is not a right. You do not have a right to play football; it is a privilege. Secondly, depending on the method in which the school does the testing, it may not invade the individual's privacy. If it is done in a very sensitive manner, and the results are not publicized, and you do it at random, it is perfectly legal. I want everyone to understand that these statements are very general. In law there is never 100 percent yes or no. Does that mean you can go back to your school and test for drugs? NO! You can do a urinalysis, but you cannot do a blood test. The reason you cannot take the blood test is because it invades a person's privacy.

An example of this is a young girl who was given a blood test. Now, not only does the blood test tell you what drugs a person is taking, it also tells all of the other things a person is taking. The young girl was taking birth control pills. She said it was an invasion of her privacy to take the blood test. The court agreed with her. You have to be careful of making blanket statements about drug testing.

If you do suspect a person is using drugs, and if you should have knowledge of this, you cannot get up in court and say, "I did not know anything about it." If you see someone on the field that you suspect is on drugs, and other players have come to you and told you that person was on drugs, then according to the courts today you knew he was on drugs. You should have known that person was on drugs if they show all of the symptoms and others have informed you they suspect that person is on drugs.

The reason football players can be tested for drugs and band members can't is this. Some football players may ask, "Why should I be tested if they are not going to test the band members?" The reason is because the courts consider that football affects public safety. They do not want someone on the football field who is in a contact sport that may not be sure what he is doing. They do not want someone on the field who may get hurt or may hurt another person.

What happens if the football coach has discipline rules relating to the team that are more stringent than the school rules? For example, the school suspends a player for using alcohol for three days, but the football coach suspends him for the rest of the football season?

The first thing to do from a legal standpoint is this. As a coach, when you have that first team meeting to start the season, you should get the student athletes to sign forms stating they will conform to the rules set forth by the football staff. Also, have them take the form home and have their parents sign it. As a football coach you have a right to determine the rules for the football team. Coaches have different rules and standards for their athletes. You want to tell your players up front where they stand on all issues. You have a right to set your rules, particularly about players on drugs, as far as protecting that person and the rest of the team. You have a right to set a reasonable rule in that area. As long as the players have notice of your rules and regulations, you have that right.

You want to put on the form: "I understand, and I have read, and fully understand, the rules for the football program." Have them sign this form and keep it on file. No kid or parent can say he or she did not know the rules. If a player does not want to sign this, then you may not want that kid playing football.

There are other coaches who are not that strict. That is not to say they are not concerned about drugs. They may give the players one chance or they may give them a warning. If the student athlete is on drugs you need to do something about it.

In a 1991 case in a New York high school, two former football players were awarded $25,000 each in a case against the coach and the school district as a result of the coach's practice of hitting players in the head and body with a tackling dummy during practice. If you have used that drill, drop it. The courts have said you are negligent if you do such action.

One thing I want to make clear regarding students signing forms: You *cannot* get students to sign a waiver that prevents them from filing a suit against the coaching staff or school for negligence. You can't walk into the locker room and say, "Here is a waiver. I want all of you to sign it. You know that football is a dangerous sport. If you get injured we do not want you to sue us. Sign the waiver." You cannot do that. The other reason for this is because most of the kids you are dealing with are minors under the age of 18. Legally they cannot sign a contract. The law states that a person must be 18 or over to understand what he or she is signing. They cannot sign away their rights.

The last area I want to get into relates to an area we all are interested in today.

WHAT ARE A COACH'S RIGHTS, IF ANY, IN RETAINING HIS JOB?

Some of you may be interested in this. A lot of the coaches have employment contracts. Most of these contracts are for one year. That is the first thing you want to look at. What does the contract state? At times the least important thing about the contract is the language. What is the intent of the party in the contract? If you are fired after one year, and they do not renew your contract, what are your arguments? One is to say that you have what we call an "Implied-In-Fact Contract." If the school board or the principal tells you that you are doing a great job and they hope you will be the coach for the next several years, etc., you have an argument, even though they did not give you a written contract that implied you had a continuing position. In the state of West Virginia that holds up more than it does in some other states.

If you do not have a contract at the end of the year, you are what we call "Employee-At-Will." If you are working without a contract you can be fired for no reason. They do not need a reason to fire that person. They do not have a contract, so they can be fired. They can fire you for any reason except for a legal reason. A legal reason is when a person says, "You fired me because I am a woman." Then you have a legal reason. "You fired me because I am black." You have racial discrimination. "You fired me because of my age." You have age discrimination. The big thing today is disability discrimination lawsuits. The big areas are mental stress and back problems. People are suing for mental stress and back problems and winning their cases.

EDITOR'S NOTE

Candace K. Calhoun presently practices law in the Pittsburgh area. She has represented both high schools and colleges in all phases of litigation. She has been published nationally and has spoken at numerous seminars. Ms. Calhoun won several litigation honors in law school, including being selected to the National Order of Barristers and the National Moot Court Team, as well as winning the George C. Baker Cup for excellence in advocacy. She studied litigation in Paris, France, and received a Certificate in European Legal Studies. Ms. Calhoun has a strong background in education and the sport of football. Her father is retired Coach Jerry Calhoun, who was the winningest coach in the state of Maryland. She is a former high school English teacher, college administrator, and tennis coach.

Chapter 6

ORGANIZATION AND MOTIVATION

Bill Curry
University of Kentucky
1992

I want to talk with you about Organization and Motivation. I hope what I have to say will have meaning to you and I hope it will help you with your program. Obviously, I have no idea about your program or where you are coming from, or what your problems are, or what you difficulties are in specifics. What I am going to say should apply in a broad-brush manner that would cover all levels of the game. I have never coached high school football. I regret that. I think everyone should be required to coach at the high school level for a number of years before moving on to the next level. I did spend 14 years in the NFL as a player and a coach. I have been in college football coaching for 14 years as well. Ironically, I have been a head coach for 12 years. My career happened backward. When I should have been painting lockers and lining off the fields, and coaching the JV's and learning what real football coaches learn, and then being a graduate assistant, I was playing center in the NFL for all of those years. I mean this sincerely. Possibly the worst preparation to be a head coach at the college level is to play in the NFL for a long time. Do you know what I learned in the NFL for 10 years? I learned how to survive as an offensive center. That was all I had time to do.

As a result of my NFL career I did not learn many of the things that some of you have learned coming up through the ranks. I got thrown into the jobs that I took before I was ready because of circumstances that I will not bore you with. So, I have had to go at the game in a different way. This has forced me to survive on learning Structure and Organization and Motivation. I have had to hire great instructors of technique in the areas that I have been so deficient in. Hopefully, I will learn a little more each year. I want you to understand that it is on this basis that I bring whatever I bring to you. But it is also on the basis of the fact that I have been at a lot of places. I have been blessed with some great jobs. I have been blessed with some of the hardest jobs ever, I think. I am sure you think this about your job as well. This is very interesting and this is where I want to start.

Yes, we are in a tough business. But I think we are in the most important business in America today. This is not because it is necessarily the most moral, or that it ought to be the most important. It probably should not be the most important. The church should be the most important. The family should be emphasized next, and then education after that. But this is not the way our society is today. What is emphasized the most in the minds of male teenage America today is sports. Because of this you and I have an awesome responsibility, like it or not. I am not here to preach morals to you, or to preach a religious sermon to you. I want you to understand that if you are a football coach in today's world, your players are going to use you for a role model. You do not have the privilege, in my opinion, of abdicating that responsibility. The way you act and behave, by what comes out of your mouth, and what is in your mind, is going to have an awesome impact on these young people that look up to coaches. They are going to be just like us. That just scares the daylights out of me. That is because there is a lot about me that is not worthy of emulation, but I can at least be working to make it better.

When I see a team on the field on Saturday afternoon, as in my case with blue shirts on with a helmet with a big blue K on the side, this is what I must feel. If that team is poorly prepared and is getting its tail kicked, that is for only one reason. It is because the head coach has prepared them that way. So understand that is where I am coming from. I do not think there is any excuse for not doing a great job at what you do. I do not think there is any excuse for the record that the University of Kentucky had last year. NONE!

Part of what I am talking about is fighting back from adversity. It seems that I have been given my share of those opportunities. So I am very serious about the things I say to you this morning. I am serious about our profession today. I did not come here to preach to you or to chastise you. I came here to encourage you to hang in there and to improve yourself. Keep loving these young people because they may not get love anywhere else in the way you will be able to love them and discipline them. You and I have a chance to create a generation of leadership that comes off the football field understanding what it means to pay the price for something in life. They need to learn to get up off their butts and stop complaining and to be a man. This is why I feel so strongly about this area.

I learned from my high school coach that it is better to be the aggressor on the football field. I owe my entire career to my high school coach for teaching me this in the ninth grade. I will never forget the day we had "Bill Curry" day and he taught me to be the aggressor when I had to tackle our fullback. I only weighed about 140 pounds, and the fullback weighed close to 200 pounds. It took me about 10 tries, but I finally realized that I had better be the aggressor or I was not going to survive the game of football. I will never forget what my high school coach did for me. He would not give up on me.

The other side of that story is about Joe Paterno. I heard this from him in a lecture series. I love Joe Paterno and believe in him. He is one of our role models in our business. He does things the right way. He told this story and I got his permission to repeat it. It is the other side of the coin. We can hurt people with the aggressive side of our game. They recruited a great player at Penn State and wanted to make a tight end out of him. They took him out the first day in pads and decided to see how good he was. They decided to do a gut check with this new kid. This is the kid's first day with the varsity. They lined the kid up against the best defensive player on the varsity. The veteran just destroyed the kid time after time. That day was the last time they ever saw the young man again. He left the team. They destroyed him because they did not give him enough time to get ready for such an experience. Joe said he always thinks about this situation when they sit down and start talking about having a gut check. They are much more concerned how they do it today. They talked the situation over the next day and concluded that the same results would have happened against any other player they line up against that veteran. That veteran turned out to be an All-American, and no one on the team could block him. No one could block him in the NFL for 13 years. That player was David Robinson. All I am saying is this. You do not have to be gentle, but I do think you have to be careful the way you handle these young people.

I am standing here today because of a series of coaches helped me survive. Starting with my dad, who was hard-nose, but did not know anything about football, and through my high school coach, they started me learning some important lessons that have sustained me through every difficult trial on and off the field. I saw this same lesson repeated in a book I once read by Victor Frankl. This lesson helped share my football philosophy. The name of the book is *Man's Search for Meaning*. It is a very short book and it is simple language. If you will read it and pay attention to it, it will change your life. It may even help you win games. He spent six years in a German concentration camp and survived. The thing I got out of the book was this: No circumstance, or situation, or no problems of life, can remove your fundamental opportunity as a human being, which is this. It is to choose how you will respond. What we are teaching young kids is how to respond. If a kid gets knocked on his butt he gets to choose if he is going to get up or not. He can choose how quick he gets up, and when he gets up he gets to choose if he is going to wipe his nose and complain, or he can get up and run to the football. Dr. Frankl said the people that survived the worst circumstances in the history of mankind were the people that made the right decisions with the choices that they had. This was true even when their options were so limited. The next time you feel sorry for yourself when you lose your best football player, think of this situation. Don't feel sorry for yourself. You get to choose how you are going to respond. That is all you deserve.

I got to thinking about speaking to a group of coaches today and I thought about the rule changes and the budget cuts going on today. I started thinking about what I could say to you that would help you in these areas. I came up with 10 Principles to get a job and to keep a job in coaching. This is what I have accumulated over my entire career. These are things that I believe in very strongly. I have two categories. The first category is what we will call CW and that will stand for Conventional Wisdom. Conventional Wisdom is the prevailing thought of the day or of the time. The next category is called CD, which stands for Certain Death. We are going to do a Thesis-Antithesis. I am going to tell you what I am hearing around the country. Then I will tell you the truth as I see it. You can take this or leave it for what it is worth. You can be sure that Conventional Wisdom is *Certain Death*.

CW = CONVENTIONAL WISDOM

T = TRUTH

CW 1. The more people you know the better off you are. Know a lot of people. "If I could just meet people like Joe Paterno and Tom Landry."

T = The truth is you had better know your players. You better know what is on their minds. Have time for all of the players and for the little guys in our profession.

CW 2. "If I can just get *that* job over there I will be happy." "THAT JOB" looks so easy and I would be so happy and I will do a great job.

T = The truth is you will be less happy with the next "That Job" because you will be looking at the next "That Job." I see this all of the time in young coaches. They are never happy and before you know it they are out of the business.

CW 3. The person that got "That Great Job" has it easier than I do. He is on easy street.

T = The truth is he has problems that you never dreamed of. His job may be twice as hard as your job is. You should be getting the picture now. The grass is greener on the other side until you get there. I am trying to share some of my experiences with you so some of you will know how to approach getting another job.

CW 4. My situation is so tough and so demanding it is not my responsibility. "It is not my fault."

T = The truth is you are totally responsible. The instant you say you are not responsible it goes downhill. When you say that about your area of responsibility, your unit loses it effectiveness. The instant you say "I am totally responsible" you get better. Never look at the other guy and think he has it easier than you do. I can stand up and say words. I can stand up and make you sad, make you laugh, and make you happy. I can put you to sleep. I have proved that many times. How can you be enthusiastic with a group of youngsters if you don't believe in them. Don't think that they do not know. You have to be totally responsible.

CW 5. My attitude will improve when I get *what I deserve.* I will do better when I am rewarded.

T = The truth is this. Your attitude is not going to change until you change it. You are responsible for how you think. You can't blame it on your mother. "Mother liked my brother better." That will not work. Maybe your mother should have liked your brother better. Looking back at my situation I am just happy that my mother kept me at all. You can't go through life as a someone that has been abused in life. Your attitude will change when you change it.

CW 6. My personal habits are very poor because I have to do something to relieve all of this pressure. "I drank all of that whiskey and I stayed out late at night to relieve the pressure." I am not talking about my habits; I am just talking about some of the excuses that I hear. People use the excuse they have to do bad things to relieve their pressure.

T = Your personal habits are a reflection of what you are. Your habits are your habits. If you have some habits that you need to change then you need to change them.

CW 7. The person that got *that great job* got it because he was *politically wired.*

T = The truth is that he got the job because he performed. He got his teams to play hard. You did not get the job because you did not get your teams to play hard. That is the truth most of the time; not always, but most of the time.

CW 8. Coaches will say, "My players are sorry people. We have no leadership." Is that what you say after a 3 and 8 season? When I accepted this speaking engagement I expected a great season. I wanted to come here and tell you how we turned it around and went to a bowl game. What do you do as coaches? Do you stand around the bar and tell people how sorry your team is? Conventional Wisdom will tell you to get around other coaches and complain about how sorry your players are.

T = The truth is the players reflect you. This is true. It may be hard, but it is true. You may be saying I am moralizing. But I will tell you, if you keep on criticizing your players you will keep on losing. This is a promise. They are a reflection of us. Kentucky was 3-8 because we had a 3-8 head coach last year. There is one thing that I can do something about and that is the head coach if we are going to improve. I said this a year ago. I think I did improve, but obviously not enough. We were 4-7 the year before. I have another chance to accept responsibility for what happened on my team.

CW 9. Conventional Wisdom says the only way I can get hired by the head coach is to harass him until he gives me a job. Or, I will harass the school board until I get hired. I will stay on the phone 18 hours a day trying to get the next job instead of coaching my team. The fact is that is certain death.

T = The truth is that you get the next job by being great at the job that you do now. Just be great. If you want to get a job, you get your players to play so great that everyone wants to hire you. That is the way you get a job.

CW 10. I do not owe my employer anything. "He is lucky to have me working for him." He owes me! Conventional Wisdom will tell you that is certain death.

T = The truth is we should be happy we have a job. *Go the second mile*. Just think in this mode for a few minutes. What if you did twice as much as your boss demanded of you. What if you were doing extra work every time you had an opportunity?

I had a kid that I was ready to kick off our team. I had every reason to kick the kid off the team. One of our assistant coaches asked me to let him work with the kid every morning during the off-season. He asked me not to kick the kid off the team until he had a chance to work with him. I asked the coach what he could do with the kid that I couldn't? This is what he told me: He said, "I am going to teach him about what he could be. I am going to find the good things within him. Sometimes we will get up early in the morning and study and sometimes we will do conditioning work. If he is lackadaisical I will work his butt off. The main thing is that this player will know that I care about him."

That kid is going to start for us next year. He did a great job for us last season because he has a coach that loved him too much to let a head coach give up on him. He did not advocate his responsibility; he went the second mile. I do not know how he got the player to get up so early in the off-season. He gave that extra effort. Do you know what I did with that assistant coach? I made him my offensive coordinator the first chance I got. If that coach would go the extra mile, then I needed to get him more involved in what we were doing.

These points were prepared for this lecture. This is what I have learned from the people I have rubbed shoulders with through the years on how to get a job and how to keep a job in this business. If you do not adhere to these principles you will have a lot of difficulty in this profession.

It is like the blind man that had a Seeing Eye dog. The dog was not very brilliant. The dog was leading the man down the street one day. A bystander was watching the blind man and the dog. He became horrified when the dog led the blind man right out in the middle of the street when the walk-light was red. He walked right out in the middle of the street with cars coming down the street. The cars started honking their horns and slamming on their brakes. They ran into each other to keep from hitting the blind man. Somehow the blind man made it to the other side of the street. When he got there he reached in his pocket and pulled out a dog biscuit. He started looking for the dog's mouth. He gave the dog the biscuit. The bystander came over to the blind man and made this comment. "Sir, why would you give that dog a biscuit after he took you out in the middle of the street with all of that traffic? This dog almost cost you your life and you are rewarding him with the biscuit." The blind man said, "I am not trying to reward the dog. I am trying to locate the dogs head so I can kick him in the rear end." I feel a lot of the coaches in our profession are using all of the opposite principles that work.

Coaches can be racists or bigots. A coach can be bigoted against some kid that may be too round in the middle. He may not run the way you like for him to run. You probably play favorites. Don't think they do not know it. If you ever promise a player that he will play in a game, and you do not get him in the game, he will never forgive you. Bill McCartney says this the best. I have learned this the hard way. Don't promise players something if you are not going to keep your word.

Before we can talk about putting together an offense or defense for a football team I feel we must take a look at ourselves. We should really take stock of ourselves. My father was in the retail sporting goods business for 23 years and in wholesale sporting goods for many years, and every year his companies took inventory. Once a year we sit down and take a look at our program. We want to make sure all of the phases of our program are better than the year before. It all starts with me. Is the head coach pointing fingers and making excuses or is he going to let the other people be the best they can be?

I think it is very important to have your own offense. Many times we try to adopt what others are running. We may see a play in our first game and the next week we try to use that play. We may not know enough about the play to make it work. Have your offense and stick by it. Make sure it works and stick by it.

We like to list our objectives on offense. Our first objective is to *win*. There is nothing wrong with winning. Coach Vince Lombardi got criticized by saying that *winning is not the most important thing, it is the only thing*. What he meant by that was this: *Winning is not the most important thing, but the will to win is*. He was right. That is the way he lived and that was the way he died. There is nothing wrong with wanting to win. We should want to win every single game, every single day, every single drill. We want to win. The objective for out offense is to win. We want our offense to think that way.

Our second objective on offense is this: with today's rules in football, at all levels, the best kind of an offense to have is an offense with *balance*. I am talking about an offense with balance as far as productive is concerned. We want as many yards rushing as passing over the total season. We do not mean this for each game. Over the long haul we want as many first downs rushing as we have passing. We will run the ball from any point on the field, and we will pass the ball from any place on the field. I have learned these things from the many people I have worked with and studied over the years. The reason I feel a balanced offense is best is because of the rules that we have today. We can get away with using the hands-on offense today. High school rules are coming that way as well. I see a lot of film and I know what I see. I do not know what your rules say, but the rules *are* what is being called. I do not think you should teach your players to hold. There are coaches that feel you can hold every play because the officials are only going to make two or three holding calls per game. We are not talking about this. We do not want to break the rules today. With this in mind, I feel you can develop a balanced offense. I know there are some teams that just run the ball or just pass it most of the time. They do one or the other and still win. I know this. This is our kind of thinking.

The next objective is this: We want to punish our opponent. We want to wear our opponents down in every way that we can. We want to demoralize our opponents. We want to do this during the play. We do not want to do this by getting up and dancing, and not by playing for the crowd. We want to be enthusiastic and celebrate each good play briefly, and then get back in the huddle and get ready to go again. We want to get ready to make another great play.

How do you do this? You do it by doing several things. You do it by controlling the *time of possession*. Joe Gibbs talks about this in his book, that I recommend. The thing Joe talks about more than anything else is time of possession. You watch his teams and you will see that they just grind the ball out. Then when you least expect it, they go up on top and hit you with a big play. Time of possession wears the opponent's defense out and keeps your defense off the field. You do this by hitting your opponent over and over. You have to win the last round. You do it by being in better condition than your opponent. These are things that you can promise your team. You can promise your players that they will be in better shape than their opponents. That is the gift you can give the players. Let them know this when you run them so much they can't stand up. You have to be careful that you do not overdo it and overwork the players.

In our first game at Kentucky against Central Michigan I made this mistake. By the middle of the first quarter my face was drained and pale. The head coach was so stupid because we were drained. We were in great shape, and we won that game in the fourth quarter because of a gut check by some of our seniors. But conditioning requires intelligence.

You build an attitude on your team that you can't be stopped. You have to instill that attitude into those players. You can't wait for a great player to come along to get that done. You have to have a system the players can build on.

We have to have a *method* to get all of this done. It is a year-round thing today. It may not be the way it should be, but in football today that is the way it is. Our quarterback is a great baseball player. I promised him he could play baseball this spring. I am going to keep my word. He still throws the football every day. He has to under-stand this. You have to have some gym rats. Don't kid yourself into thinking you are going to have a great offense if you do not have people that are willing to work at it.

We have a great basketball team at Kentucky. We like to shoot the three-point shots at Kentucky. We have a great coach. He makes them shoot the three-point shot and play defense like crazy. If we could get our football team to play defense like the basketball team does we would be great. I heard one of our big basketball players on TV the other day, and he shoots the three-point shot very well. They asked him how he could shoot the three-point shot so well for a 6'9" player. He explained that he had to shoot 300 of those three-point shots in practice every day, all year. I can assure you he is a good shot.

Coach Rick Petino learned his basic approach from Coach Vince Lombardi. I am trying to learn from Coach Petino. I am amazed that I am trying to learn from a coach that learned his basic approach from a coach that I played for. It is a singleness of purpose that keeps us going. So, our methods involve a year-round program.

In our off-season we have divided our program into phases. Phase One is our Strength Program. It includes our Quickness and Power areas. This part of the program is done in the weight room. We want to make the players bigger, stronger, and faster. We want to make sure there are no steroids involved. The tests are so expensive, and you may not be able to test for steroids. If a player gains 40 pounds in two months there is something wrong and you will need to check that player out. He could screw up his life. Check him out because he is just trying to please the coaches.

Phase Two consists of nine sessions. We do it when the whole team can be there. It is divided up into three distinct sections. If you will ask any Georgia Tech, Alabama, or Kentucky football player if he likes the program under Coach Curry you will find all of them had one thing in common: they all hated Phase Two. Phase Two is a gut check. We set it up so it does not eat up all of their time. It lasts one hour and five minutes. There are three segments in the program. We get three-minute breaks in between the three segments. We give them Form Running, Endurance, and Quickness Drills. It is just plain agility drills during the Quickness Drills. Endurance may be running the stadium steps or running around the track. We cannot do any football-related drills.

Phase Two is also a period that we call One Fail – All Fail. When they start to get tired you will find your leaders. If they quit in the drills they will quit in the fourth quarter. When we are doing a drill and someone is not doing the drill the way we think he should, you stop the drill and point out the player that is not getting the job done. Everyone must start the drill over and do it again. Everyone has to pay for that one player who is not getting the job done. What happens when 10 players do their job in a game and one players lets down in a game? That one man is a member of the team and if one man fails the team fails. It teaches them it is a team game.

The skill work is fundamental. This is very important. You have to work on skills every day. We just do not have enough hours to work on all of the skills. People used to tell me that Homer Smith was crazy for laying down between our center's legs to check the center-to-quarterback exchange. He did that before the Auburn game. I told them that Homer was not crazy, because he was doing what he was told to do. I never saw anyone do that before Homer did it. However, I have been seeing Daryl Dickey, our quarterbacks coach doing it recently now that I have been mentioning it frequently to him. He lies down between each center's legs and watches to see where the ball hits the quarterback's hands. Doesn't that make sense? How hard is that? You get dirt on the back of your shirt. People think you are nuts, but it works. There is no magic. You have to have players who are willing to work.

Practice is the next phase of our program. Develop a real offense. We run on and off the practice field. We run in and out of the huddle. What does that do? First, it makes the players think you are crazy because they watch the pros and they do not do that. I do not care what the pros do. I was with the pros for a while. A lot of the things the pros do could be done better. We run on and off the field because it saves you some time. You have more time to call your plays. You get to the line quickly, and get to the ball and get down quickly. Why do we want to do this? So our quarterback can break the huddle with 18 seconds on the 25-second clock. We want the quarterback to be able to see what is going on with the defense. The quarterback's today are so sharp they can actually run the game if you will only give them a chance. If you will train them in small doses you can train them to call the right plays. He can't do this if the line is not down and set to go. Give yourself some time to run your offense and you will be amazed at how well you can do. Also, it bugs the opponent to get demoralized with a team that runs to the ball all of the time. That is the way I was taught to play the game.

It is the same way with conditioning in practice. Some days we will run so hard in practice I will not make them run at the end of practice. That will fire them up. The next day they will work even harder. You have to work with them and make sure they know how it works.

We run a drill every day that we call Formations. We feel it helps to be able to run a lot of different formations. We do a few simple things from a lot of formations. If you have watched the Redskins and 49ers you have seen that they do a few things a lot of times. They do a lot more with the passing game, but you and I do not have to do that. We run a lot of formations so the defense is always thinking. If you will practice it five minutes a day it is amazing how much you can get accomplished simply by going through formations every single day. We put our players on the sideline. We work on this with our offense and defense during this drill. When we call for a certain formation we want the right personnel in the game. The defense has to get their personnel in the game to be ready to play. We do it for about five minutes each day.

We also work on field position during this drill. We will put the ball on our 1-yard line. We tell them we must have a first down in this situation. We tell them we want to get one first down so we do not have to punt from the end zone. The defense will tell their people that we have to stuff the offense here to make them punt from the end zone. The next time we may put the ball on the 20-yard line going in. We tell the offense we want a touchdown. The defense wants to stop the offense with a field goal or less. We make them think *field position* in this Formation Period. It is a very helpful drill for us.

Every day we *walk through* what we are going to do in practice. I got this from Homer Smith. This takes 20 minutes from our practice schedule. We do not have all of the time in the world. We take 20 minutes and walk through everything we are going to do that day. We go through the cadence and walk rapidly to the right place. We want them to finish in perfect blocking position. We want them to end up in a perfect *fit*. The whistle blows and we get back to the huddle quickly. It is amazing how many reps you can get in for this 20-minute session. If we have our huddle down where we want it we may not huddle. We may just run from the line of scrimmage. Homer Smith used to tell them that he wanted 100 reps in this session. It is almost like going full speed if you just make them take their proper routes and go to the right blocking angles. Then when you get into your regular practice you can run full speed and not waste time. We use Walk Through very efficiently.

Repetition – Repetition – Repetition. We believe in the religion of *repetition*. That is what we believe in. We have not had enough reps to be a good football team at this point, but it is only a matter of time. It is the coach's responsibility to get them ready. I am on the coaches constantly to get quality repetitions. The definition of a football coach is this. It is a person that can take a problem on the practice field and make it disappear on the game tape or film. A football coach is a person that can take these principles and take a player on the field with a problem and make it disappear from the film. If you are not doing that you are not coaching. If a player comes back out to practice and has the same problems he had the day before, then all you are doing is reinforcing the bad habits. You can practice bad habits and you can get good at those bad habits. It takes times to break bad habits.

Don't let an assistant coach sit in a meeting and tell you that a certain player can't play. Do you know why I do not like to hear that? Because I know there were coaches like that on every team that I ever played on. I know they would tell the head coach that Bill Curry could not play for them. I would find this out later. I do not want our assistants to think this way. If we get in a staff meeting and we have a new coach that I have not had a chance to discuss this point with, it is funny when that new coach says something to that effect. "I will tell you one thing, that Jones kid cannot play for us." All of the other assistant coaches just about fall on the floor laughing when he says that. They know what I am going to say. "If he can't play, then why do I have you here as an assistant coach? If he can't play, then I do not need you. I do not need you to tell me he can't play. I need you to teach him to play."

I was coaching for Pepper Rogers in my first coaching job. I was at Georgia Tech and we were running the Wishbone. I was coaching the offensive line. We were watching the practice film. We had a big, lazy offensive tackle. Pepper asked me why the weakside tackle did not sprint across the field to the safety like he is supposed to do. I said, "Coach, I have told him 50 times to sprint to the safety." He reached up and turned off the projector. He said, "You did what?" I said, "I told that tackle 50 times to sprint to the safety." He said, "That is really wonderful, Bill. Do you know what that means? It means I can fire all of the assistants because it would mean all you would have to do would be to tell the players what we want done and they would do it. Coach Curry, I want someone that will coach that tackle and make him sprint across the field to that safety. *Do you understand me*?" I said, "I think I have it coach." That afternoon I got that big tackle by the face mask, and we sprinted together to that safety. We did it over and over until he got it right. Later he played in the Pro Bowl eight times as an offensive lineman. It was not because of me. It was because we had a head coach who would not let me shortchange that player.

The quality of repetitions is very important. You must make it happen on the practice field. It means everything in coaching.

Finally, I want to talk about our Practice Organization. This is a very basic practice plan. Many of you may be doing this with your organizations now. It really makes sense to the players. Today the players expect you to explain things. Those of you that are about my age can remember when we used to run out on the field and the coaches would tell us to *do it*. We would try to *do it*. Today they will ask you why you are doing something. If you will tell them before you go on the field why you are doing things they will do them. They are 10 times more dedicated than we were. You really do have to explain things to them today. This is how we have or practice sessions set up.

ORGANIZATION

1. Individual

2. Group

3. Hookups

4. Combos

5. Team (11-on-11)

This is how we work it. The first session is our Individual work. That means the position coach is going to work with the different positions he is coaching. He is going to work on stance, starts, and head placements, etc. They are going to work on the techniques for each individual position.

The second area is Group work. This is defined as groups of individuals from the same side of the ball. The right side of the line will be working on the plays to the right side. The other side will work on the plays to its side of the line.

Next, we go to Hookups. Now we work on Offense against the Defense. We will work 1's on 1's most of the time. We put into practice the individual and group techniques in this session. Every day we have some type of Hookup drill with 1's on 1's.

Next we go to our Combo Drills. This is combinations of offensive units going against defensive units. This means Pass Shell, and our 7-on-7 Drill. At the same time we are having our Inside Run Period, with Best-on-Best. I know high schools may not have the numbers to do this, but you can use other players instead of Best-on-Best.

Our last session is our Team Drills. If you are going to have a balanced offense we have found that we need more 11-on-11 work. We put more of our time in this type of work than we used to. Everything is done according to situations. Don Shula did a great job with us on a First Down Drill. If you play for Don Shula you learn that you must have 4 yards on first Down. On defense you learn that you have to stop the offense for less than four yards on first-down plays. We went at it full speed all the time in that drill.

Obviously we work on short-yardage situations in the field. Then we work on Goal Line. Then we work on Passing Inside the 20-Yard Line. If you are a passing team you know it is tough to score when you get down to the 20-yard line because the field is much smaller. That is what happens to teams that have 500 yards passing but only score 10 points. They lose because they have not practiced when they get down close to the goal line.

Next we work on third-down drills. We work on third-and-3; third-and-4; third-and-5; third-and-6. Now the players can start thinking in situations. They can get in a game and know they have to make the plays on certain situations. That is our basic organization.

I learned this point from a high school coach last year. We went down to Florida last November and played a great Florida team. We played a great game, but we did not win. But we were the team that was fresh in the fourth quarter. I think it was because of something I learned from a high school coach last year. We tried to sell this idea with our team.

"Men, we know that you hate to do all of those gassers and sprints and running around the field. We know that is not a part of football. But, if you will run in practice and run between drills the way we urge you to do, it will pay off later in the season." Several times during the season I would call the players up at the end of practice and tell them they did not have to do conditioning because they had run enough during practice. I had to stay after them sometimes during practice but they were in great shape. No one believed me until we got into the game against Florida in early November and it was hot. We found out we were the fresh team. That was exciting for me to see because I know it works. You might experiment with it. You know your job. I am going to do a better job with this in spring practice. I want to sell the idea that we are going to work on conditioning during practice so they do not have to line up and run 50 gassers after practice.

Chapter 7

THE INTANGIBLES
IN FOOTBALL

Pat Dye
Auburn University
1992

I want to talk about a few things that you probably already know about. You old-timers for sure will know this, and if you young coaches don't know it you need to know it. These are some important aspects about the game itself and about some things that are important in winning. If you are coaching football you have an unbelievable responsibility. You can give your kids something worthwhile. You have an opportunity to influence more lives in the right direction than any group in the country. This is because of the nature of the game of football. You can do more with them than their parents can do with them. You can teach them lessons that they can't learn in Sunday school, in the classroom, or anywhere except out on the football field in the dirt, sweat, and blood. The lessons they learn in football will stay with them the rest of their lives. For everyone I can teach at Auburn, the high schools can teach at a younger age. Not everyone has the opportunity to go to college and play football.

I am in coaching today because of my high school coach. I love the game of football. Football has always been easy for me. I grew up on a farm working 16 hours a day, from daylight to dark. When I started practicing football for only two or three hours day it was much easier. I feel like I have been running downhill all my life in football. Football came easy for me, but football does not come easy for all young men. Not everyone has the opportunity to grow up on a farm with a dairy or grow up in a working environment sacrifices must be made and a disciplined life is necessary every day. Those are the things that you can instill to a youngster that are very important to him and will be important to him as long as he lives.

Coaching makes a difference in football. Coaching makes a bigger difference in football than any other sport because you are dealing with more individuals than any other sport. No other sport has 11 people working together. Baseball has nine men and basketball only has five men working at one time. Football has 11 players working at once that you must get synchronized and playing on the same page. They have to have the same heartbeat and they must have the same common goal. Everything being equal, the best-coached football team is going to win. Players make a difference. Coach Don James of Washington did a great job this year. I am sure the first thing he would tell you is the fact that he had some great players this year. The same is true at Auburn. I feel that I have done my best coaching job when I have had my best players. We were named Coach of the Year in 1983. In other years we won the SEC championship. We did a good job of coaching because we did not screw them up too bad. Those were the years that I got the most recognition. We had more players make All-American and All-Conference then. Players do make a difference. But, everything being equal, coaching also makes a difference. To me, a well-coached football team is one that wins all of the games it is supposed to win and some of the games it is not supposed to win.

I have a list of things that I call *The Intangibles in Football*. You can call them anything you want to call them. They do not have anything to do with X's and O's, but they have a tremendous impact on the game of football. I am not a coach that thinks you have to have an All-American at every position to have a winning team. I am a coach that feels that you must have impact players, but you have to surround those impact players with winners.

THE INTANGIBLES

1. **CONDITIONING**—You can put this before everything else. One of the other coaches talked about his year around program. If you do not have a year around program and you can't have one, you are handicapped. If you can have one and you don't have it, then you are handicapping your football team. A year around program where you are upgrading the players physical ability is a must if you expect to win championships and if you expect to compete at the top level. You must develop *speed, quickness,* and *strength*. You need a year-round conditioning program. You can think about any phase of football and conditioning as important. If you are a better-conditioned football player you are going to be able to play harder and longer. If we are not the best-conditioned football team

in the country at Auburn, whose fault is that? That is my fault. If you are not the best-conditioned football team in the country, then that is your fault. Because you do not have the organization, and because you do not have it instilled in them and your program, then it is your fault. You have to sell them on the fact that they can be the best-conditioned team in the country. This is very important and don't underestimate this point. Be able to play harder at the end of the game than your opponent. Most close games are decided in the last two or three minutes of the game. You do not want to be out there with tired people.

2. **FUNDAMENTALS: BLOCKING AND TACKLING**—We may have great players but we still must teach blocking and tackling. I can recall the first scrimmages we had at Auburn. Someone had called me up and asked me how many tackles we missed per game. We had never counted them before. We missed so many in this one particular scrimmage that we went back and counted them. We missed 33 tackles. The next day we tackled for 1½ hours. We had every tackling drill you can imagine, and we made up a few. We became a better tackling team. A missed tackle is 5 yards, or 3 yards, or 10 yards, or a touchdown run. The same is true with blocking. The fundamentals the game is played with are important. If you do not come off in a stance, and explode off the ball and use proper technique, then you are not using the right fundamentals. If you do not teach him how to take all of his physical ability and use it to win on each play, then you have handicapped him. Don't assume a young man is going to come out there and know how to block and tackle. You have to teach them how to block and tackle. You have to spend time with them every day on this. It has to be a way of life that you are going to be the best fundamental football team on the field when you go out there and play.

Catching and Passing the football are important. They go back to fundamentals. I have seen kids that could not catch a *cold*. But through hard work and concentration, they have learned to be good receivers.

3. **MISTAKES WILL GET YOU BEAT**—Earlier I heard a coach talking about simplicity. Anything you teach to your team that you can't get taught well enough to keep from making mistakes on, then you have too much. By mistakes we are talking about missed assignments. Missed assignments mean missing a block or getting beat deep. It is important to understand your assignments, responsibilities, and your role in that 11-man scheme.

The second part of this is *penalties*. That is a mistake. You teach them not to get penalties. You don't hit a man in the back and get a clipping penalty. Holding is a tough call. The way we play football today we are using our hands all of the time. However, we have a legal way to use our hands. If you get the hands outside the shoulders you are going to get called for holding. Offside— that is another mistake. If a player jumps offside it is because you have not disciplined him enough to stay on side. If the defense is vulnerable to jumping offside on an irregular snap count, then you have not taught them to stay on side. Don't jump his butt on Friday night about being stupid for jumping offside in the game. The stupid person is on the sideline, the one that did not teach him better. You have to work on it in practice enough so he is disciplined enough to keep from jumping offside. If you prepare him properly he is not going to jump offside on a long count.

4. **PLAY HARD**—There are a lot of people that do not understand what *playing hard* is all about. A lot of players think they play hard, but they don't. I am talking about playing the game with everything you have in your body from your head to your toes, with your heart and your soul, and your guts, and everything the Good Lord gave you to work with. *Intensity* and *contact*! I believe you can teach those things. They are going to play the way you coach them. Everyone wants to play well and everyone wants to play hard on Friday night. It is on Saturday afternoon for us. But there are no miracles out there. They are going to play on Friday night or Saturday afternoon the way they have been taught on Monday, Tuesday, Wednesday, and Thursday. The same thing is true for you at your level. We may have our players in a more confined environment, but you can still do the same thing. If you are organized and utilize your time and work on the intangibles of the game you can get them to play hard. It has nothing to do with X's and O's. It does not matter if you run the Wishbone, the Run-and-Shoot, or everything in between. It does not matter if you use a 4-3 or an 8-Man Front on defense. All of that is immaterial. These intangibles are important regardless of what you do scheme-wise.

5. **BUILD TEAM UNITY**—The first thing you are trying to do is to *build team unity* and *togetherness*. This is very difficult to do. It is very important. You have kids from all kinds of environments and all kind of backgrounds. You have kids that have problems at home. They have problems there and problems here. Their biggest concern may not be your football team. It may be a girlfriend. You have a wide range of individuals and it is your respon-

sibility to bring them together and form a team. You have to form a team that cares about each other and one that has compassion for one another, and one that is going to be unselfish. You are dealing with all kinds of people. You may be dealing with a kid that has a big ego, or with a quarterback that wants to throw the ball 50 times a game, or with a tailback that wants to carry the ball 50 times a game. You may be dealing with a wide receiver that wants to catch 10 passes a game, or with a defensive back that wants to play offense. It may be an offensive lineman that wants to play defense. There is a wide range of problems you are dealing with as far as these individuals are concerned as to what they feel about themselves. It is important for them as far as what they feel about themselves and what they want.

When you start to develop a team you have to find someway to get their minds off themselves. You have to get them to put the team number 1. You have to be able to do that some way. As long as you have a quarterback that is running the ball when he wants to be throwing it, you are not going to be effective. If you have a tailback that is upset because he is blocking instead of running the ball, then he is going to be less effective. If you can get everything centered and concentrated around the team concept you are going to be better off.

The way I have been effective in getting everything centered on the team concept has been by trying to make every individual on the team feel that he is special. They are special to us. From the managers, to the trainers, to the guys that are not getting to play, to all the other players, everyone is special to the success of our football team. It may be an offensive guard or a defensive linemen. He has his place on the team and it is damn important. If you do not think it is important you ask him, or you go ask his mother and father. It is an important position. Naturally, he does not play a glamorous position. But, to the success of the team, making a critical block is very important. He has to believe this.

I wish I could coach every football team where all of the players on the team had the personality of an offensive lineman. Do you know what? That offensive lineman does not care if you run the ball or pass it. He does not care who scores, how many times a back runs the ball, or who catches the passes. He does not care about any of that. He is interested in one statistic. He is interested if you *win* or *lose*. When I played football I also played with both hands on the ground. Some of you former backs may not understand what I mean by that. But a lot of my personality comes from this line of thinking. That offensive lineman will be the happiest player in the dressing room when you win. How many of you have been in the dressing room after a win and you look over in the corner and see a little wide receiver that did not catch a pass that is pouting? I will kick his rear end. I want them all together when we win. If that wide receiver had made the football team based on his blocking ability, then he would be happy, too. We have had to go through that at Auburn.

Two years ago we could not made a first down. We did not have a very explosive offense. This was in 1989. We beat LSU 10-6 and Florida 10-7. We were biting and scratching to have a football team. We couldn't do anything offensively. Finally I told all of them that they were going to make the team based on their blocking ability. I told them we were going to run the ball and that we were not going to pass it. We lined up against Mississippi State and we ran the ball, and then we would punt it. Then we would run it, and then we would punt it. Then we would run it, and then we would punt it. The score was 0-0 at the half. They booed us when we went off the field at the half. We came back out the second half and kept on running the ball. We won the game 14-0. But you would be surprised how those little wide receivers got after their blocks the next week. Do you know that those receivers started running their routes better and they started catching the ball better. We starting executing the passing game better. Our whole offense got better because they were not as concerned with all of the other things. They worked a little harder on some of the other things they had not been doing very well.

It all starts with you when you go on the practice field. It doesn't matter if you are the head coach or an assistant. You better have your act together when you go on the practice field. Don't you be thinking one thing and the head coach thinking something else. If you have one coach in charge of the running game you better have your act together. If there is any separation between that person and the head coach the players will know it. They will be the first ones to notice something like this. They will ask what they are doing on the field when the coaching staff does not know what it wants to do. If you have division on the coaching staff soon you will have division on the team. If you have one coach pulling his players one way and a second coach pulling his players another way, then you have chaos. If that happens you have an impossible situation. It is bad enough to get the players to play together as a team, but if you can't get the coaches to-gether, then it is totally impossible.

6. FIVE CRITICAL THINGS THAT DETERMINE IF YOU WIN OR LOSE—
The number 1 thing that determines if you win or not is *turn-overs*. When you turn the ball over on offense with a fumble, interception, fumbled kicks, or have a kick blocked, it is critical. Turnovers! Just as quick as a turnover will lose a game for you, it will win a game for you by creating those turnovers on defense. That is the number 1 priority at any practice at Auburn. We want to protect the football and to be sound in the kicking game. We want to be in position to prevent the turnovers. We want to pro-tect the football from an offensive standpoint. Defensively, it is just the opposite. We want to create turnovers and force the mistakes for the offense.

The second area is *penalties*. Again, it is a matter of discipline. If you have a player that is undisciplined he will get a penalty if you do not convince him that he can play hard but still not get those penalties. The key is *discipline*.

The third area is *critical downs*. Win the critical downs! What are the critical downs? Anytime there is a change of possession when the ball is to change hands is a critical down. I would not say that third-and-15 is a critical down unless the game is on the line. That may happen sometimes, but you do not necessarily try to make the first down then. You may want to run a Draw or Screen Pass. But you can punt the football and still play defense. However, when the game is on the line you'd better have a play that you have worked on in practice that will give you a chance to make a third down-and-15 to go. Still, the *possession down* is the third-and-4, third-and-5, and third-and-8. It may be third-and-1, 2, or 3. You may get in the fourth-down category—fourth-and-1, fourth-and-2, or fourth-and-3. Those are critical downs where there is going to be a change of possession of the football.

Fourth, *keep a drive alive* or *take the ball away from an opponent*. Any time you are on the goal line is critical. Win the critical downs. It is very important to *win the kicking game*. Win all phases of the kicking game.

The last thing is to *win the fourth quarter*. This goes back to what I said about conditioning. There is a way around conditioning if you want to take the easy way out. You may have the ability to take the easy way out if you have a lot of players. By that I mean in numbers where you can play a lot of players. That will help conditioning. If you have enough players to play fresh players all of the time they will perform much better. If a player never has to play tired he will perform much better than a tired player. If you do not have enough players to keep them fresh, then you'd better have a well-conditioned, mentally and physically tough football team.

Chapter 8

KEYS TO SUCCESS

Jim Herrmann
University of Michigan
1998

In 1995 and 1996 we had good defensive teams. We were good, not great. This past season we had a great defensive team. What was the difference? The difference was this: Everyone on that team who went out on the field and played for Michigan played for each other. They played for the guys on the sideline. Everyone played together. There was not one day before practice that I had to go into a meeting and rip someone for not performing and giving effort. *Not one day*. Those kids came ready every day and they knew what their roles were. We told them what their roles were and how important they were from the first man to the last one on the defense. We told them how important they were. How did we do that?

I was on a cruise last summer in Alaska. I sat down and started thinking of how I was going to pull this team together. I thought a long time and was getting nothing but blanks. I was getting worried because when the cruise was over we had to get back to work. All of a sudden I reached into my pocket to get the key to my room. My key didn't work. I got an idea. I thought I had something I could use.

I went back and got a sign made that was 12 feet by 12 feet. We had a special sign company come in and make the sign. We put the sign in the defensive room on the wall. It is a huge sign.

The kids reported for practice but I never said a word about the sign. We started our two-a-days and I could see the players looking at the sign. I could tell they were thinking, "Coach is nuts. What is he doing with a sign of a *big key* in here?" What does the key mean? Finally we got going into the two-a-day session where I wanted to get into a theme of what was going to bring our team together. Later that night I walked into the meeting room and talked about the KEY on the wall. "There are 12 notches on that key. The first 11 notches represented the starters who go on the field. It represented all of the players who start. Then there is a 12th notch on that key. The 12th notch is represented by the second-team players who are the back-ups, third-team players, and the coaches, and everyone in this room is represented by that notch."

Then I proceeded to talk to them about how that key was designed to unlock a lock. If one of those 12 notches on that key is shaved the key will not work. "You can stick the key into the lock and turn it but it will not open. *No one notch is bigger than the other notches.*" Charles Woodson's notch is no bigger than the notch of the last player on our team. They are all the same. So the kids had something to identify with. We spent some time talking about the key.

That same night I gave every kid an individual key. This is what it said on each key: "Michigan Defense—1997." It also had his number on it. If it was a coach it had his name on it. It had the GA's name on it. Every player on the defense got a key. Coach Carr came in the room with us that night and he got a key.

Next I proceeded to take a box and painted it with our name on it. I put a padlock on the box. I had a man make me keys that fit that padlock. I called a scout team player up front and asked him to put his key in the box. He put the key in the box and turned it and it clicked. The lock opened. I locked the box again and called Charles Woodson to come up with his key. He put the key in the lock and it unlocked the lock. I locked the box back and asked Coach Carr to come up. I said, "Lloyd, unlock the box." He put the key in the lock and unlocked the box.

After Lloyd sat down I said, "Men, what you have just witnessed is what this team is all about. My key is no more important than your key. If I don't carry my key I can't help the team unlock the box." At that point I took my key and opened the box. I took a red rose out of the box. It was beautiful. I said, "We talked about our goals in the spring. On January 1, 1998, at 4:30 EST we are going to be in Pasadena, California, playing in the Rose Bowl." That rose remained in that box and each day we would bring in a new one. I would see players go in the room and unlock the box just to smell the rose.

Men, the point I am making is this: You must have some direction. They have to understand their roles. Each player knew his role. They understood that we were all a part of the team and that we were all important. We knew we all had the same importance and that is when our team came together. If you watched the way they played you know they were together. I was proud to be their coach. I never had to ask them for effort. Never did I have players come to me about playing time. Never did I hear anyone complain about the stats they had compared to another team member. If you have those problems you are dead and you will never win.

That is the first thing we did last year. That is how we started the season. We all have keys in our pockets. We probably never think about them until we stick the key in the door at home. You turn the key and stick it back in your pocket and never think about it again until the next time. You would be sick if you put the key in the door and it didn't work. That is the way we are. That is the way football is. That is how you develop a team. That theme helped us through the season. Football season lasts a long time. Those kids get beat up and they get tired. You have to be able to get them to focus back in on what is important. Every once in a while I would get them to look at the key on the wall. "Look at your notch, look at it hard." They would focus back on why the meeting or practice was important. They could not let their teammates down. If they filed their notch off they could not go to the Rose Bowl. That was our goal. Those are some things I thought helped us last year.

If you ever have a chance, read the book *Into Thin Air*. It is a great book. It is about a team of climbers that went up Mt. Everest. They had to stop at each camp as they went up the mountain. If you have a season coming up where you know it is going to be tough, you need to read the book. See what they did, and how they focused in. Those are the little things that help you win.

Last year we sat down and asked what we wanted to accomplish in spring practice. As a staff we looked at all of our film in 1996 and asked these questions: What do we want to get out of the 15 days of practice? What do we need to concentrate on? What were the things we were good at and bad at? We wanted to find a couple things we needed to do to get to where we were this past year.

Everything we did had the date of January 1, 4:30 EST at the top of it. You can never remind the kids enough where we want to go. Everything we handed out to them had that date at the top. That would be the time in Michigan when we would go on the field at the Rose Bowl. We spelled it out for them.

We expected great effort. Sometimes you can leave that by itself and you do not say anything about it. That is the first thing we tell our kids. "I am not going to coach effort. That is not my job; that is your job. You can help us by giving great effort." After that we talked about the 15 practices we had for the spring.

We wanted to develop a dominance over each ball carrier through an assaulting gang-tackling defense. That is how we played last year. They had an attitude. In 1996 we had a good average on yards per run. But do you know what? The son of a gun came out the backend every time. We did not knock the ball carrier backward and knock his head back. That was the kind of attitude we wanted to gain in spring practice.

What did we do to get this attitude? We did Eye-opener Tackle Drill with the full team. We did not split up. We sat there and let their peers watch them tackle. It is amazing when your peers are watching you how much better you will perform. It is amazing to see the players who shy away in this drill. You can find out who your tough players are in this drill. That was the attitude that we wanted to develop this spring because that is what we needed to do to win.

I talked to an NFL coach the other day and this was the first thing on his board. It was this point and third-down efficiency. We wanted to average three turnovers per practice for a total of 45 in those 15 days. We had a huge board made up with practice 1 through 15. It has slashes all the way across so we could write in who forced a turnover in that practice. In practice we got nine turnovers. We had a total of nine strips, or interceptions, or fumble recoveries in that practice. Then we wrote down the kid's name and the drill it was in and we put it on a film. We saved the film and did not show it to them that first day. The next day we had eight turnovers. The offensive players were starting to get upset because we were not even tackling them. We were stripping the crap out of them. They were getting upset because their coaches were ripping them. It helped our team both offensively and defensively.

After the second practice we put all of the films of the two days of turnovers on for them. We put it to music. You know how meetings can drag on? You see the kids and their eyeballs are setting back in their head. We put the tape on and put their music on the tape. Now it was a challenge for everyone on defense because they want to get on the turnover film. We ended up with 72 turnovers in those 15 practices. That was an emphasis for us.

Did it carry over to the season? In some ways, yes. We had 24 interceptions. Where we were lacking was in fumble recoveries. We only had four recovered fumbles. That will be a point of emphasis for us next year. Why did we only have four recoveries? We looked at our game films and found 30 plays where our man was in position to make the tackle and did not break the arm down. The ball was sitting in the man's arm and we did not strip it out of his arm. If he gets the arm down the ball comes out and we get one. Who knows how many we could have had? This spring we are going to get after it in terms of ripping the arm and getting the quarterback's arm off his shoulder. We have to get better in that area. But you have to emphasize it to them and you have to give them a goal. They have to know the goal and they have to be able to see it.

Football is changing today. Everyone on the team must be able to communicate with each other. Everyone from the wide halfback to the short corner to the nose man has to communicate. It is imperative if you want to be a good football team. In 1996 we had a lot of this. "I did not get the call." Bull crap! Who is supposed to make the call? If he made the call, get the call. That is how you have to be with them. You must communicate. They must understand how important it is to communicate so that men can get lined up. You can't win if you can't line up. This year we only had a handful of those situations. Why? Because of communication. All it takes is for one man to make a mistake. So it is important to communicate.

We told them we were going to find the best 11 players on the defensive team. We told them we did not care what position they played, we were going to find the best 11 players and we were going to get them in the football game.

When we started our 1997 season we started with a group we called our "Speed Group." It consisted of three true freshmen. It consisted of one player who had just switched over from running back to play linebacker. It consisted of a redshirt freshman. They started that first game. They were a part of that first 11 with speed, and we promised them we would get them on the field. In that first game the most experienced player we had was 37 snaps. It was a part of our plan to find our best 11 players.

We nailed it down and gave them something to look at. That board stayed in that room right up front. I would refer to it every single day. It was the same that we did with our season goals. One of our goals was to hold our opponents to 30 percent or less on third-down efficiency. That was our goal. We ended up with 27.5 percent. That is what the offense averaged against us on third down. If you do that you are going to win. That was a goal and I emphasized it every day.

You have to show it to them and keep it in front of them. If you don't, how are they going to know what is important? No matter what part of the season you go into, you must show them the objectives. "What are we trying to do here? What are we doing as coaches for the players?"

Let me give you a couple of thoughts. These are the things I learned from Coach Bo Schembechler and Coach Bill McCartney and Coach Lloyd Carr and some of the people I have been involved with in terms of *what it takes to win a championship*.

This is what it takes to win a championship. I talked to Bo the other day. I told him I would be addressing a business group and then I would be talking with you. He said, "Jim, remind those coaches that blocking and tackling are the most important things they can coach." Here was a man who was one of the greatest coaches who ever lived and he is telling us it is a simple thing. Do you know what? It's true. Why were we a good tackling team? As a defense, every Tuesday and Wednesday we tackled as a team. We did not break off into groups and tackle. Every kid saw the other kids tackle. We do a string-out tackle drill and it was a competitive drill. They saw themselves tackle. It was the same down at the other end of the field. The offense saw their players block. We cannot forget how important blocking and tackling are in football. We get involved with X's and O's. We cannot forget about the basic fundamentals.

The next point is that *defense is knowing where your help is*. You can draw up a million things, but if the players do not know where the next player lines up and where his fit comes into play you are in trouble. You need to look at the word fit. "Where do I *fit* in this defense? Where do I belong?" If you do not understand that as a player, you may not understand it as a coach. You can draw all of this up on the chalkboard, but if he does not understand you need to look at what you are doing. The players must understand where they fit in the defense and where their help is coming from on the defense.

One of the best terms I have ever heard in helping on the ball and keep it inside is *inside and in front*. Keep the ball inside and in front of me, as long as they don't break a big one on us. We only gave up one big run, and that was a 54-yard touchdown against us. Why? Because the free safety did not keep the ball carrier in front of him. That was a key point.

Let me talk about Sudden Change. In 1996 we lost three games in the Big Ten. In all three of those games there was a sudden change in the fourth quarter and we let our opponents score. How are you going to win if you do that? You are not going to win. We went back and said *sudden change to us is going to be big*.

I had one of our assistant coaches come up and give us a lecture on sudden change. Coach Brady Hoke spoke to them during two-a-days. He did a fabulous job. He took this huge jar of water and filled it up halfway with water. He put the jar on the table. He started out his talk and after a few minutes he said, "Hey Charles, what is that on the table?" He responded, "A glass half empty." Brady went on and continued to talk. Later he said, "Glen Steel, what is that on the table." He responded with, "It is a glass that is half full." He went on to talk to the squad and at the end he concluded with this thought. "It is how you perceive what you see or what you are in." One player said it was a glass half-empty. One said it was a glass half full. How do you perceive sudden change?

This year we only gave up two touchdowns on sudden change. I have to qualify that because one of them came on the 1-yard line. We gave the ball up on the 1 and they went in and scored. We had two situations where they scored after a sudden change. All of the rest of them we stopped. To me, that is critical. Sometimes we just send our kids on the field and they are not into the game. We have to get jacked up about the situation.

To me, enthusiasm is what defensive football is all about. Our kids were jacked up. Our kids came together as a team right after the Colorado game. They understood that they were something special. We got after Colorado. From that point on the enthusiasm toward our defense took off and then it was fun to coach them. Every day those kids wanted to know what we had new for them. That is what we want. To me, enthusiasm is everything.

I really believe in the 3-way go. If you put the player on the field and you tell him his position is a 3 technique, and you tell him, "You line up in that position and you play against that big guard every single snap." If you do that you are screwing that kid. I would not want to play for you. It is not fun to get your butt kicked every play. We must have a way to defend ourselves. We want to give the players three ways to go. He can go inside one time and outside the next. Don't let them sit there in the 3 technique and get their butts kicked in. We can expect 70 snaps per game. We can't have them sit in one position for the whole game. You must design some things where you can give them a chance, and you must understand how that works within your defense. That is what we did. We gave our guys a 3-way go.

I am going to ask you a couple of questions. To me this is important. Let me talk about personnel. We have three down linemen that are for sure down linemen. We have a player that we call a "Twiner." If you are a coach you know what that means. He is big, but he is not big enough to play in the line. He is okay as a runner, but he is not much as a dropper. He plays one of our outside linebacker positions.

Our philosophy is that we are a 3-4 front. We have three down linemen and four linebackers. We have to help the "Twiner" by controlling where he drops. We do not want him on a wide receiver on the wide side of the field. Now, he is good over into the boundary or the inside hook position. We do some things to help him out a little. But that is our base defense.

In our coverage we try to come out and line up in a Two-Deep Secondary alignment. If you watch our film you will see how they move out and up and in to disguise some of the stunts that we are running. Sometimes a disguise is as good as a Three-Way Go, because you are showing one thing and then you are giving them something else.

I have a friend who sent me a book to read this summer. It is a real small book. The text is 2000 years old. The name of the book is *The Art of War*. A Chinese man wrote it. Some of you may have read the book. The main topic in the book is this: Show me an overload here, so the person you are at war with feels he can escape here. Then all of a sudden you ambush him because you are really strong where he thinks you are weak. That is the whole point of this book.

That is what we do in terms of that odd front. To look at an odd front the offense has no clue where we are going to be. You could be Fire Zoning from the weak side, or the strong side, or the middle. You could be playing a straight base defense. That quarterback asks his coach what is going on. The coach tells him one thing and all of a sudden something else happens. He gets hit upside the head. That is no fun.

So when you look at your defense and draw up all of your fronts you should consider how to disguise all of your coverages. Find out what complements each other in your defense. You need to look at that when you put your package together.

Chapter 9

BUILDING A PROGRAM

Johnny Majors
University of Pittsburgh
1994

When I get ready to play certain teams I like to find out if there is some special way to prepare for that team. When I was at Iowa State we were getting ready to play Notre Dame. I called Bud Wilkinson to ask him how to get ready to play such a team as Notre Dame. This is what Bud Wilkinson told me: "Johnny, this is the way I approach it, always. Every time you have a big rival like Notre Dame or anyone else that is considered a rival game, anyone that is worth anything is going to get cranked up to play hard. I always talked to our team as we approached each game as if we were playing team X. That means to play at your fullest potential each week and not overlook some team that you think you are going to beat." If we are playing a team that is 1-AA and we are a Division I school, the worst thing we can do is to overlook that team. Bud went on to say that he always got his teams to try to play up to their fullest potential regardless if he was playing Notre Dame, Nebraska, Iowa State, or Podunk U.

Another thing Bud talked to me about was very important and I will never forget it. He said, *"The Will to win is very important, but more important is the Will to Prepare to win."* Most coaches like to win or they would not be in the game. The big task is to prepare to win the game each week. They must learn to practice like they play. You play like you practice. If you practice with pride you will play with pride. If you practice with enthusiasm you will play with enthusiasm. Practice does not make perfect; *perfect practice makes perfect*. We have never had a perfect practice. We are human and we make mistakes. However, we have had some near-perfect practices with some of our better teams. They knew how to practice with tempo, and they knew how to practice techniques and fundamentals. We have coaches that strive for the perfect practice.

I have been very fortunate in having some good assistant coaches over the years. I have had some coaches that were not so good. I hope the coaches that have been in our program have learned something worthwhile. I know I have gotten a lot out of the assistant coaches that I have hired. When we do well I know why we have done well. I had a great mother and father. My father was a terrific coach. I played high school football for him. He was always my number 1 counselor. He died about 12 years ago. I called him about every major decision I ever made. He never bossed us around. We had five boys and one girl in our family. My mother was a schoolteacher. They never made much money but we had a great life. We drove an old car for a long time but we had plenty to eat and we had plenty of balls to play with. We had plenty of council, love, leadership, and discipline in our home. My father would always say this to the little guys, "You do not have to play to please me, but if you play I expect you to give it all that you have."

My father also taught me something that I never forgot. I told my first Iowa State team this. "We are going to play with Pride and Enthusiasm. We will never learn to lose. We will never give up. If we never learn to lose, we can learn to win." That means acting like a winner. It means practicing with enthusiasm and effort. It covers the way you act when you go away on road games; the way the players treat the people in the restaurants. I am proud of the fact that I have never had a team that was called down for its conduct in a restaurant or on an airplane. About 90 percent of the time when I get off the airplane the people will tell me that our group was about the nicest group they have served. I do not mind bragging about them. They say the same thing about us at the hotels that we stay in. I am sure in the 26 years of coaching I have had a few players that threw a mattress off a bed, or threw a pillow at someone. But they paid a price for that mistake. We want our players to play within the rules and to give an effort. We want them to act like winners and never learn to lose.

At the present time there are six individuals on the Dallas Cowboys that have been a part of our program. Jimmy Johnson was on our staff at Iowa State the first two years we were there. He was only 24 years old when I hired him. Another coach for me at Iowa State was Jackie Sherrill. He was on the first eight football teams I coached. He was at Iowa State and came to Pittsburgh with me. Jackie Sherrill in now at Mississippi State. Joe Avazanno is at Dallas. He was with me for 11 years. He is the special teams coach at Dallas. The Cowboys' personnel director is Larry Lacewell. He was my defensive coordinator at Iowa State in 1968. Bruce Mays was an administrative assistant at Pittsburgh and Tennessee. The head trainer for Dallas, Kevin O'Neil, was the assistant trainer at Pittsburgh and Tennessee before he went with Jimmy Johnson at Oklahoma State. Larry Campo is the defensive backfield coach. He was with us at Pittsburgh. Dave Wannstedt played for me at Pitt in my first year there and I hired him for his first coaching job. All of these people helped me get better as a coach. They were good, young coaches. I feel they learned a lot about enthusiasm and practice tempo. I learned about practice tempo from Frank Broyles of Arkansas as much as anyone. That is practicing like you plan to play: "The Will to Prepare."

You have to know yourself and you have to know everything about your opponents that you can know. You must have good scouting, and you must have good film sessions. I still say film, but it is video now. We are not allowed to scout next year. We have to do all of our scouting by video. You need to know every weakness and every strength of your opponents. What is the old saying? Run your best back behind your best blocker at the weakest opponent. Sometimes they may not have one as weak as your best player. Determine what the opponents do best and what you do best. You must make an intelligent and stable game plan. Larry Lacewell worked for Coach Bryant a few years. Larry said Coach Bryant always said, "You rush a poor passer, and against a great passer you pray." You have to know what you can do and what you can't do.

We have *Game Maxims* I learned as a player. When I played my first game at Tennessee as a sophomore my coach got up and wrote these points on the chalkboard.

GAME MAXIMS

1. The team making the fewest mistakes will win the game.

All things being equal, this is true. You do not want to beat yourself. You don't want to beat yourself by fumbling the ball away or by jumping offside. You can coach discipline and you can coach someone to hold on to the football.

2. Play for and make the breaks. When a break comes your way— SCORE.

Be opportunistic, tackle the ball, teach the team to pursue, and teach them to intercept the ball correctly. Don't do foolish things when backed up in your own territory. The shorter distance they have to go for a touchdown, the more they are going to score on you. If they have to go 80 yards they have to be a lot better than you are. This is true at all levels. A statistic that I like after the score is the turnover ratio. Other than being undefeated I would rather be the number 1 team in America in turnover ratios each year. That means we give up fewer fumbles and interceptions and we cause more fumbles and interceptions than our opponents. At the top level the teams that are in the championship games are the teams with the best turnover ratio. We want our players to put two hands on the football going in and coming out from the goal line. This is also true in critical game situations.

3. If at first the breaks go against you, don't let up. Put on more steam.

These points apply to the real world. You have to talk to your team about losing a fumble. You have to tell your defense to try to force the fumble at times. This comes from leadership, desire, guts, and it comes from the coaching staff instilling toughness in the players.

4. You win football games with people.

Players win football games on Saturday. Coaches prepare the people.

5. Players must have techniques and fundamentals to get the job done.

6. Press the kicking game for here is where the breaks are made.

7. Carry the fight to Allegheny Tech and keep it there the entire game.

(It is 60 minutes in college and 48 in high school.)

I first saw these maxims on a blackboard in 1954 at Tennessee. They stuck with me ever since. Our coach at Tennessee was fired after two years and Bowden Wyatt came in as head coach. He used the same maxims. They had gotten them from General Bob Neyland when they had played for him at Tennessee. I started coaching after graduating and went to Mississippi State and later I coached at the University of Arkansas. In my first game at Arkansas as a coach I walked in the dressing room just before the game and on the chalkboard were those same maxims. They were a little different, but basically they had the same message. Frank Broyles had gotten his maxims from Bobby Dodd at Georgia Tech. Coach Dodd had also played at Tennessee.

The more football has changed the more things don't change. We have seen the Veer, the I-Formation, Offset Backs, the Wishbone, Split Backs, the Wide Tackle Six, The 4-4 Defense, and the 4-3 Set.

There are certain things that never change. When I first started coaching I came across a book by Colonel Earl Blaik of West Point in 1959 or 1960. The name of the book was *You Have To Pay The Price*. It was a wonderful book. Colonel Blaik was taking about playing for Colonel Daily when he was at West Point. Colonel Daily's Game Maxims were very similar to what we just covered. They had been passed on from Army to Tennessee to Arkansas and to Georgia Tech. These points can be traced back to 1914 and 1915. We may use different formations and different sets but football is still very similar to what it was many years ago. I go over these maxims with our players before every game. We cover them just before we go out for the coin toss each game.

Most of us have problems when we take a new job. When you succeed a coaching legend it can lead to more problems. Many coaches do not make it when they follow a legend. Coach Tom Osborne took a tough job. Taking over after Bob Devaney was tough. If you take a job at a school like Iowa State, which was called the Coaches' Graveyard, it is tough to turn the program around. I have a tough job now at Pittsburgh. We were 3-9 last year. We have a lot of work to do. We are going to get some new facilities.

When I first talked about taking the Iowa State job I talked to Darrel Royal of Texas. I always had a lot of confidence in Darrel Royal. I had talked to Frank Broyles and I was not sure if I wanted the Iowa State job or not. Frank suggested I talk with Darrel. I went to see Darrel and we had breakfast together. We talked about some things in general and then I told him that Iowa State had a lot of problems up there. He said, "Johnny, if they did not have any problems they would not be looking for a head coach. There is no easy head coaching job."

I think I have been very fortunate in that I have been on both sides of the fence. I have been in some tough jobs. I was at Tennessee when we lost and when we won. We won all of our games my last year except the bowl game. My dad took a coaching job at Huntland, Tennessee. It was a small school with only 30 in the graduating class. There were only about 300 people in the town. We lived in the small town of Lynchburg, Tennessee, the home of Jack Daniels, whose spirits travel worldwide. I had a lot of experience in what to expect as far as winning and losing. I was the starting quarterback at the age of 14. I had a lot to do with the success of that team. We won 1 and lost 9. We lost the first game 58-0, and we lost the second game 75-6. We lost the third game 65-7, and we went downhill from that point on. My dad was driving back and forth 22 miles to coach that team. It was hard getting started. A year or two later we won 30 and lost 1. After me and my brothers left the team won 40 straight games. I learned the difference between winning and losing. I went from one extreme to the other. I played at Tennessee and was able to coach there. It was tough coaching at Mississippi State. It was great at Arkansas. I went to Iowa State and it was tough coaching there.

I know what it is to win and lose. I know what it is to coach at a school where it is tough to win, and I know what it is to coach at a top-notch program. I know that something will bring you back if you have the right stuff in you. As discouraging as it is to lose, you must instill in the players to never quit and never give up. How many times have you had a tough game where you got beat 40-0? I know I have had to face a squad that was looking to me for leadership after losing like that. Many times I have stood outside the locker room door and taken a deep breath before I went in to address the squad. I walk in and try to put on a good face. You tell them that we are going to make things better. We have to bounce back. You have to give it everything you have. We do not want any coach making excuses. There is a reason why you lose games and there are reasons why you do not get a recruit sometimes. We do not want coaches making excuses.

I have always talked to our staff about surrounding themselves with good people. This is true not only in hiring assistant coaches, but in other areas. Choose a good banker and a good minister. Surround yourself with a good wife. Surround yourself with good friends. I do not want any nay sayer around me. I do not want any negative people around me. I either change them or get away from them. A few years ago my wife went to Oxford, England, to study in the fall. We played four games and we lost three of them. One evening after practice I called up two of my good friends and invited them to go to dinner with me after practice. We went to a nice place to eat and got seated. We were not there five minutes until one of the friends said, "Boy, are they upset downtown about losing those three games." The other friend said, "Yea, I am hearing it too." I said, "TIMEOUT! I came to dinner with two friends to get away from all of that negative crap. I asked two friends to come to dinner with me so I could enjoy the evening. I do not want to hear any more of that crap or I will leave and you two can buy your own dinner."

I will not bring negative people in my home. I do not want negative writers in my home. Some of them that are that way are not worth a dime. Some of them are very professional. I am not going to bring any nay sayer into my confidence. If a writer has to write about a team and that team is not doing very well, I can understand that. He can be objective when he writes about a team that is not having a good year.

I read the paper from front to back. I like to keep up with what is going on in the world. I do more scanning now than I used to. If a writer is negative I will not read that person. If you do read those negative writers, they will effect how you feel about your staff, fellow coaches, players, teammates, and about yourself. If a friend that you trust tells you something, don't get mad. If you can't trust a good friend, who can you trust? Don't bring negative people around you unless they help you win.

I want people that are enthusiastic on the field. I do not want someone that is a buzz saw on the field, but does not do any teaching on the field. We like to teach on the board before we go to the practice field. Teach the players on the videos. I do not want a coach on the field that talks all of the time. I do not want a coach that talks all of the time and keeps the players standing around all day. I want coaches that coach on the run, correct, and move. I do not want a coach to stop every fourth play to talk to one player and hold all of the other players back. As the head coach I have that privilege. I am not going to talk very long. I am going to make my point and move on. We want to keep the flow going. We want them in and out of the huddle. We correct on the move. Don't be the one that slows the tempo down in practice. When we take a break we can talk to them. I can't stand slow, sloppy practices.

Say what you mean, and mean what you say. If you say 'break down,' say it with authority. I do not want cookies that repeat the same things over and over. Make sure the players understand what you want and see to it that they make the corrections. A good coach can make them line up with their heads up and in a good stance. We can teach them to step with the left foot or the right foot. We can teach them about angles and body position. We can teach them about leverage and rotation and pursuit. Say what we mean, and mean what we say.

If it is to be, it is up to me. I talked about football being a team game. For everything that has happened to me good, I know why it happened. I had good coaching, and I coached with some good people and for some good people. I have had some good players play for me. When we do badly, I can blame myself. I have been around some good people in my life.

I have to make a lot of talks. My wife still corrects me on some of the things I say. I make mistakes. If I interview a coach I want to interview his wife as well. I want to see her to see if she is the type person we need in our program. My dad liked to chew tobacco as well as anyone. He was a great man, and I loved him. Now, we have a rule in the NCAA that you can not smoke or chew tobacco on the practice or game field. I think it is a good rule. I do not want that around our program. I have had some great friends that liked to chew tobacco. There is a time and place for that. I do not want an assistant coach going to see a recruit with a chew of tobacco in his mouth.

I want a coach that has good manners. I do not want them to be chewing gum in the living room. I want them to dress nice. Some people say they do not look right in a coat and tie. I have never felt right going into see a recruit in a school or in his home without wearing a coat and tie. You need to look as neat as you can. I try to have good manners. I try to project what my mother taught me about table manners. I think it is important how we go about coaching our players on these things. We have to teach them more than just blocking and tackling. We have to teach them to live in the real world.

If we have a meeting at our place I want them to fill up the front of the room. I want that front row filled first. I do not want sunglasses and I do not allow hats. I want them to know how to act when they go into Westinghouse or US Steel to interview for a job. If they go see a high school principal I want them to say, "Yes, sir," and "No, sir."

The Winning Edge

I got most of this list from Frank Broyles. I think every good coach has a list of The Winning Edge. Football is a game of inches. It is the little things that get you beat. Inches make feet, and feet make yards, and yards make first downs, and first downs make touchdowns. Frank Broyles would talk to the team about The Winning Edge for 30 minutes five or six times a year. He would explain how teams could win football games with the points related to The Winning Edge. Now, I do not like long meetings. I use a little of The Winning Edge every chance I get. We talk to them throughout the day and in practice. We talk to them about how to practice. I place a lot of emphasis on The Winning Edge in the preseason every year. We cover how to drive the ball off the goal line, how people score more when they can back up a team on the goal line. We refer to these talks as The Winning Edge talks. They are the little things in football.

I have had a few young men on our staff that had bad English. I have advised them to go sit down with an English instructor and work out a program to help them improve. I did not let others know this was taking place. I did this to help them improve in their profession. One of my goals is to meet with a speech instructor and see if he can help me in organizing my speeches a little better. We can learn a lot by just talking to English teachers.

Two things are important in organization when building a program. You need to have a checklist for every coach on the staff. I have a list for all areas I am responsible for. I have a checklist for all of my personnel. My lists have grown through the years because of the mistakes I have made. I have certain things on my checklist that I want to get done by a certain time in the year. Let me give you an example.

I was coaching at Arkansas in 1964. I was in charge of the defensive secondary and the punt returners and the punters. Ken Hatfield was a senior safety for us at Arkansas. He led the nation in punt returns that year. He made All-American. We were playing Tulsa and we were in a tough game. We were ahead 14-9 at the time. Tulsa had fourth down and about 10 on its own 20-yard line. I looked out on the field and saw that Ken Hatfield was backed up deep to field the punt. I was trying to get him to come up and play his regular position in case Tulsa faked the punt and went for it on fourth down. They had no timeouts left. All we wanted was the football. He could not hear me, and he ended up lining up deep to take the punt. He caught the ball and we won the game. But I can tell you this. On Monday we corrected that situation. What we should have run was our Punt - Safe - Peter. We should have stayed in our regular pass defense and played our Cover 3. Monday I put that in my checklist. Everyone on our staff has a checklist.

If I have a change of coaches I will go over my checklist with the new coach that comes in. I will go over the checklist and go over the drills that I want him to use. If he has drills that he wants to use, I have him go over them with me. If I like them I will let him use them. I will listen to what he has to say. I like to go over all of those things to save time later on.

Another thing that we do that I think is helpful is to have an in-house calendar. We can go back and look at the things we did last year to make sure we do not forget something we need to do this year. We list everything that is important that we must do. It takes a lot of worry off your mind. It allows us to be more productive and allows more time to think.

We all know what Murphy's Law is: if something can go wrong it will. It doesn't catch up with you until it catches up with you. It is pretty simple.

It is important to cultivate and work with other people in your community. We all need booster clubs. Work with those people and get them involved in your program. Don't forget to say thanks to the custodians and the school cooks. Don't forget to thank your athletic director. The more I work the more I know that I do not want to be an athletic director. Everyone wants the athletic director to do something for him. It is the same way at our place. It is good to say thanks to the athletic director. I know all of the custodians' names at our place. I know the cooks by their first name. I know all of the student trainers at Pitt. We have about a half a dozen of them. It is important to say, "Thank you; I appreciate your help."

It is important to know who you answer to. I am going to listen to the athletic director. I may disagree with him, and I will go tell him if I do. But I am going to listen to what he has to say. I am going to do what he requests. Don't have too many people that you have to answer to. Don't allow boosters to do you too many favors where you are obligated to them.

I do not allow other people to talk about other coaches on my staff. If one of my friends criticizes one of my coaches in public I will put a stop to it. The most important thing you can have is loyalty. Loyalty and honesty are a must. If a coach will tell me he made a mistake and that he is sorry and does not try to cover up, I can accept that. Football is a great game and we must keep it that way. I am very fortunate to be a part of the game. Make the most of what you have, and make as few excuses as you can.

I will leave you with two axioms. We were 0-6 to start the season in 1988. I talked to my dad and another friend about it and this is what they advised me to do. *Make the least of what is gone, and the most of what is to come*. I went through a dramatic situation in the last year or so. I went through a job change and I have five heart bypasses. I am alive and I have a job. I have a tough job. I have a job that is exciting, and so do you.

The last axiom is this. *Failure will never overtake us if our desire to succeed is strong enough*. If you have the right desire, as I have, we will never be beaten down very long. We may have a couple of bad seasons, but if we have a desire to be better, we will play better. We will continue to coach with pride.

Chapter 10

BUILDING
A WINNING ATTITUDE

Glen Mason
University of Kansas
1993

When I get introduced, they always talk about how I have been a part of a turnaround process at the University of Kansas. Kansas was not very good when I got there. The first thing I talk about before I start talking about offense or defense is attitude. We all talk about attitude. I am amazed at the business meetings I go to because they talk about attitude first. If you can't conquer that in the turn-around process, it doesn't matter what you do on offense, defense, or in the kicking game. We have to talk about attitude. I thought I knew something about attitude when I was an assistant coach. Then I got an opportunity to be a head coach at Kent State University. That is where I really learned the meaning of the word *attitude.* I got the job at Kent State in some unusual circumstances. The head coach there had died suddenly during spring practice. There were only four days left in spring practice. I had to keep the coaching staff that was there. The program was in bad shape. The perception of the program was terrible.

Four days after I got the job at Kent State, I got a letter from a friend of mine who is the editor of *Scholastic Coach* in New York City. I had written some articles for him. When he wrote me, this is what he said: "Dear Coach Mason, Congratulations on your new position as head coach at Kent State University. However, why would you ever take that job? Didn't you realize they have lost 55 of their last 66 games?" Now, that made an impression on me. I wrote him back promptly. I said, "Dear Bruce, Thanks very much for you recent letter congratulating me on my new position at Kent State. Why in the hell didn't you tell me all of this before I took the damn job?"

111

I found myself in a situation that was not very good. But what do you do once you are in the job? We had four days of spring practice left. We only had 87 players. I did the only thing I could. I decided to interview every player before he went home for the summer break. I brought all of them in and had a long talk with them. I asked the normal questions in this situation. Before I would let them go, I asked each of them this one question: "Are you a good football player?" Not one of the 87 players answered yes! Most of them were shocked. I got answers like this: "I guess I am pretty good. I have never given it much thought." Not one said he was a great player. I had spent the past eight years at Ohio State, and every player at Ohio State thought he was great. They players who started thought they were great, and the ones who were not starting felt the coaches were giving them a hard time. You know how that goes. The players and confidence at Ohio State were never questioned. Not all the players who went to Ohio State were All-Americans or played for teams that were state champs. When they signed on at Ohio State, they thought they were great, regardless of the background they came from. This was reinforced by their parents, their coaches in high school, the people in their community, and their local media. Why? Because everyone has the perception that you have to be a great football player to play at Ohio State. When they get to Ohio State, the students and faculty have the same perception of the football players there. "You have to be a good player to get a scholarship at Ohio State." This is not true. Not all of the players at Ohio State are great; they all think they are great.

I can think about my own experience when I first started coaching. After you get out of college, you do not know a lot about coaching, but you want to give it a try. Before I got to Ohio State, I worked at a lot of small schools. I coached at Allegheny College, Ball State University, Iowa State University, and the University of Illinois. We did not win a game when I was at Illinois. I was not sure I was a good coach when I was at Illinois. I was just trying to keep my job. All of a sudden a great thing happened to me. The phone rang and it was Coach Woody Hayes. He said, "I have an opening on my staff. I need you to coach the outside linebackers. Are you interested in the job?" I said, "Coach, not only am I interested, I will take the job." I left immediately for Columbus. I got to Columbus in five hours. I went in, took off my Illinois coaching shirt, put on the Ohio State coaching shirt, and was ready to go. I started thinking to myself, "Boy, I must be a great coach." Do you know how I knew I was a great coach? Because everyone knew that Woody Hayes only hired great coaches. He hired me to coach the outside linebackers at Ohio State, and I had never coached defense before in my life. I was an offensive line coach.

I was at Ohio State for three days, and my phone started ringing like crazy. People from Texas, Florida, and New York wanted me to come talk at coaching clinics. They wanted me to come and talk at their clinic on outside linebacker play. Why did they want me to talk on outside linebacker play? Because they knew Woody Hayes only hired experts to coach at Ohio State. It was ridiculous, but it was a perception, and it affected my attitude and my confidence.

Now, I had talked to those 87 players at Kent State, and they did not think that they were any good. My first official function as head coach at Kent State was to go to the Mid-American Conference Kickoff Luncheon. It is a great event. It is the biggest event that they put on in that conference. They bring in all of the media and the coaches from all of the teams. They have a write-in vote to see who the media thinks will win the conference. Before the luncheon, they get each head coach to get up and tell all about his team for the upcoming season. I got up and I didn't say very much. How was I going to say much about 87 players who did not think that they were very good?

After we ate, the emcee got up to tell everyone how the voting had gone for the conference. He was very dramatic. "Picked to win the league by an all-time vote and picked to go undefeated: Miami, Ohio, with 5442 votes." Everyone clapped. I even clapped. If they had let me vote, I would have voted for them.

"Picked to finish second in the MAC is Toledo." They went right down the line; 3, 4, 5, 6, 7, and 8. I was not expecting to be picked first, but I was beginning to wonder how many teams were in the MAC. Finally, he got to the last team. "Ladies and gentlemen, another all-time record-setting vote. An all-time low, picked to finish last, and picked not to win a game, with only four votes: Kent State." Everyone clapped. I stood up and waved. I did not know what to do. I have a little pride. I was embarrassed. I could not wait to get back to that team.

I called a meeting the first day that we could meet for fall practice. The college president was sitting in the back of the room during our team meeting. I got up there and told them what had happened at the luncheon in Toledo. They laughed, and that really ticked me off. I told them the only thing wrong with this team was its attitude. "Our chances of finishing *first* are a lot better than finishing *last*." I finished with that statement, and I walked out. I went out the backdoor, and my president stopped me. He said, "Coach, how could you tell those kids that they have a chance to finish first in this league?" I replied, "I guess I got mad, and it just came out." I knew we had a problem. I kept thinking that I had gotten myself in a jam. I knew what the problem was. The main problem we had was the players' attitude. That is the one area that we have a chance to work on with our players.

What was going to be the solution? We had to come up with a plan to improve the team's attitude. Let me tell you how I approached the situation. All of a sudden, it hit me. I was always amazed at one certain group of people. We all went to high school with some of the guys who never made a big hit in school. They were good guys, but they all had the same traits. They would stand on the corner and smoke cigarettes. They could not pass English, they could not get a job, they could not get along with their parents, and they were doomed for failure. Then most of them would finally disappear for about 10 weeks. Do you know where most of them went? They would go to the Marine Corps. They would come back with those funny-looking flattop haircuts. All of a sudden, these guys would come back, and they were squared away, mentally tough, and disciplined. They were guys who knew what they were doing. It was unbelievable. Ten weeks earlier, they could not get along with their parents and they could not get a job. They couldn't do anything. They came back, and they were all squared away. What happened? They changed mentally in the Marines.

I have always been impressed by the Marine Corps approach. They are always loyal to the Marine Corps attitude. They take them to Parris Island and work the heck out of them. They work them so hard that they want to kill themselves and they want to quit. But finally, they make it in the Marine Corps. They feel good about what they have accomplished. We decided to have the Marine Corps approach at Kent State that year.

Our approach at Kent State would be based on three things. One, there would be no tourists allowed. We did not want anyone going along for a free ride. Each player had to pull his own weight. Two, I would set the tone by the strong. The strongest person on the team was going to set the tone. Everyone else was going to try to catch up with him. I did not want to try to find the average and pull the weak players up and the strong players down. The third point was that everyone was going to make a big time investment. I approached them with this idea: "If you really put something into it, you will fight hard to keep it."

We started our two-a-day practices. I wanted to be sure that our players knew what our approach was for the season. I am big on setting goals. They have proved that people who set goals achieve more than people who do not set goals. People who set goals and write them down achieve more than people who just set goals.

As soon as we got into fall practice, I got the team together and told them that we were going to set our goals for the season. I told them that we were going to set our goals and we were going to write them down. I told them that we had to be realistic. "You guys are going to set the goals, not the coaches. You have to achieve the goals, not the coaches. When you arrive at the goals, you come and get me, and we will discuss them." I walked out of the meeting and went outside to get a cup of coffee. Before I could drink the cup of coffee, one of the players came and got me and said they were ready for me. I said, "You are done already?" They assured me that they had set their goals and wanted me to go over them. I walked down the aisle, and I started thinking. "These kids are trying to impress me. They are going to say that they want to win the conference championship. I will have to bring them back down to earth." I sat down and waited for them to read me their goal for the season.

"Our goal for the 1986 season is to beat Toledo!" I said, "Beat Toledo? What kind of goal is that?" I just left Ohio State, and our goals every year were in this order: (1) win the Big 10 Championship, (2) beat Michigan, (3) win the Rose Bowl, (4) win the national championship. Beat Toledo?

Toledo was our first game of the year. I had 87 players, and their goal was to beat Toledo. I am thinking, "This can't be. What happens if we play Toledo and we lose? What are they going to say—'Coach, we will see you next year'? What happens if we beat Toledo? 'Hey Coach, we made it. We are done for the year.'" I asked them whether I could talk them into setting another goal. They insisted on keeping that as their goal.

We played Toledo, and the game came down to the last seconds. I sent in a freshman kicker to kick a field goal in the last minute to win the game for us. We beat Toledo! Our locker room was wild. I was jumping up and down. "We made our goal for the year." I was a big success. The players thought that I could do no wrong. The pressure was off. We went right on down the schedule and got down to the last game of the year, and we had a chance to win the conference championship. We had come that far with 87 players who did not think that they were very good.

The week of the final game, I got the team and everyone involved together to tell them how we were going to win the championship.

This is what I told the group. "We are playing Western Michigan University on Saturday. They have only won two games. Their head coach will be fired before or right after our game. The weather in Kalamazoo will be terrible. It will be about 22 degrees, and it will be windy and snowy. They will have nothing to play for, and we will have everything to play for. We will play very conservatively. We will let them make the first mistake. When they make the first mistake, we will capitalize on it and get ahead. They will have nothing to play for, and we will win the game going away. We will win the championship and go to a bowl game." That was a great plan, wasn't it? The only thing about it is that it did not work. They did not make the first mistake.

All year we were very aggressive and loose in our play. We got in position to play for the championship, and we decided to play conservatively. We got beat. I went in the locker room, and our players were crying. I started crying. Then I got them together and told them how I felt.

"When we started, you had a terrible attitude. We lost the championship today because another person had a terrible attitude. It was my terrible attitude. I learned a long time ago that when you want something, you do not wish for it, and you do not just hope for it. You have to take it. You don't play conservatively when you have a chance to win the championship. You have to take it. We did not do that today. I cost us that championship. I promise that if we ever play for another championship, we will not be conservative. We will start the game with a triple reverse pass."

We talk about attitudes and the decisions we have to make. I really believe that confidence is a choice. We have an opportunity to make a lot of choices in our life. Confidence is one of the things that we have a choice in making in our lifestyle. You are not born being confident. It is something you go through. We sell everyone on this idea. I have to sell myself on the idea at times. Why do I say this? How many times have you heard someone say something like this: "I knew we would play well this week because we always play well against South High School"? "I knew we would play well today because we always play well in the snow"? "I knew we would play well because we always play well when the coach eats his Cheerios before the game"? Then it can work conversely. "I knew we would not play well. We never play well against those guys." "I knew we would not play well. We never play well on the road." Those are mental things in the decisions that we make. There is a way that you can have confidence and have a choice in those things. We try to get a hold on those things in our program.

There is a psychological commitment that I want my players to make. There are three things they can do. When we ask them to do something, they can tell us three things:

1. I am going to do it.

2. I won't do it.

3. I will try it.

I tell our players that two of those things are acceptable, and one is not acceptable. When they are asked to do something, we want them to respond positively. If they say that they are going to try to do it, they are leaving themselves an out. You either *can* do it, or you *can't* do it. If you can't do it, then fine, we will do something else. If you say you are going to do it, then we are going to do it. "I'll try" will not work. We do not accept that.

There are five things that work in dealing with players. First, you have to believe in your game play or system. Whatever you choose to run on offense or defense, you have to believe in it. I hate to hear an assistant coach say something like, "Boy, they have a great offensive attack." They are trying to say that their attack is better than ours. Bull, we had a right to run their type of attack. We believe that our attack is the best way do it for us. The way we do things is best for us.

Second, we believe in positive self-talk. When you come to our place, you see signs all over the place. You will see signs such as this: "Beat the Little Man." I use to have a doll that I called the Little Man. I would hang him up all over the place. There were times when most of our players thought about quitting our program, when we were working hard to establish things the way we want them. I jog every day. I hate jogging, I really do. A sportswriter once said to me that he was sure that the jogging made me feel good and that it gave me a chance to do a lot of thinking while I was jogging. I assured him that there were only two things that I thought about when I jogged. One, I thought about stopping, and the other thing I thought about was quitting. If I finish the jog, I am successful. If I stop, I get beat. I talk to that Little Man all of the time. When I am jogging, I can feel the pain. I start talking to the Little Man. I start telling him that I can make it and that I feel good. The same thing happens to the players. They have to talk to the Little Man. They have to tell themselves that they do not feel the pain.

Third, the other side of that is positive visualization. We see ourselves being successful. We do not want them seeing themselves getting beat. You have to control this. You have to program them to see success. When that Little Man starts talking to them, it has to be positive feedback. They may have to talk to themselves out loud, but it must be positive.

Fourth, you have to trust your ability. You can't press. Just because you are playing the top team in the league, you can press too hard. You have to let things happen.

Last is prepare to be successful but be ready to adjust. Mistakes and setbacks. Don't coach the players *not* to fumble the football. You know they are going to fumble the ball. Everyone fumbles the ball at some time or another. How are you going about to prepare the players when they do fumble the ball? We know they are not going to be playing if they fumble too much. I am talking about the player who is your best back. Is this going to affect him mentally?

How many of you talk about sudden change? When you fumble on the 5-yard line, you expect your defense to go in the game and stop them right there. Our defensive men are just like firemen sitting around at the fire station. They are sitting there, waiting for the bell to ring to go put the fire out. They don't gripe and complain. They get out there to get the job done. They yell "Fire" and run like hell! They may not like to be in those situations, but you have to do them. How have you prepared them for those sudden situations? You have to work on those things mentally. I believe that you can affect a person's mental outlook on those things.

Let me give you another example of what I am trying to get across to you. When I first went to Kansas, we had a great pole vaulter. He was great. He was preparing for the Olympic team. His whole life was spent up to this time in preparing for the Olympics. He graduated and had one year to go before the Olympics. He was clearing 18'6" when he was a senior at Kansas. He got married after he graduated and got a part-time job. He was still preparing for the Olympics. He started getting ready for the international competition leading up to the Olympics, but suddenly he started having a problem. He could not vault as he did before. Now all he could clear was 17'1". Finally, he got to the point where they stopped inviting him to the international meets. He started thinking about quitting. He was ready to give it up.

Our sports psychologist got involved and started working with him. The pole vaulter went in one day and started telling the psychologist that he was ready to quit. "I am married now, and I have a part-time job. It is not really fair to my wife. I should quit the team because of the part-time job. I am not on the team anymore, but I am still out there using the track and using the coaches' time. I am taking away from the other track members. I am over the hill. I am too old; I have lost it. I am not going to make it."

The psychologist went to the track coach and asked him what the deal was. The coach said that he could not explain the situation. "He is bigger, faster, and stronger, and he has better technique than he has ever had. He is just not getting as high as he was before. It has to be mental, because it is not physical."

The psychologist went to see Scott and told him that he wanted him to do three things: "One, go to your wife and tell her exactly what you told me about quitting the part-time job. I want you to go talk to the coach and track team, and tell them what you told me about taking up their time and using the track. Then I want you to come back and see me."

He came back to see the psychologist. He asked him whether he talked to his wife. He said that he had, and this is what she said: "She did not care about the part-time job. She wants me to go to the Olympics more than I do. She doesn't care whether I work at all, because this is something I have worked for all of my life." What did the track coach and track team say? "They want me to go to the Olympics. They do not care whether I take up the track all day long." The psychologist told Scott that he wanted him to get his best friend to explain to him why he should not quit pole vaulting. He asked Scott who his best friend was. "My Dad is my best friend." "No, he is not your best friend." "My brother Jimmy." "No, no." "My wife?" "No!" "Who is my best friend? *You* are your best friend. You sit down and write yourself a letter and explain why you should not quit." That next day he came in with a seven-page letter explaining why he should not quit.

Let me tell you what happened. Later that week he jumped 18'1". The next week he went to the Melrose Games and took second place with a vault of 18'4". Soon he was up to 18'8" in Los Angeles. The next week he went to Europe and jumped 17'1" because he lost his pole. The next week, back in the U.S., he jumped 19'0". Nothing changed except the way he was talking to himself. The only thing that changed was what he was thinking about at the end of that pole. He heard the Little Man telling him to quit. "Part-time job; you are over the hill." He did not want to quit. He had to prepare himself to be successful, and he made the Olympics. That is an amazing story.

I have had an opportunity to coach at a lot of places. I had a chance to coach with Woody Hayes. That was really a great experience. I learned two lessons that are very applicable. Woody would talk to you about being a coach as well as a teacher. The big difference in our job as teachers is this: When our pupils go out and perform on Saturday, everyone knows who his coach is. If they do not perform well, they want to blame the coach. Those same kids go to English class, and if they do not perform well, they blame it on the students and not on the teachers. Accountability is different for coaches. We used to talk about being a teacher all the time with Woody. In teaching, it does not matter how many times we go over something with someone if he does not understand what we are trying to teach him. In teaching and coaching, the only thing we are interested in is the bottom line. The question is, did you get the job done or not? We measure results.

The other thing Woody talked about a lot related to communication. Our ability to communicate is important. We make the mistake at times of thinking, "Because I said it, they have it." Communication is a two-way street. It takes two to get the job done. If it is more important to you, you had better make sure that you communicate with your players, no matter what it takes.

We talk about perception. Perception has a lot to do with our jobs. I learned about perception. I had a great opportunity to take our team to a bowl game this year. We had not been to a bowl game in a long, long time. The bowl game was in Hawaii. We went over there. We were practicing one day, and a man came up to me and told me he really liked our team. He invited our team to his house for dinner. I told him we had a big team, and he told me he had a big house. We went over to his house, and it was beautiful. I went to the reception before the party and looked everything over. He had a swimming pool out back that was filled with sharks and alligators. When the team got there, he showed everyone around and finally came to the pool. He stopped at the pool to tell the team why he had sharks and alligators in the pool. He told them that he had worked hard all his life to gain his wealth. There were two things that he attributed his success. Those two things were courage and guts. He put the sharks and alligators in the pool to remind him of the courage and guts it took to get where he was today.

He told the team that he would give them any amount of money they wanted or anything they wanted if they could swim across the pool with the sharks and alligators. He would give them anything he had if they successfully swam across the pool. He had no more finished talking about the pool when we heard a big splash. We looked down, and there was our second-string quarterback in the pool. He started swimming for his life. He made it across the pool and climbed out unscratched. The man went over to him and congratulated him for his bravery, courage, and guts for swimming across the pool with the sharks and alligators in it. He asked him want he wanted. He said, "Heck, I just want to know *who pushed me in the pool.*" Perception is more important than facts.

I think you have to know where a coach is coming from. When I first got into coaching, I did not have a philosophy. There was not a place to start. When it got rough, there was no place to go back to. We have a philosophy at Kansas. It is very simple. It has to be something everyone can understand and everyone can tie into.

On offense, we talk about being able to attack a broad front. We can attack every hole on the offensive line. We can attack all of the passing zones, run and pass. We can attack all of the areas. We have a play to attack each of those areas. We are fundamental. We evaluate our players every day on stance and starts. We are going to take what the defense gives us. I do not want to be stubborn and say, "I will run this play regardless of what the defense does." We want to take ball control and use it for consistency. We want to tie that in with the ability to have the big plays. You must have the ability to have the big plays. If you have big-play talent, that is fine. If you don't have big-play talent, you had better find a way to get big plays into your offense. We want to utilize talent. If we have a person with great speed, we want to get the ball in his hands.

We want to eliminate mistakes. There are four areas where you can eliminate mistakes.

1. Missed assignments. That is teaching. It may be too complicated for them.

2. Turnovers. I am talking about quarterback decisions. Keep the turnovers to a minimum.

3. Lost yardage plays. Get the ball back to the line of scrimmage. Control the line of scrimmage.

4. Penalties. You have a chance to control penalties. There is no excuse for delay of game. That is a coaching mistake. Twelve men on the field; who do you blame for that? That is a coaching

mistake. What about false starts? That is lack of concentration or lack of conditioning. A late hit we can live with. That is aggressiveness. We are going to eliminate those things that we have a chance to coach and discipline.

We have to be flexible on offense. Our offense has to be able to adjust. We will see all kinds of defenses, and we have to be ready for them. Our offense must be great in short yardage and in short-yardage situations. You tell me a down that is more critical in a game than third-and-short. If it is third-and-1, get the yard or you will have to give up the ball. If you get it inside the 10-yard line, you have to come away with seven points because it is too hard to get it back down there. Last, but not least, we have to be physical. Whatever we do, we want to be physical. We play physical football at the University of Kansas.

Let me talk about defense. Take away what the offense does best. Every offense does something well. Take away something they do well. Do what you have to do to stop their best play. If you don't, you will see it all day. Just like offense, we will coach fundamentals. We are not skiing coaches. We have certain fundamentals for each position. We teach the fundamentals. We move on the ball. Once we get there, we have to be able to tackle. When teams do not play well, they will say, "We didn't tackle very well." If it is that important, you had better be working on it all of the time. You have to work on tackling. We must stop the cheap touchdown and the big play. You have seen it before: You play good defense for several downs, and then they make a big play on you. Don't give up the big play that breaks your backs. You have to be able to stop the third down-and-short. We have to coach them to be physical on defense. I do not know whether you can take a kid who is not physical and make him tough, but you can improve his technique. If they are not physical, they will go to the offense at Kansas.

In our kicking game, there are a couple of things that we like to do. We all talk well about the kicking game. I never have enough time for the kicking game. One of the things we want on our kicking game is consistency. This is especially true with our punter. The most important play in football is the punt. We average more than 40 yards every time we punt the football. That is important. I can live with a punter who kicks it 40 yards every time. I can't live with a kicker who kicks it 70 yards one time and 20 yards the next time. We want consistency from the kickers. If fundamentals are important in the offense and defense, why aren't they important in the kicking game? We teach fundamentals in our kicking game. We coach the heck out of it, and we evaluate the kicking game. We want to be organized on the kicking game. All of our coaches are involved in the kicking game. They may only have to work with one player. We want to motivate our kicking-game players. We do not put that in our offensive and defensive objectives. We may overlook this on our kicking game. We want to motivate them to be just as good on the kicking teams as they are on offense or defense.

The other thing I am a firm believer in is making the players better, regardless of the level they are on. I learned this lesson at Allegheny College. We only had two coaches. We handled all of the coaching duties. It does not do you any good to gripe about how bad the players are. They are all you have, and you have to work with them, regardless of their ability. Coach them and make them better. Make them as good as they can possibly be.

I think that they go through certain stages in development. First is learning the assignment and learning what to do. If you are an offensive lineman and you do not know who to block, it is tough. They get confused. You have to get them through those stages. After they learn who to block, we go into the how-to-block stage. Then we take them into their techniques. After they know who and how to block, it becomes a habit. They do not think about it. When we get players that know who to block and how to block, we want them aggressive. Then you have a good team. It is our job to get them through these stages. I will ask the position coaches what stage a certain player is in. "How do we get him to the next stage?"

The other thing I believe in is our formula for success. It all starts with a positive attitude. Nothing can be accomplished by being negative. Every player does something well on your team. Put them in that situation where they can do a good job. If they have a better attitude, they will work hard. We all work hard on the things that we are good at. If you believe as I do, "Hard work leads to success; more success leads to better confidence; confidence leads to more success. Hard work leads to . . . " We just keep going around and around. This is an individual approach that we use with all of our individuals. By doing this with individuals, we improve the team. Get the players to the point where they feel good about themselves. This is a coach's responsibility.

On the other side of the coin, I tell the players that they have a responsibility. When they leave the University of Kansas, they should be a lot better than they were when they got there. Part of it is a coaching burden, and part of it is the player's burden.

There are four areas that I think all players can improve in.

■ First, every player—short range and long range—has the ability to control this improvement. Each player must develop an attitude that, when it is a full-go situation, he will not be outhit or outhustled. They may not win the battle, but they will get after them. It is easy to talk about. It is easy to do for one period. It is easy to do for one day or a week. None of us runs all of our drills full speed every day. However, there comes a time when we blow the whistle and say that we are going full speed. They have to understand the difference. They have to let it kick in and get after it.

■ Second, we can control conditioning. We tell our players that we will be the best-conditioned team on our schedule. We can buy into this. You can sell them on this. It will be to our advantage late in the ballgames. They have to do it. Only they know whether they are giving it their all when they are running sprints at the end of practice.

■ Third, they must become better technique players. I tell the offensive line that they have no chance unless they have good technique. The players on defense are bigger, stronger, and better athletes. That is why they are playing defense. They can legally use their hands. They must have superior technique to play the offensive line.

■ Fourth, they must be smarter players. They must understand what the whole system is about, not just their individual assignment. They can study film and learn more about the opponents.

Take those four things and study them. Attitude! Never be outhit or outhustled. Be in better condition than anyone you play. Use better technique than the other team you play. Be a smarter player than your opponent.

If you are playing a team that has more talent and it is doing those same things, then you are going to get your fanny beat. If you are playing a more-talented team that is not doing those things, that is where you can gain the edge. The only thing we are interested in is how we are going to improve. Don't sit around and worry about how you are going to win. Who can give a definition of how you win? You can't. Worry about things you have a chance to control. Worry about improvement. How am I going to be a better player? How can each player improve? If you improve the part, the whole will get better. If you improve the whole and it is not good enough, so what? You are still doing your job as a coach. Your job is to improve the players.

As a head coach, I want to organize a staff that understands the building plans and is committed to carrying those plans out. It is as important for the staff to know my plans as it is for me to know them. The staff will be the leaders. They will set the tone. They will be in the classrooms when the players walk into a meeting. I believe a staff must be the type of people that the players can look up to and respect. A positive attitude must prevail on our staff. It will be a realistic attitude. They must have a burning desire to succeed. You know what I am saying. I want coaches that show enthusiasm in their work. I am not in pro ball. I do not want to be in the pros. I believe in the excitement of the college game. I want my coaches excited about what they are doing. We must have the attitude that our way is the best way. We are not saying that it is the best way in the world, but it is the best way for us.

We have done a good job in some areas. We have done a good job offensively the last five years. We did not have great personnel. We have improved each and every year. There is a process that we have gone through. There has to be a systematic plan for success. The system we have used was been a big reason for our success. One of the things that I try to do with our players is this: I do not want them to tell me where they are; I want to know where they are going. That is the same way we approach our program. I keep track of where we were and where we are going.

We chart our offense, compare the last five years, and see what we have accomplished. You have to sell your players that what you are doing is right. How did we improve over those five years? Here is the process that we went through in those five years. We go through our game play each week. We use 18 things that we make sure to go through in setting up our game plan.

Formulating the Game Plan

1. What are our base run and pass plays versus their favorite defense? Those plays are in our game plan; we know that we are going to run them.

2. What kind of automatic system do we need? We pick out our best plays that we want to use each week. We throw out the bad plays.

3. How are we going to handle the blitz? We want to know what our blitz control package is going to be.

4. How do we stand on personnel? Do they have better personnel than we do? We want to know how good the opponents are.

5. We want to know what the down tendencies are. You are going to find out where they blitz you from. We use computers, but I am not a big computer coach. I like to have a gut feeling for the plays.

6. What are they going to do when the formation goes into the sideline? What kind of adjustment are they going to make?

7. What happens when we use flankers and motions? Do we want to use it or not? If we don't gain an advantage, I do not want to use motion.

8. What happens if you flip-flop your tight end?

9. What happens if you put your tight end in motion, compared to flip-flopping him?

10. What will they do if we play two tight ends?

11. How do they adjust to the one-back set? Teams see this a lot today. In fact, that is not a big problem today.

12. How do they adjust to trips?

13. How do they play the option? We have the option in our attack to keep the defense off balance. Which option are we going to use?

14. How are we going to get big plays? You have to work on this. Does it have to be a flea flicker? Reverse? We look for the big play.

15. We must anticipate the game-plan change. We have an opponent defensive coordinator. He knows what defense our opponent does best, and he anticipates what they will try to do differently each week. I hate those "what-if" coaches. We want to be prepared for any change they may make in the defense.

16. We must have a plan for the weather. I do not worry about the weather, but you have to have a plan for bad weather.

17. What happens if our key player goes down? We must be prepared for this. Do we continue with the same game plan, or do we change? There is a key man on your team. You have to be prepared for this.

Chapter 11

LEADERSHIP
AND TEAM CONCEPTS

Bill McCartney
University of Colorado
1992

Each year we have a theme with our spring clinic. The theme this year is the One-Back Attack. We will discuss how to install it and how to defend it. When we talk about the One-Back Attack we are talking about spreading out the defense. We are spreading the defense out where they are vulnerable in a number of areas. To me that is the most difficult offense to defend today. We have some early thoughts on this and I will cover some of these thoughts as we go along.

To begin with I want to talk about leadership. Individuals that can get the attention of other men fascinate me. I am fascinated by those that have that extra dimension to them where by they can get scores of men to do unusual things for them. As this talk develops you will see that several people got my attention.

The first person is considered the number 1 leader in our country today. That person is General Norman Schwartzkopf. I have not heard him speak, but I do know that he has an interesting lecture. In his talk he talks about Rule Number 13. He says this is the most important rule for all great leaders. This is what rule 13 is. *Every great leader must take charge*. Then he goes on to say that the second most important rule is number 14. Rule 14 is to *use good judgment*. A great leader takes charge and applies good judgment. The obvious question is this: What were the first 12 rules? General Schwartzkopf said those other rules do not matter if you *take charge and use good judgment*. I suggest to you that those are the two great ingredients of every great leader. He is totally in charge and he uses good judgment. He is always thinking things through before he does anything.

Every year as a coaching staff we select a theme for our program that is peculiar to our team for that year. This past year this was our theme: the former prime minister of Great Britain, Benjamin Disraeli, said, "The secret of success is constancy of purpose." In other words, when you have a sheer purpose that everyone agrees on it is the key ingredient to the success of this year's squad. To never lose sight of this purpose has tremendous power in it. This past year was a year of transition for us. We had played for the national championship for two consecutive years. We had graduated a lot of players. If we were going to repeat as Big Eight champs we would have to reach deep and use all of our resources to make it work. This helped us zero in on what we were going to have to do if we were going to be successful. When we went about selecting our *purpose* this is what we selected. We only have one sign in the new facility in our coaching office. This is what it says: *greatness is achieved through the discipline of attending to detail*. If you have seen anyone do it over a period of time, like Michigan has done over the years, it is because they attend to the little things and to the details. It is because they have labored to the details.

I got this from the *Rocky Mountain News*, a Denver daily newspaper, two days after the Super Bowl. I want to read this to you.

> A few days before the Super Bowl, assistant head coach Rich Pettibone tried to put his finger on what made the 1991 Washington Redskins unique. "This is a selfish game, full of selfish stars," Pettibone explains. "But, every once in a while a team gets caught up in a team concept. When that happens egos get submerged, and everything is done for the good of the group." Such was the case with the Redskins, Super Bowl Champs after Sunday's 37-24 mashing of the Buffalo Bills. "This team really had great chemistry," said Coach Joe Gibbs. "The players really had a great feeling for each other. From day one, I rarely got upset with our team. I very rarely had to deal with off-the-field problems. It was truly a team effort and not a bunch of stars."

Let me tell you what I think it was with the Washington Redskins last year. I believe it was *Joe Gibbs*. I believe Joe Gibbs is an extraordinary leader. I believe Joe Gibbs is a person who takes charge and uses good judgment. My high school coach had that same dynamic quality to him. We responded to him. We wanted to please him so much. Joe Gibbs is the same type of guy. If we are all honest we know that even in high school, football has become just like Rich

Pettibone said. It is a bunch of *egos*; a bunch of selfish guys. That is what we promote with our athletes today. That is what the news media does when they celebrate these guys beyond what the other kids in the school get. It is not any different on the college level. At our level it is the same players that the news media want to interview. After awhile those players do not think straight.

Bo Schembechler, Joe Paterno, and Joe Gibbs are guys that know how to keep players focused. They have that tremendous ability to keep the team focused. After five wins someone asked Joe Gibbs what he attributed the great start to. This is what he said: "Everyone on our team knows his role, and he has accepted that role." There are certain guys that can get that done better than other guys.

Athletes are lauded and celebrated for their talent and not their character. This is a mistake. It is a mistake to keep calling attention to a guy that has tremendous skills, but is not a very sound person. We make that mistake all of the time in athletics. We cater to that selfish kid. We send a wrong signal to our team when we do that. Our players do not respect us as much as they should because of this. We must stop doing this in football. It is not getting any better. It is only a handful of coaches that can keep this in perspective. It is tragic for a team not to call out its men of character. Those are the athletes we should be parading to the front of the room. Those are the ones we should be setting up as an example.

The thing that Bo Schembechler always did when I was at Michigan was this: he always took the player that had the greatest attitude and then he started working with that player. He started coaching that player. When you do this you raise the standard of the whole team.

Do you know one of the biggest problems I had when I went to coach at Colorado? Our players *thought* they were working hard. The standard was so low, they did not know what it was to work. When we did have a few players exert a little more effort, that became the standard. That was too low, and I kept trying to tell them we did not work very hard. They did not know how to work hard.

There are two types of men. *There are men who live by preference; there are men that live by conviction.* I am talking about value systems now. Men that live by preference, their values are negotiable. It depends on the predicament or the situation that they find themselves in. Men that live by conviction, their values are nonnegotiable. They are not up for debate. There is a certain honor about them. They will die for certain things. What has happened to men like that?

Where are the men left that will die for all the right things? The men that enjoy the longevity of this profession are the ones. Preference weakens under pressure; conviction gets stronger under pressure. It intensifies and resolves like tempered steel. Here is one thing that you can be sure of, and it is true in this room right now. People who live by preference always dislike those who live by conviction. They resent them. They do not want any part of them, because they expose them. They touch the bases and do the things right. Those are the type of examples kids need today, more so than in the past. They need people that do things right around kids. They do not compromise their language or their values around kids. Kids can respect them and they can appreciate those types of people. *Fame can come in a moment, but greatness comes with longevity*. This is what separates Gibbs, Paterno, and Schembechler. You may be able to do it once, but can you do it again. It is harder to maintain than to obtain. If you can't take it, you will not make it.

Let me talk about some Principles of Leadership. These are not my principles, but things I have learned over the years. You can take them to the bank because they are good every time. Let me list them for you.

LEADERSHIP PRINCIPLES

1) Knowledge always translates into authority. Football coaches need to know this. Football coaches want titles, authority, and rank. Some of them do not pay their dues to earn these rights. My advice to any young coach is this: Go gain a monopoly over a certain source of information that is important in the game of football. Then you can become authoritative. You will become an in-market coach. You will be in demand. You must have the information. You can't do it any other way. It is true in every line of business. It is true teaching in the classroom. The person with the most information is the person that is in the position of authority.

2) Decisions always translate into energy. Do you know there are coaches in this room that cannot make a decision? Do you know that indecision is a curse? George Washington said it many years ago. "Eternal defeat always attends the man of indecision." Let me tell you the right way to make a decision. It is like going back to General Schwartzkopf in taking charge and using good judgment. The way to make a decision is this: you listen to the advice and counsel and wisdom of those who should know. Listen to those that have a vested interest in what you are seeking. Then you must detach yourself and then *you make the decision*. Don't

put the decision to a committee. You must make the decision. You know if it is the right decision, even if it is going to be painful. If you will do it, the rest of the team will follow. Every tough decision I have had to make as a head coach, I have gone against the grain of the entire staff. They did not want me to make that decision. They wanted me to do the more acceptable thing. But every time that it has happened I knew that I had to make the decision along. I did not get any support in making those decisions. I know that is the only way to go about doing some things.

3) Committees do everything by compromise. Leaders don't compromise. It takes 100 years to grow an oak tree. It only takes 15 minutes to cut it down. You cut it down by compromise. You cut it down by taking shortcuts. Do you know how we do it as coaches? When we have a player that is in trouble and we want to bring him back on the team, we let the team vote on it. They are going to take the shortcut and take him back most of the time. We can't put such decisions in the hands of the kids.

4) Mediocre men want authority, not accountability.

5) Talent must undergird the talent or the talent will cave in. It is like a submarine. The pressure has to come from the inside. This is what happened to us this year. We started out 2-2. Against Stanford we did not play very well. We came to the fourth quarter and it was hot. The game was on the line and we turned it down. It was there for anyone to take, and we turned it down. We have a sign in our dressing room: *The Pride and Tradition of the Colorado Buffaloes Will Not Be Entrusted to the Timid or the Weak.* That is what the sign says. I went in and covered up that sign on Monday after the Stanford game. I told them the sign is a farce. I told them I could not look at that sign. "I can't look at you and the sign at the same time because we turned the game down at Stanford. Now, we are at a time of recoining in our program. Are we going to go back to the way we used to play? Are we going to play all out all of the time?" What we did was to start all over again. The kind of drills we ran were the kind of drills you run on the first day when you first put the pads on. I was right in the middle of every drill. I was begging for a fighting heart. I was begging for a kid that would fight and claw until the last second. We went on like that in practice until I was about ready to lose them. A famous general once said, "A wise general does not send his troops to battle every day." I was in danger of violating that rule. We had an open date and we let up after a week and a half.

Let me tell you what happened to our team. They had a chance to cash it in or they had a chance to respond. Most college coaches do not handle situations today like we handled that one. We were at a crisis. We were ready to become mediocre again. We were going to be like a lot of other teams where we would win the games we were supposed to win, and lose those we were supposed to lose. We came out to play Missouri in the next game at home and we played with *fire in our eyes*. We played with great intensity. It carried over when we went to Norman, Oklahoma. We knew it would be a new test away from home. When we went to Oklahoma we went right after them. That is the only way you can play Oklahoma. The point is we could have caved in, but responded in a positive way.

6) People want to know how much you care before they care how much you know. The thing we have going with kids today is this: they are not going to put it all on the line unless they are convinced and satisfied that you are really interested in them. If they know that you approve of them it makes a big difference. We have a sign up on our chalkboard for our off-season program for our coaches. I have asked our coaches to do these three things every day. Show our players that you enjoy them one-on-one. Show them that you value them, and show them that you approve of them. Take time each day with them. Players need this today more than ever because of the home situations we are facing.

7) Ambition is most mature, not when we know what we want and know how to get it, but when we understand what we have and how to give it. Let me explain what I mean. Stanford, Harvard, and Carnegie did a study that showed 85 percent of the reason why you get a job, keep a job, and move a head, has to do with people skills and people knowledge. Listen to this because it is the best thing I have said today. This is the most legitimate thing you can take home with you. *Concern for others is the foundation for leadership*. It is the cornerstone for leadership. *Concern for others*! If you do not display that then you are missing a great chance for leadership. Let me show you why that is true today.

Take the word *integrity*. This is the dictionary definition. It is a strict inherent to a set of moral values. There are six of these. See if they are true of you as you relate to your players. *Utter Sincerely - Honesty - Candor - Not Artificial - Not Empty Promises - Not Shal-*

low. A man of integrity is a promise keeper. When he says something his word is good. He is a coach that the players will respond to today.

I am not sure if Michigan State or Hawaii did this study. Let me share it with you. It is a survey to see what was the most influence in a person's life. This is the way the survey came out.

Look what has happened. TV was just getting started in 1950. Look at what has happened with the church. Today, peers have the most influence on individuals. My question to you is this: Why is the home fourth today? Could it be because no one is home? Could it be that there is no trust in the home? Could it be that the word in the home is no good? Do you know where the young people go today for help? They go to their peer group. They go to guys their own age. They get their best advice from people that do not know any more than they do. That is why in coaching we must be giving the players an alternative. The key word is trust. They come in and see the coach and they know they can trust him. When we recruit players it may take them two years before they will trust us. They will test me for two years before they give me the benefit of the doubt. It is only then that they can begin to trust. They have been so disappointed time after time in their home.

Philosophically, this is what I believe. Teams with talent do not always win. I believe *morale is to the physical as 4 is to 1*. It is four times as important that your morale be right as it is to your physical ability. I feel our players proved this from Stanford to Oklahoma this past season. We did not do anything in that two-week period of time except change some attitudes. I believe the difference in winning and losing is in the heart of a man.

We do not meet with our team as a full squad from the end of the bowl games until March. Then we have what we call March meetings. I call all of the players into a meeting that has an amphitheater effect. Now we have one of those rooms in our new building. I do not invite anyone to that meeting except the returning players. There are no student managers or other coaches. I do not want any diversions. I want every eye focused on me. I have thought long and hard about what I am going to say at that meeting. That meeting is going to set the tempo for the team for the next season. We are going to take inventory for the team for next year at that meeting. First Corinthians, 14:8 says, "If the trumpet blast is uncertain, who will prepare himself for battle." I quote scripture because I believe scripture is true. I find that I can make a point with this technique every so often. I plan to have this March meeting next Thursday. We ask our players these three questions:

1. Who are we?

2. Where are we going?

3. How are we going to get there?

For the team that won the national championship the year before, I went back and got the notes we presented to them at our March meeting. Keep this in mind: the last time I had seen them we had lost to Notre Dame in the Orange Bowl 21-6. We were undefeated and Notre Dame had lost one game. If we had won that game we would have been national champs. At halftime the score was 0-0. With two minutes in the half we had 180 yards and they had 45 yards. Let me tell you what happened at halftime. Our locker room was very subdued. We were within 30 minutes of a national championship. We were commiserating over what might have been, instead of recognizing that it was an even game and that we had a chance to go out and gain a victory. What went on in the Notre Dame locker room is that they must have circled the wagons. They came out and took the game to us. They took what was ours right from us. We should have had more incentive to win. We had more to gain and we had more at stake. They took it from us. Keep this in mind as to what happened as we approached our March meeting after that loss to Notre Dame.

This is how I approached that meeting. I started with *who we are*. I said, "We are the Big Eight defending champions." We had 23 seniors coming back. I feel the greater number of seniors you have the greater capacity for leadership. The reason for this is because those guys have paid their dues. If they have the right attitude and display the right kind of perspective for our team it is contagious. There is tremendous resources in the seniors.

Where are we going? Big dreams create the magic that stirs men's souls. You have to give the most competitive players something significant to sink their teeth into. You have to give them something substantial to get them going. This was our goal; back-to-back Big Eight championships. We had not been able to do this in 100 years of Colorado football. Furthermore, we recognized the fact that the Big Eight champion often plays for the national championship. Five out of the last 10 years this has been true. We knew that if we won the Big Eight Championship the other things would be out there for us. I put the following down for them to see. I put down Oklahoma and Nebraska and no crap. By that I mean this: You may have the same situation in your conference. These two teams traditionally rule the Big Eight Conference. I told them they have abused us over the years and it has taken its toll on us. I really believe the only way to play with teams like Oklahoma and Nebraska is like this. I feel you must go nose to nose and mustache to mustache with them. You have to look at them and tell them, "I am not taking any of your crap. I want your butt tonight." Until your players have that type of attitude for 60 minutes, you are not going to beat the big teams. The only way to face those teams is go face-to-face with them. We beat them back-to-back this year only eight days apart. We have to play them eight days apart again this year. It will not be as easy to beat both of them this year. It is not going to be as easy next year because it happened last year. The reason we beat them both last year is because we went right after them.

The next point is: How are we going to do this? Basically, this is what we said. "Men, we have to come to grips on why we lost the game to Notre Dame in the Orange Bowl. How are we going to solve this problem? We were within one half of winning the national championship. I said, "I want to tell you why I think we lost that game. I am sure all of you have your own reasons. I think we lost because I think Notre Dame was mentally tougher than we were." Now, down deep in my heart I knew it was me. I knew at halftime that things were not right. I had been in enough locker rooms to know that something needed to be done. I did not know what to do, and I did not do it. If I had it to do over I would have done something. I would have thrown a chair across the room, or stood on top of a table, or something. I would have done something. I tried to make the necessary adjustments and go out and play the second half. I knew that things were not right. I sent them back out for the second half hoping we could win. I told them that Notre Dame had what it took to win that game and that Colorado did not.

A goal is a dream with a date attached to it. There must be a day of reckoning. When you set a goal you must have a way to measure the goal and you must have a time when the goal must come to bear. I told our players that I had looked at our schedule and I saw that we had six tough road games. Again, we play Oklahoma and Nebraska back-to-back. However, Nebraska is the last of those road games. We had not beaten them since 1967 in Lincoln. Men, that is the *day*, when we will find out if Colorado is tough enough to win a Big Eight championship. We went to Lincoln and we were behind 12-0 at the half. However, it was different this time. It was a bitter cold game, played in a rain. We went in at the half and no one sat down. No one slumped over. We had a pep rally at halftime. It was hard to get them together to make the adjustments. They knew the game was on the line. We got the wind in the fourth quarter and we were still trailing 12-0. You achieve what you emphasize. Wherever you put the greatest emphasis is where you get the greatest returns. That is where it came to bear. We scored 27 points on Nebraska in the fourth quarter. That was the most points ever scored on Nebraska in one quarter. Our men rose to the occasion.

We came back and played the same Notre Dame team in the Orange Bowl again. We trailed Notre Dame at halftime. This time it was different in our dressing room at the half. Now we were mentally right. I say the Morale is to the Physical as 4 is to 1.

I believe that when those kids sit in those March meetings the perfect attitude they could have would be this. They would look at me and say, "Coach me! Take me beyond myself, and take me where I can't take myself." If a player is thinking like that he is thinking clearly. Then he has confidence in his coach. Then he knows if he will subscribe we can get the job done.

I believe you train the mind. I believe the mind is supple and flexible. Let me give you an example. I got this story out of *Sports Illustrated* 26 years ago. It is a story about Tommy Nobis, the All-American linebacker from Texas. This is the main point of the story. Nobis told about his feelings about losing a game. They were getting ready to play Arkansas and those games were tops in those years. Tommy Nobis went on to say that he could not stand the thoughts of playing a game and not giving 100 percent. He was afraid that he would make a mistake and his teammates would see how he played. He said the worse feeling was to think he could play in a game as big as this and not give 100 percent on every play. He went on to say that he worried about those films. He cared about the way his teammates felt about him. He did not want them to see him not giving his best in a game. He said he kept telling himself, "Don't dog it; don't dog it." Now, I read this article to my players. I want them to see the film on Monday, and I want that film to be a *day of reckoning* for them.

A lot of coaches will split the team up to watch the film. They divide up into three or four groups to see the films. I do not believe in that. The dynamics that exist when one man influences the others is valuable. You destroy this if you split them up for the film. There is tremendous pressure and leverage on every player that gets into the game when you watch the film as a group. Then after you have seen the film as a team you can break down into small groups. The power that is in the room when you watch films as a team is tremendous.

Let me tell you what Eddie Crowder used to tell me about Bud Wilkinson. I wanted to know about Bud Wilkinson. He won 46 or 48 games without losing. I wanted to know what he did. This is what Eddie told me Bud would do. When the game was over on Saturday no player or coach would see him again until he had seen three films on the next opponent. He would look at those films until he was satisfied that the only way they could win the next game would be to have an extra effort in practice the next week. Bud Wilkinson never lost to a team that he should not have lost to. If anyone ever beat him everyone knew it would be for all of the marbles. Bud would go into a coaching meeting on Sunday where they would be a 24-point favorite for the next game, and he would start in on the assistant coaches. He would let them have it with both barrels. We all want a little slack as coaches.

This has been my experience working with the game plan. If a coach puts together a great game plan where he knows in his heart that the team was hitting on all cylinders, and he had something to do with it, there is nothing like it. But, do you know what happens? He doesn't coach as well the next week. That is my opinion. Do you know why? Because he has not convinced himself that it was all on the line again. That is what Bud Wilkinson could do. It is individuals that must make it happen. I could have done something at the halftime of the Notre Dame game that we lost. I have to live with that. It is individuals that make the difference. The best definition of leadership I have ever heard is this: *Leadership is a powerful, positive presence.* Under that definition anyone can lead. The last player on our team can lead. He may never play in a game because he is not good enough. But if he brings an upbeat spirit and a positive attitude he has something to offer. Conversely, if he is complaining and he is not playing, he is pulling us down. I can't have this. If I have players that can't play for us that are going to be on our team we are going to sit down and talk about the situation. I tell them I want them to understand their role. They must be part of the solution and not part of the problem.

I think Lou Holtz is a special person. When he talks I listen and write down what he says. This is what he does. When they won the national championship a few years back when they beat West Virginia in the Fiesta Bowl their theme was *Count On Me*. He was asking everyone on the team and every coach to say, "You can count on me. Coach, you define my role and tell me what you expect of me and you can count on me."

Coach Holtz asks every player three questions.

1. Can I trust him?

2. Is he committed to excellence?

3. Does he care about others?

The key word is *trust*. The first person the players must trust is *you*. If they can't trust you it will never work unless you have them out- numbered. The last question is the most important of all. Does he care about others or does he just care about himself? Does he expect special treatment on this team? That is where Bo was good. No one got preferential treatment with him.

One more thought and then I am ready to close this part out. Men follow men. All down through history strong men have led weak men. All the great stories in history are traced back to a man that had a thirst for victory that could not be quenched. He would not stay down. You can't suppress guys like this. People like this may lay down and bleed awhile, but they will get up and fight again.

I believe everyone in this room has big-time problems. Some of us have problems that would bring us to tears if we told them. But do you know that everyone on your team has problems? The youngest player on your team may have more problems than the other players. There are two types of people related to their problems. There are people that focus on the problems and people that focus on the solu- tions. When you focus on the problems it saps our strength and destroys our initiative, and it fatigues us, and it depresses us. If you will concentrate on the solutions you immediately get energized. You get excited, elevated, and you draw people to you. If you are always complaining you are spacing people. If you are upbeat it makes a big difference. Let me give you an example.

The last two years I have lost two offensive coordinators. They have gone on to head coaching positions. It is like losing a big game. It is painful, but it is not the worst thing that can happen to you. But at 2 a.m. you wake up and you realize that you have lost the game and a knot comes in your stomach. Is it just me that has that feeling? Well, that is the way it is with me when I lose a great coach off my staff. But, let me tell you what happens. You have to start looking for some- one that could be even better. I start looking for a solution. Immedi- ately, the knot starts to untie. Things get back into perspective.

I want to stay on the *cutting edge*. I do not want to be the last coach to figure out the best offense to use. We can look at the high school quarterbacks today and find that they are throwing the ball much better than they did before. The important thing that is important in coaching is knowledge. It is what you know that is important. I had always believed you win football games by running the football. But all of that is changing today. There is no market on age as far as coaching is concerned. It is information that counts. Who has the most information and who can communicate that information is the important thing in coaching. Who takes charge and uses good judgment is important. It does not matter how old the coach is or how young he is. Look at Dick MacPherson and David Shula as good examples. Today we have teams that line up with no backs in the backfield. I want to stay on the cutting edge.

Why change offenses? We were punting too much. The defenses were attacking us. They were operating on our side of the line in the formative stages. We were inconsistent against teams with less talent. Do you not want to play this game on your toes instead of on your heels? When you get the ball don't you want the defense on their heels? When we are on defense we want to be on our toes coming after them and dictating to them what happens. That is the way I want to play the game. The two college teams that were 12-0 this year played the game like that. They play on their toes and they are dictating what happens. That is my observation.

Let me tell you about two guys that are having a lot of success. First is Don James of Washington. A few years back Washington played Arizona State and the game ended up 34-33. After the game Don said he would never get in a game again where the offense would be able to determine what they were going to do before the ball was snapped. He changed his defense to keep the offense off balance.

Dennis Erickson was the head coach at Wyoming at one time. He was 6-5 that year. Washington State came in and tried to hire him. The people in Wyoming did not want to let him go to Washington State. "Keep him; pay him what you have to, but keep him." He left and went to Washington State. In two years he beat USC. In two years Washington State is a heavyweight. He goes to Miami and they have been outstanding. It is *that man*. The guy has something to him in my opinion.

Here is another person that has something to him. It is Sam Jankovich. He was the Athletic Director at Miami that hired Erickson. He hired Jimmy Johnson before that. Now he is with the Patriots. He hired Dick MacPherson. How do you figure that. He got the young guy in Erickson and then he hires the old coach that might be over the hill. Listen to what he says. He talks to football fans about his Pyramid of Success. I have three points that he makes about football. First, the obvious thing is that you win football games with the defense. He went on to say that 90 percent of all football games are won by scoring 17 points or more. Second, the next most important ingredient in a football team is to have a superior team pass offense. That is essential. Third, coaching the passing game is the hardest thing to do in all of football. You know, as much as I hate to admit it, he is right. I believe this is true. I subscribe to this theory.

He went on to talk about hiring coaches. He said if he has two candidates for a coaching position he looks for energy and enthusiasm in the coach. "I look for the guy that does not burn out. I look for a guy with staying power. He coaches at the end of the season with the same energy as he has at the beginning of the season. That is the reason I hired Dick MacPherson." That is the same type of person as Jimmy Johnson of the Cowboys. Sam went on to say that some coaches are 70 going on 20, and other coaches are 40 going on 60. Age means nothing, and I believe that.

How do you change your offense? Don't turn me off. We must learn from the past. Let me tell you what I learned from the past. We changed our offense once and it saved my job. As I think back, this is the situation. We went to the Wishbone then. Teams were using the Wishbone and beating teams that they were not supposed to beat. We did not have the players to beat people. We took advantage of what the offense allowed us to do best. The first year we just put in the system, and we just lived with it. We did not try to use everyone's best idea. This is the point I am trying to make to you: when you put a system together don't try to compile everyone's best plays. It doesn't work that way. You must go to an offensive system to win, all other things being equal talent wise.

We went out and recruited a lot of good tailbacks. The Wishbone is a quarterback-fullback offense. So we had to adjust our offense to take advantage of our great tailbacks. We did not do it the first year. We changed it so we could play with the great teams on our schedule.

Now that you have a system you must do some research. Knowledge always translates into authority. I am telling you that I do not have the in-depth knowledge of the One-Back Offense that many of you have, but I am going to get it. I know where the resources are and I will get it and I will study their films. That is what I am saying to you. Don't do it on your own. I am not smart enough to do it on my own.

You must have repetition. We made our change before the bowl game. We felt that was the best way for us to win the bowl game. It turned out to be a disaster. But now we have the spring to work on our offense. Then we have 29 practices in the fall to get our offense down. I am not going to screw our team up on offense. We have won the Big Eight three years in a row and I am changing offenses. "If it ain't broke, don't fix it." I will not leave a stone unturned. I may lose my team by changing offenses. If we don't win next year the players may look at me and say, "It is his fault because he changed our offense." I still want you to know that I believe you win games with the running game. History tells us this.

Take a look at most defenses. They like to line up with four defensive backs. When a team puts three wide receivers in the game it forces the defense to put five defensive backs in the game. The package the defense spends all of their time with is not the package you end up using. You may say that you can sub one man for another and cover the formation. It is not that simple. The things that we do best on defense is with four defensive backs. Most teams with a One-Back Set try to get us in a mismatch. We do not have a chance against the mismatch. They put us at a disadvantage.

Here is one observation I make as I watch a lot of film. Most defenses do not reroute receivers. We let them run their patterns where they want to. The more receivers in the game the more rerouting problems we have. I feel we must have a package with traps and brackets in it so we can take away the great receiver or the favorite receiver.

The next question we must ask is this. If there are two safeties in the game, who is the extra man in the box? Let me explain what the box is. A box to us is the number of men from the tight end to the opposite tackle. The offense has six players in the box. The defense has six players in the box. Any time the offense has as many players in the box as the defense, the offense should win. The offense dictates; the defense can't stop them.

If we played a team that lined up in the I formation and could not throw the ball very well I would line up and play them with nine in the box to their seven men. I would stuff the run and make them beat me with the pass.

Any time there is only one free safety back deep the defense is going to outnumber you in the box. However, they will be one-on-one on the flanks. It does not matter how you cut it, but basically, there are two or three men that are one-on-one when there is one free safety.

This is my point. This is one solution to playing the One-Back Set. I think the soundest strategy is to play with a Nickel in the game. We want to match skill on skill at each of the positions. We do not call the right linebacker Roger or Louis anymore in this defense. I call him *Dime*. That regular linebacker had to come out of the game when we bring in our sixth defensive back. That is where the Dime is going to play. Now, I have a chance to build my defense from day one as far as where the Dime is going to play. On down and distance situations I am not afraid to put him in the game.

Now I can trap or bracket on either side. I can take any receiver and trap him or bracket him. I have that in my package. Now we can take one of our Safeties and put him in the box to play the run by the time the ball gets to the line of scrimmage.

The thing that is happening is this. Those linebackers will move around. You can't tell if they are coming or not. They are all over the place.

Let me get to my next topic, *how to get up for the big game*. One thing Michigan does is to put certain teams in red letters on the calendar. They had not done this at Colorado when I got there. When we put Nebraska in red letters it was a significant statement. Now, Nebraska writes about it every year.

Next we use T-shirts to motivate our players. T-shirts are cheap and we can get them printed anywhere. You can get them if you plan right. Our players are less apt to fall for the T-shirt promotion than your players are. However my players will fall for this every year once or twice. It is not the T-shirt that counts, it is *what is on the T-shirt that counts*. Before our Nebraska game, when we beat them in the fourth quarter, I asked our players on Thursday before the game what color Nebraska was. They all responded that they were Red and White. I asked them why they called their great defense the *black shirts*. Black is our color. I told them to pass out the T-shirts. This is what was on the T-shirts: *The Real Black Shirts*. That is all it said.

We decided to arrive in Lincoln on Friday at night before the game on Saturday. We decided to let our 60 player wear the Black Shirts when they got off the plane. That was big news in Lincoln. This was the Real Black Shirts. Now we had to back this statement up. It motivated our team tremendously.

Also, for that game I told our 60 players that would make the trip to Lincoln that I have ordered 60 autographed game balls for them. I explained to our players that I had heard somewhere that we spend 86 percent of our time thinking about ourselves. If you can get people to stop thinking about themselves, and to start thinking about others, there is a whole new energy source to that person.

In order to get on the plane they had to agree to do one thing. "You have to take this autographed football and call someone on the phone or go visit someone by midnight tonight, Thursday, and you have to dedicate this game to them. It may be your Dad, or someone else. If it is your Dad I want you to find the words to tell him you love him. Tell your Dad you love him and tell him you will prove it by how hard you play at Nebraska on Saturday. Tell your Dad you are going to give him an expression of your love by sending him a game ball with the final score on the ball. Tell him you will mail it to him on Monday." Each person was going to do this with a special person in his life. The next day they came back with some unbelievable stories. All 60 of them told their story to different coaches and players. It was a perfect excuse for the players to tell someone special that they loved them. There is tremendous power when you can get the players to quit thinking about themselves and to play for someone else. Football is an *ego*-type game. It is a selfish game.

If you really want to get them ready to play a big game try this. We were going to play the number 1 team in the country and we were going on the road to play them. On Thursday night I told them who would travel. I told them they could not get on the airplane until they came to my office and sat down and got into my face and told me what I could expect of them in the game. "Until I can see it in your face and in your eyes, I am not buying it." I had a signup sheet and had them come in for three minutes each. I had all 60 players pick a time to visit with me. They came in and I asked them what I could expect in the game from them. They would say things such as this. "I am going to play like I have never played before." Before they could say anything else I would say, "I am going to hold you to that statement." We shook hands on their commitments. After all 60 players walked out of my office I told our staff that we would play sensational that week. I told them not to give them any pep talks before the game. I told them to line them up and they would play their hearts out. That is what we did. Do you know why we played so hard? It is because when a competitive kid puts it into words, and looks you in the eye and tells you what he is going to do, there is more power here than you can imagine. A man will deliver on his word.

I have used the telegram when I was in high school coaching. They were expensive so I delivered them myself. I would have them printed, but each player got a different message. It was something special to each player. We had played two tough games in a row, and we really needed something to pick us up for that third road game in a row. I gave each player a special message. I took the telegrams to their homes. I put it in their mailbox. When they got to school the players did not talk about the telegram. I could see it in their faces; it was a great way to communicate what we had to do to win the game.

Next is the *Home Visit*. This can be dynamite. You know you have to have a great game out of a certain player. You call him up on Thursday night and ask him if you can come over to visit. What can he say? You go over to his house and you ask him if there is someplace where we can talk. This is what you tell him.

"I am so proud of you and what you have done for our team. I am here to tell you that you must play your greatest game tomorrow. I know you will, but I am just here to tell you that we are counting on you." That is about all you need to say. It only takes a couple of minutes. Then you are out the door. That player is going to do his level best to play to the utmost of his ability.

I want to stop with this next point. When I was at Michigan we used to have an assistant coach talk to the defense each week. I had never heard Lloyd Carr give a fiery speech. If we wanted someone to give a pep talk it was Bo, Gary Moeller, or myself. That was the way we did it then. We decided early in the year that each assistant coach would take one game and talk to the defense. We were getting ready to play before the game. This was Saturday morning and we were getting ready to meet with the offense and defense and then go to the stadium for the game. Lloyd Carr gave our defense this talk.

Lloyd Carr has a soft voice. He started off in his real soft demeanor. He said, "This is what it is going to take. Every player is going to be challenged to the point that everyone will have to come hard on every play. I know I can depend on you. I tell you what will happen when we go all out." Then he shifted his demeanor and his voice became loud and strong. "We will have Michigan helmets going BANG - BANG - BANG." All he did was to portray what was going to happen when the Michigan helmets started going after our opponents. I never saw Lloyd like that before and neither had our defensive team. Lloyd single-handedly lifted our defense another notch that day.

My point is this: You have to time those things up and use them. Everyone has to contribute. Everyone has a role to play. When everyone plays the role the way Lloyd did it can lift you for a big game.

Chapter 12

THE IMPORTANT THINGS ABOUT FOOTBALL

Joe Paterno
Penn State University
1992

I want to tell you about some of the things that I believe in. I have been coaching 43 years at Penn State. I was an assistant for 16 years and this is my 26th year as being the head coach. We all want to do a good job. I thought very seriously about what I would say to you. I am not going to try to cover the individual steps for our tailback or the techniques we use with our quarterbacks, nor am I going to tell you about the great passing game we have at Penn State. Instead, I want to tell you about some of the things that have helped us over the years.

I want you to understand the type of kids that go to Penn State. My wife and I have five kids. My first four kids all went to Penn State. I want you to know one thing about Penn State. I had four kids in Penn State at one time and none of them lived at home. It cost me more money in one year than I had paid in all four years before. I told them all that they had to do a good job or they would hear from me.

Let me talk a little about *what I think coaching is all about*. Hopefully, I will not boar you with what I have to say. I will not talk long. I will give you a chance to ask questions and then perhaps we can shoot the bull back and forth about different things. I have been trying to think about the things that have allowed me to coach for 43 years and have some decent luck.

I think it all goes back to 1955 when I heard a lecture by Bud Wilkinson, the former Oklahoma coach. Most of the things I will talk about the rest of this lecture probably were covered by Bud Wilkinson in his lecture that night. I may add a few things that Paul Bryant, Paul Brown, and Vince Lombardi may have said to me that have had an influence on my coaching career. I think Bud Wilkinson was the founder of modern coaching. Bud was the guy that probably got us headed the way we coach today. When I heard Bud talk it was down at Oklahoma where they were having spring practice. I had never been around a situation such as that. I played football at Brown University. I had a great experience at the spring practice at Oklahoma. Bud Wilkinson had complete command of everything that I thought coaching was all about. They had a coaching clinic right there on campus and had over 1000 coaches there. So what I am trying to tell you is that some of the things I am going to tell you are not original from me.

At the clinic in Oklahoma Bud Wilkinson talked about "What Makes the Best Coach?" This is what Bud said: the one that makes the fewest mistakes, the one that does the best teaching job, and the coach that is the best organized. As I look back, these are my feelings about Penn State. I do not feel we have made a lot of mistakes, and that is in preparing our kids for the games and playing the right kids in the right positions. We have not made a lot of mistakes in handling kids. We may not have been brilliant and we may not have done anything innovative, nor did we stun the world; but we did not make a lot of mistakes. The one thing that I would brag on is the fact that we have been good teachers. When I say *we* I am referring to our staff. I think we have been *organized*. We do not waste time. We know what we want to do. The X's and O's are not the most important thing in football. You need to understand that fact. There are 22 variables in a football game. There are 22 players on the field at one time and they are variable. All of us, if we want to be successful, must be salesmen. You have to be a salesman to the point that when your team loses a game the blame is not placed on you, the head coach, the assistant coaches, or the offense, or the defense, or on the formations you use. Rather, they blame it on themselves. The errors that I want to talk about with you are the same five errors that Bud Wilkinson talked about when I was visiting Oklahoma in 1955.

There are five basic *errors* that I want to stress. They are:

1. Errors in Teaching Methods

2. Errors in Tactics and Strategy

3. Errors in Judgment

4. Errors in Your Off-Field Relationships

5. Errors in Developing Morale

The Errors in Teaching Methods all relate to this common mistake. Of the above errors, this is where we do the poorest job. Failure to use time effectively is the most common mistake we all make. We fail to recognize the importance of the time factor. We do not make effective use of our valuable time in planning. I used to be good with time. When I was a young coach I knew in December what I wanted to do in June. Now, I may not know until March what I want to do in June. I am not eating "humble pie" or anything like that, but when I was younger and did not have as much to do, I could make plans six months ahead of time. That was before all of these demands came from the university and the success that has gone with our program. I think you need to plan to be successful.

At times we give too much attention to one thing in teaching football. If you are spending too much time on one thing it creates boredom. Once kids get bored, you can forget about learning; learning flies right out the window. The minute you start teaching something that is boring to the kids, you are wasting your time. You might as well go out there and let them start kicking the football around, or let them play soccer, or do something else. You can work on physical conditioning if you want to get something out of those things, but that is about it.

I think football players have a very short attention span. Football is not a very complicated game when you break it down to the individual player. It is *not a very complicated game*. This is the reason a player can play pro football that has never played the game before. It is not a hard game to learn one-on-one. It gets to be a hard game when we have to coordinate everything. Our job is to make sure everyone is on the same page. It is very easy to get bored. You have to hold to a time schedule. I am on my coaches all the time about the amount of time we are spending on drills. If we say we are going to spend eight to 10 minutes on a drill, we should spend those eight to 10 minutes on the drill. If we go out there and spend a little less than 10 to 12 minutes on a drill and it looks like we have gotten enough out of the drill, then I will blow the whistle in a hurry to end the drill. Get the heck out of that drill and get to something else. I am not going to go over the time schedule.

Many times we fail to explain the purpose of the drills. Why are you running a certain drill? You cannot beat something into a kid's brain unless he understands what you are trying do. Tell the player why he is running a drill, what you are trying to get accomplished, and then I think he will do a better job. *Explain why* and then *show how*. I think we make errors in the way we teach in the sense of teaching progression. You can't teach a player to block before he learns his stance. You can't expect the offensive lineman to come out of his stance properly, keep his hips low, his head up, and hit into a defensive man with his shoulders square if you do not have a teaching progression. I do not care what you do with him, he can't do it. You must have a proper teaching progression. You must know what you want to teach. It is not that complicated, really. Unfortunately we are all impatient. We can't go out on the field for more than two days without putting the pads on. The assistant coaches all want to know when are we going to start knocking the crap out of each other. We do not need that. We need a proper teaching progression.

I think we have too many detailed instructions on the field. Even on our level we have too many instructions on the field. Many nights I have walked off the field and felt that we could have gotten more done on the field had the assistant coaches not been talking too much. How much can a kid learn when he has a helmet on, he has a headache, he is sore, and he is tired of practice. You are trying to give him some attention about details and he doesn't hear one thing you are telling him. I do not think you can do that much instruction on the field. You do the how and the why on the chalkboard, with videotapes, films, and you can even go out and walk through things. You can walk through most details before you even get started in a practice. Teach the assignments before you go on the field, and you correct on the field.

We do very little teaching on the field. We have too much demonstrating by assistant coaches. I think we are on the field too long most of the time. I think you are better off with a team that is not tired. How long do you practice? That is up to you. That comes with experience. Bud Wilkinson said if one of his assistant coaches looked tired and it appeared that they were practicing too long he would cut practice back. I think all of us practice too long. I think you have to cut down as the season goes along. I thought we did a great job of coaching this past year, but we still practiced too long at times. I thought we did a good job considering the way our schedule was set up. We practiced from August 1 to January 1. We were six months playing football. We played some big games and some that were not so big, and then we had more big games. We had to pace our football team. We were constantly worried about pacing our players. You can't get them ready to play big games every week. You have to be intelligent enough in your mind where you can't take anyone for granted. You can't say that team is easy; the minute you say that team is easy the entire squad will feel that way and your staff will feel that way. You have to drive yourself. I do not think you can drive your football team the same way you drive yourself.

Players do not understand you sometimes when you are pushing them. You must tell the players that they have to go to class, and that they have to be ready to play, and all of the other things that go with playing the game, but you still have to pace the team. I thought we did that very well this past year except for the Southern Cal game. That game was not a matter of not being ready to play. We just got a little fatheaded for that game, and I could see it coming. But other than the Southern Cal game, we did very well. We played very well against Miami and actually had a chance to beat them, but did not. I think how long you practice and how hard you practice has a lot to do with the type of season you have. I would think it is more critical on the high school level than the college level. This is true when you are dealing with 16- and 17-year-old kids.

The second error I feel we make is in *Errors of Tactics and Strategies*. You very rarely win a game because you outsmart another team. As coaches we may think we win games because of tactics, but we rarely do. To win games you have to outblock people, outtackle them, outhustle them, and you physically beat them down. A lot of you may not know who Red Sanders was. He was one of the giants in our coaching profession. He coached back in the 1950s and his ideas still have an influence on us today. Red Sanders used to say, "Intimidate them Physically; Outmaneuver Them -- The Hell with That." Red Sanders and Woody Hayes were too peas in a pod. If they were at a clinic such as this, they would show you three plays and they would spend three hours going over those three plays. We don't have many coaches like that today. They would never get excited about the first drive in the game. I do not like to score easy, early. I really don't. We have gadget plays that we like to use, but I do not like to use them early. If you run the gadget play and score easy, what do you do? The other team doesn't think you are better. All you have done is just to trick him. You have not knocked him down, and you have not run over him, and you have not blocked him, and you have not tackled him. We are not playing chess. We are in a physical game. I think you must understand this point. If there is anything I have stuck with in the years that I have coached, it is this point. I hope you do not mind me saying "I" because I mean our team.

I have been able to survive the coaching profession and I always believe it has been because of this fact. I believe football is a game where you always have to make the other team say "Ouch." I would like to hear the other team say, "Don't hit me anymore. I don't want anymore of this crap." Every good team that I have been associated with has had the determination that it would come out and pound the opponents until they would say "Ouch." You can't do this by looking cute. You have to work at the game and make it physical. You have to block and tackle and hustle and have a bunch of kids that believe that something good is going to happen. You have to know what you are going to do. A fancy way of saying it is this: You have to have a clear-cut philosophy. You must decide on what you want to do offensively and defensively. You must do things that will suit your personnel. This is truer for you in high school than it is in college for me. In college we can recruit. If we want a three-wide receiver offense, we can go out and recruit three wideouts.

You have to make up your mind what your kids can do. Don't let the fans tell you what to do. How many of you have been down on the sideline and are ready to make a call and then start worrying about what the fans are going to say when you make that call? If that is the case, you are not going to be in the game long. I am sure you have been in games when the clock is running down and the fans want you to throw every down? I have said to myself many times, "They have been playing good defense, so I will take it to the opponents one or two more times and not try to get it all at once." About the time we start running the play the fans start booing. Now, we have 96,000 of those Boo Birds. Boo! I don't want that crap. Sometimes you lose then you have to put up with that crap. You make up your mind what your kids can do and put it together and stay with it; stay with it; stay with it. The minute you start screwing around with it you get lost. Then you do not know where you are, who you are, what kind of football team you have. I have seen some big-time coaches come into college football that I thought would be outstanding coaches. However, they did not have the kind of success they thought they would have early and they get all screwed up. They change their offense from week to week, and they change their defense from week to week. I know one coach that is as good as any coach in the country today. As good as his program is, he had a lousy year because he could not settle on one defensive scheme. I will not get into who it is, but I am sure he will never do that again. He got himself out of whack and he did not know what he wanted to do. He thought he could do magic with the X's and O's. You can't do that. Don't have too many plays and too many defenses.

If I were to be critical of Penn State football I would say too many plays and too many defenses. If Coach Sandusky would spend more time with his wife he would have less time to come up with all of those stunts on defense. We have too many stunts and too many plays. I am responsible for the offensive plays, but I am an old man and I don't have that much time to spend with my wife. Sandusky has more stunts that we have plays.

The next error we make are *Errors in Judgment*. Be realistic about your players. Be realistic about your players and their ability. When you get up on the chalkboard and start drawing those X's and O's, stop and write the names of the players in those spots where those X's and O's are on the board. For the X end put down the player's name, his height and weight, and his speed. It is humbling to do this. Everyone wants to run the offense that Miami is running today. If you draw in the speed for the Miami X's and O's you see that they run a 4.3 and a 4.4. Now you write your players' times in the X's and O's; 4.8 and 4.9! Now, perhaps you will not get too carried away with the X's and O's. I think we are all guilty of this error.

When the chips are down, make sure you get the football to your blue-chip players in the game. This falls in the area of an error of judgment. If I were coaching high school football I probably would play some players both ways, but I do not think there are that many players that can go both ways. Let me tell you about Rip Engle and the story he told me when I first started coaching for him at Penn State. Rip Engle had been the head coach at Waynesboro High School and only lost 10 games in 12 years. He left Waynesboro and ended up at Brown and was my college coach. He hired me at Penn State after my senior year. When we were driving down to Penn State one day I asked him the difference in football at Waynesboro High School now and when he coached there. Waynesboro had not won 10 games in 10 years since Rip Engle left them. This is what Rip Engle said. He pointed out two important things to me.

In general this is what he said. Number 1, you only get three or four players that can make a difference in high school. As I look at Waynesboro today, I find those three or four players are not on the field when they need them. When the game is in doubt, they need to be on the field during that time. He said the other thing is the fact that they cut players from the team today. When he coached he never cut a player. He would go up to kids and ask them to come out for football, and they were encouraged to stay out for the team.

They were not cut from the team. By doing this there are always a couple of kids that will make the difference in the program.

Paul Dietzel said this to me one time about Billy Cannon. This is going back to the middle 1950s when LSU won the national championship. Paul used to tell me what a great player Billy Cannon was. I asked Paul Dietzel what makes a great player? This is what he said a great player is: *a great player wins the game when everyone else is tired*. I have tried to apply this to the great players that I have coached. They ask me why we did not get the ball to our great backs more. "Why didn't you get the ball to Curt Warner more?" Because I wanted those players ready when the game was on the line.

The point I am trying to make is this. Coaching is a judgment in your material—what you have and how you use your players. Don't panic! Don't be like the fans. Don't get nervous. It is a 13-6 game and everyone gets upset. When we played Tennessee in the bowl game this year I wasn't worried. We were down at the half 10-7 and I felt good. They should have been ahead 17-0. Basically, we felt they could not play as well the second half, and we felt we would play better the second half. Don't panic. Football games are played for four quarters. Play the entire game. It is a game of attrition. You have to wear teams down. If you have saved your ace, you may have a chance to pull the game out at the end when everyone else is tired. I feel we have won a lot of games at Penn State with patience. We have been patient and we have been able to make that clutch drive when we had to make it. We want our best players in there when they are fresh.

Errors in Your Off-Field Relationships is the next area of discussion. I talk to a lot of high school coaches and perhaps I do not understand what coaching entails as far as obligations are concerned in the other areas and in the schools. I would say that your relationship with your faculty, while it may not be the most important factor involved, it will have a lot to do if you are to be successful. The environment your kids are in will have a lot to do as far as winning and losing. When the faculty respects the players and cares about them and encourages them, then the kids are going to do a better job for you. I learned this from Rip Engle. He would go to every single faculty function. The faculty of Penn State is very, very supportive of our football team. They are extremely supportive of our program. Our kids feel good about the fact that they are supportive of our program. There is a respect that they get in the classroom. The players are not out of the main stream of our student body. This makes my job much easier. We have an interesting faculty and they are interested in our players. We are all educators. I will talk about this more when I wind up this talk.

The worse thing that is happening in high school football today in the state of Pennsylvania is the fact so many coaches are not teaching in the high schools they are coaching in. I do not think the educators today understand what a tremendous, positive, impact a good coach can have on a high school. The coach can watch their kids every day, and see how they look and how the players treat the other students and teachers. I think it is vital for the coaches to be around the other kids in the school. I am not saying this the way I would like to say it. I walk around on our campus and our kids identify with those things. They will stop me and say, "Hey Joe, how is everything going? That was a great game, Coach." They do this because they want to identify with me. In most of the programs that I go into that are successful over a long period of time, the student body identifies with the coach and the faculty identifies with the coach. They respect the coach. He is a colleague; he is a fellow teacher. When you have that type of respect, you make your whole program better. I may overemphasize some of these points, but I am not overstating this point, believe me.

I think your press, radio, TV, and other media relationships are important. We all think the media are a pain in the back, but most of the media people are great. Handling the media is just about the toughest area I have to deal with. It does not matter if we like it or not, but people get their impression of you by what people say about you, the way you look and the way you talk, and what people write about you. They get their impression of you from those areas. They determine if you are a bright, young, progressive coach that is going to go all the way or not. They can provide the image that you are the person that has put the program together and that you are a strong disciplinarian. Your values are important to the school system and the kids. The media will give people certain impressions of you. You cannot get to everyone in your community and every parent in your community. I can't.

I wish I had more time for the media. I would like to do more with the media. I think you have to do more with the media that are important to you. I know you have a newspaper in your hometown, or a TV station, or radio station. You should let them know what you are doing. I do not expect for you to hurt your football team. I used to meet with the media that covered our football game every Friday night until about eight or nine years ago. I would try to explain what we were going to try to do the next day. Everything was off the record. I figured those people had such a tough job and needed a story that perhaps I could help them. I would tell them things like this: "We are going to open up with this type of play. If it works we will come back with this type of play. The key in the game tomorrow will be if we can block so and so." I would put the things that were off the record on the chalkboard. I did this until one night they started talking about the time when I would retire from coaching. I asked them if they were trying to get me out of the coaching profession. I just turned around and said, "What do you want me to do, turn this game over to Switzer and Sherrill?" This was off the record, and I was not trying to be smart. I and had no intention to ridicule Barry Switzer or Jackie Sherrill. There was *one pipsqueak* in the group. He could not wait to tell Jackie what I had said. As most of you may know Jackie Sherrill and I had a few words over the incident. I assured him that there was nothing more to the incident. Since that time I have not been able to build that type of media relationship. I do not do that anymore. The regular media that used to enjoy that type of atmosphere were the ones that lost out on a good thing.

I am sure you do not have that type of problem. I hope there are one or two media people that you can trust and tell what you are going to do. I was shocked at what happened to me. I am a product of the media, I really am. I am a product of the media. The media have always bragged on me and made me look better than I am. I wrote a book just to let the people know that I am for real and that I am not a saint. I am not what people make me out to be. Because I always felt for the media, and I spent time with the media, and I really felt for them and wanted them to do the best job they could do, they always leaned over backwards to help me out. I am giving you this information as a person that has had some real experience in this area. I am sorry I do not give the media the time I use to give them. I will have to work on this now that we are going into the Big 10.

Errors in Developing Morale is the next area. Football begins with morale. In our game, if you do not have the heart and the mind, it does not matter if you can have everything else. You may beat me one week, but if I am going against you enough times I will beat you. Football is primarily a mental game. You must have the heart for the game.

If you do not have many rules, you do not have to enforce as many penalties. If you have a rule and someone breaks the rule, you'd better be prepared to enforce it. You must have the guts to enforce the rules you set up. Don't put those rules down unless you have the guts to make it stick. Make the rules and then make it very clear as to what you are going to do to those who break the rules. Don't be vague. Once you say you are going to do something and you are challenged, and you do not do what you have said you will do, you will lose your credibility.

You must have discipline. Discipline creates pride. Pride creates morale. I could go on and on about discipline. Vince Lombardi said, "We are going to work you so hard that you will never surrender." That was the same motto for the Marines.

I think you must be interested in your kids. Every one of your kids is different and they are unique and they are special. You must show an interest in them, and their studies, and all of their other interests.

Coach your own way. I am up here telling you the way I feel. Tommy Prothro was another coach that I respected as a young coach. He used to say, "Nobody's coach was as tough as he thought he was." Be your own boss and listen and learn. I learned from Prothro and Bryant, and I learned from several coaches, but each coach had a different impact on me. I learned that you have to be yourself.

I want to try to wind this down and let you ask some questions. I think we have to say to ourselves every once in a while, "What is a coach?" I feel strongly about our profession, I really do. I say this to you as serious as I can. The one thing I want to do before I get out of coaching is this: I want to do the best I can to make sure our profession is respected and that our game of football is appreciated. I feel we may be in danger in this area. I am all for the President's Commission and the NCAA. I feel it is very proper that they have institutional control over all athletics. For them to do certain things in our programs without having dialogue with our coaches is wrong. We have made a commitment to young people that very few people have made. Very few people are willing to spend the time, nor do they have the energy and ability that coaches have that are working with our kids in our society today. There are very few people that will go home every single night and try to figure out what they can do best for the people they are responsible for. There are very few professions that will do this. I know there are some individuals that will do this. I know that teachers do the same thing. College and high school coaches spend thousands and thousands of hours on the game. I am not talking about the pro coaches because that is a different game. That is a business, and I do not mean this in a demeaning way. I am talking about the players that are 14 to 18, and those that are 18 to

23 years old. There are very few professions that have made the commitments that we have made to young people at our own personal sacrifice and expenses. If we all got into coaching for the money we get paid, we would be in trouble. If we ever sit down and figure out how much we get paid per hour, we would ask how dumb can we be? I think we should feel good about ourselves and our profession. I do not want people berating coaches. If there is anything I want to get out of coaching it is that I want them to understand this fact. I want them to know what we are all about.

How are we? Number 1, we are teachers. We are educators. We have the same obligations as other teachers. I do not think we should ever forget that fact. We probably have more influence over young people than anyone. This is true for not only the kids you coach in your high school. The way you walk about that school and the way you conduct yourself around that school affects those young people. We have more influence over them than anyone except their families. In a lot of cases we may have more influence over the young people we work with than their family. Teaching an academic subject is not easy. I am not going to berate that aspect. When you say 2 and 2 are 4, you are saying 2 and 2 are 4 for every kid. If you talk about the Warsaw Pact, every single kid is on the same wavelength. When you say Warsaw Pact, you can be sure you are right. But when you get into coaching you literally have to get to the souls of these people. We are dealing with emotions. We must give them commitment and discipline and loyalty. Those are the things that make a difference in one person and another person's life. We can not underestimate this fact. We are teaching them realities of a competitive life.

We must teach kids to come back from defeat. What do we do? We get beat, and then we grab hands and say, "Let's go. Next week we will come back and do a better job." They do not get this from other aspects of our society. We are trying to get them ready so they can make a difference in this world. We must get the very best people and we have a demanding responsibility to make them work to reach their potential. *We get the very best people, we really do!* I tell our players each year that they are the best group on our campus. Somehow we have to make them reach their potential.

Our kids look to us for examples. They look to us for poise and class and how to handle adversity. When your team is behind at halftime what do your players do? They look to the coach for encouraging words and hope and inspiration. They look at the coach to see how he handles adversity. We have a lot of monkeys on our back. Some of you may not be sure the kids are looking at coaches today, but they are. This is particularly true for those that can't find this from their parents. We are role models perhaps, but in a lot of ways, we are *heroes*. My high school coach was my hero. The thing about this profession is the fact that every kid is different and everyone is unique. There is a different way in responding to us. It would be easy if we only had one standard way to get to all of the kids. However, there is no one way. We must understand this fact. We must treat them all different; and on the other hand, we must treat them all the same. We can't have one rule for one kid and another rule for another kid. If you do that you will get them all lost. You want to treat them different, and at the same time, you want to treat them the same. You have to make each one of them make the same commitment but by different people. We have to be understanding, and we have to be tough. *You must know the difference.* You must know that they have problems, but you still must be tough. You must be sympathetic, but demanding. Just because you sympathize with them, it does not mean that you can be less demanding. The minute you start sympathizing with them and you do not demand of them, then they go downhill.

We must be fair. However, it is not enough just to be fair. You must appear to be fair. There is a big difference. You can sit around a staff meeting and say we have been fair to a certain kid. However, the kid may not know this and he may not feel this way. Not only do you want to be fair, you want to appear to be fair. You want to be consistent. That has to be the most difficult thing. It is important for you to be emotional, but some way they have to know what to expect out of you. *You'd better be consistent. You must understand that the kid is going to love you one day and hate you the next. You can't let that worry you.* That is part of coaching. You go out there and drive them and drive them. They will hate your guts. If you punish them for breaking a rule, they will hate your guts, but they will *love you* the minute they have some success. The minute he realizes what you are doing for him he will love you. You have to understand this.

We must understand that we are dealing with people's lives and not our own egos. We are not in coaching to see how many games we can win so we can get on the Coach of the Year Clinic and all of that stuff. Perhaps that all comes with coaching, but you must take care of the kids and once you realize you are working with their lives, you will get those other things. We are there to help our players reach excellence and not just win games. All of us need to understand this fact. I can get up here and preach it over and over, perhaps, because

I am a survivor. Hayden Fry said to me one time, "*You do not even know what coaching is all about.*" I asked Hayden why he would make such a statement to anyone. This was his response. "*You have never been fired.*" Hayden Fry had just been fired from SMU. Right after he said that, I assured Hayden that I was glad I had not shared that experience with him. We all have to understand that we will get fired if we don't win. However, you are really a winner if your kids know you are for them. I do not see a lot of coaches get fired because they are not for the kids. They get fired for other reasons.

You can't coach just to make money. You may not make a lot of money, but you can make it. I make more money than I ever dreamed of making. I get more money than I deserve. Some people have accused me of not liking Jackie Sherrill, but I really do like him. When Jackie Sherrill went to Texas A&M to coach, an interesting thing happened. Our vice president for business called me into his office and asked me if Penn State was paying me enough money. I said I didn't know. He asked me how to find out the answer. I told him to call Michigan and find out what Bo Schembechler is making because Bo and I are about the same age and we have had about the same amount of success. He called Michigan and I ended up with a $25,000 raise out of it. I love Jackie Sherrill. The point I am trying to make is the fact that you can make more money in other professions.

If I would had a chance to make more money by giving up coaching, I would never quit. I never would give up the satisfaction that I have in working with our players and seeing them do things that they never dreamed they could do. This is true both on the field and off the field. I have been able to say to a group of players something like this: "Hey, we are going to be better than you ever thought you could." It was an experience for me to be able to say to a group of players before the season ever starts that we are going to work you so hard the next two weeks that you will wonder why you ever got into this crazy game. Then I would say to them, "Some day you will come back to Penn State and some day you will get down to the Rathskeller and start drinking beer. Then you will start telling lies about how good you guys were when you were playing at Penn State. Then you will start talking about your old coach. Do you know what men? You will never be able to say 'Joe was a great guy and a swell coach, but he was too easy on us. He never made us work hard. We could have been a great team if Joe would have worked us harder. Joe was too easy on us.' No men, that will not happen. You may come back and say, that damn Joe. Do you remember the day he almost killed us when he worked us so hard? It was so hot and

Joe just kept driving us on and on. Men, you will never be able to come back and say that because I will never sell you short."

Ten years after kids are out of school they will write me letters. Some of them will say they never expected to write the letter. They will say things such as, "I didn't believe it when you said it, but I do now. I hear it now. Pay attention to little things and big things will take care of themselves. Keep hustling and something good will happen." They talk about discipline and appearance and things such as that. If I never got paid a lot of money, those letters would have been satisfactory for me. That is what I would say to those of you tonight. I will say it to all of you that are really committed to the profession of coaching. We are in the best profession in the world. I know doctors must get a lot of satisfaction out of what they do but that is keeping people alive. I think that is great. Also, there are other professions that give a great deal of satisfaction. But we are teaching our kids to be better than they ever thought they could ever be. *Coaching is great and yet many coaches do not feel this way*. I feel that way, but we won our last game.

Chapter 13

DEVELOPING A COACHING PHILOSOPHY

Joe Paterno
Penn State University
1996

I have a lot of people ask me, and a lot of young people write me, and they want to know how I have been able to stay in the game of foot-ball for so long. I was an assistant for 16 years. I have been a head coach for 30 years. I was not a very good head coach my first year. We were 5-5 that first year. I lost the first game of the year in my second year. I was a good assistant coach, but it looked like I would not make it as a head coach. I had to make some decisions after that first loss my second year. I had to do some things that I did not believe in. We were playing people who were not very good football players. In those days you could not play freshmen. We lost to Navy in the first game. Navy was not very good, and neither were we.

The next week we had to go to Miami in the third or fourth week of September. We knew it was going to be as hot as it could be. I had to make a couple of tough decisions. It was a Saturday night game in Miami. We took the team to Pittsburgh and spent Friday night at the hotel next to the airport. We flew to Miami on Saturday morn-ing and put them in an air-conditioned hotel that was within walk-ing distance. We never let them get outside. We put them in an air-conditioned bus and took them to the stadium. We went out on the field in pregame without pads on. We warmed up for about 12 minutes. We got them back inside so they did not know how hot it really was.

We went out and started the game with the kickoff. I started the same old players we started the first game. After two plays I sent in two sophomores on defense. They had never been in a game before.

On the next play I sent in two more sophomores. We ended up playing with eight sophomores in that game. None of them knew that they would be playing that much in the game. We kicked the crap out of Miami. You know how it is; as the years go by, you can say you kicked the crap out of everyone. Then if you lost a game you can say it was because an official screwed you. We ended up beating a real good Miami football team. That was the turning point in my coaching career. I had made up my mind that I was going to be a good football coach or I wasn't going to be a good coach. If my judgment of people and my evaluation of the situation were not right, then the heck with it, I was going to get out of it anyway. Basically, that is how I got started.

I developed a philosophy of coaching from that point on. I gave a clinic lecture 27 years ago. At that clinic talk, I talked about Penn State's Winning Philosophy.

I have made some notes to prepare for this lecture. I started thinking that you might want to know about some of the things I believed in 28 years ago when I was just getting started as a head coach that I still believe in today. As I looked over some of the notes, I found that some of these factors have not changed at all. I will quickly go over them and hopefully you will get an idea that will help you in your program. Some of this material may be repetitious to you. But, it does not hurt any of us to get together and go over some of the things that are really important that we sometimes forget.

I really believe that a *coach is a teacher first*, and then a *strategist*. Coaching is creating in practice the situation the player will face in the game. He must be able to see the situation until he can react to it by rote memory. You should devise the practices so the players will go through situations that they will face in a game. You must go through it so many times that they can react without thinking about it. They must be able to do it by rote.

I think football is basically a morale game. If you do not have good morale, you do not have a chance to win. You cannot play as well as you are capable of playing. If you have good morale you will play as well as you are capable of playing. That is all you can ask your kids to do. If you are a good teacher and you are able to teach what you want done, and you are able to get done in practice what you want, and you have good morale, then you are going to play good football. You may not be as physical as the opponents, but you are going to have a chance to win the game. If you do not have good morale, your team will never have a chance to reach its potential.

If you look at the coaches who are successful on your level or on my level, the coaches who are consistent winners, they always say that they win because they get good players. There are some things that are involved in this. These teams always have good morale, and the coaches believe in some of the things I am going to say.

I think morale is made up of three qualities. First is *pride*. We talk about this all of the time with our athletes. This is something you must nurture and work at to be successful. We do not want kids wearing earrings and goatees, and all of that. It is not because that we are so opposed to that. It is because of a sense of pride that the players are making a sacrifice to be a Penn State football player. If they want to party and run around, they must make a decision. If they look around and decide they are willing to make some sacrifices, they can be a part of the team. These are all little things. We keep challenging them. If they want to be a part of this team, they must make sacrifices.

I have told this story many, many times. My brother George and I both graduated from Brown University. Now, my father had run away from home when he was a kid. He joined the army when he was young. He joined General Pershing with the Infantry down in Mexico. They were chasing Poncho Villa down in Mexico in 1916. When World War I broke out, he went in the Infantry with Pershing. He was involved in most of the great land battles. But he hated the Marines. He absolutely hated the Marines. He thought the Marines were a bunch of softies. He said the Infantry did all of the dirty work and the Marines got all of the credit. He had been in all of the battles and the Marines had captured the imagination of the people and got all of the credit. He hated the Marine Corps.

I had been in the service prior to going to Brown University. George got out of Brown and went home and told my father he was going to join the Marine Corps so he could go to OCS. He wanted to be an officer of the Marine Corps and serve for two years and then get out by being in the Reserves. He did not want to go into the Army or Navy. My dad said, "How could you do that to me? You know I hate the Marine Corps." My brother replied, "Pop, they are not going to get me into Infantry. I am 21 years old, and I have a degree from the Ivy League." My dad looked at him and said, "They will get you, too." My brother replied, "Not me, Pop."

George goes down to Quantico Marine Base for 17 weeks of basic training and then he comes home. My dad cannot wait to get a hold of my brother. My dad was a typical Italian family man. We had a great family life. The family would come in on Sunday and we would eat all day. My mom would cook all day. It was a lot of fun.

My dad was the type that loved to get into a discussion with us. If I said Democrat, he would say Republican. He always got things going. If I said welfare reform, he would say no. He could keep things going. He just couldn't wait to get in a discussion with George about the Marines. George got ready to go to Mass and he was wearing his Marine uniform. When he came down the stairs to go to church my dad said, "Don't you have any other clothes?" My brother replied, "I am going like this dad."

After church we came home and my dad started in on George. "I guess you found out what a bunch of bums those Marines are. They wear all of that brass. I am glad they did not get you sold on them." This went on for about 20 minutes. George still has his uniform on. He had his jacket off, but he still had the tie on. Finally, George could not stand any more. He said, "Knock it off! The Marine platoon is the greatest fighting force on the face of the earth." My dad almost had a fit. He could not stop laughing. He said, "They got you!" I have never forgotten that.

The Marines did a good job on George. When he walked into Quantico they told him they were the greatest fighting men in the world. They had to make a lot of sacrifices to go through boot camp. He had to get up at 4 a.m. They made him do things that no one else had to do. "*You are a marine!*" This is the spirit I am trying to get on our football team. You are a *Penn State football player*. I do not give a damn what anyone else says, we are better. "You and me, we are special." I think you have to build that kind of pride. You have to start with this attitude. If you do not have good morale, you will have problems.

You must have loyalty. You cannot compromise loyalty. It is not what they can do for themselves, it is what they can do for the organization. I heard Lou Holtz say one time, "Not everyone can drive the bus." He is absolutely right. You are going to be called upon and you are going to be part of the answer.

When looking for assistant coaches, Coach Bear Bryant once said, "First, I want coaches where coaching is so important to them that they cannot live without it. Secondly, I want coaches that are loyal." We cannot sacrifice loyalty. Our profession is so tough, and we are so tough to the public, and there are so many decisions that we have to make about people and our relationship with players, we cannot have people working with us that we cannot trust. You must be able to trust each other. If we are playing Miami for the national championship like we did in 1986, and we get down on the goal line, we must be able to trust everyone. If we are behind late in the fourth quarter like we were this year against Illinois, you have to be able to trust people. Your people must be willing to make those kinds of sacrifices and commitments for the betterment of the team.

Today when I was coming down here I picked up a *USA Today* newspaper. I was passing time so I read the paper. I saw the story on Rick Pitino talking about his University of Kentucky team. He talked about unselfish players on the team. He talked about "*we* and *us*." It is the Team First for Kentucky. That is the best kind of loyalty. You can take it any way you want, but loyalty to the program, teammates, and coaches is the most important.

The third thing about morale is *Discipline*. It is hard to have discipline all the time. You have to work to have discipline. It must come from within. Unless a kid wants to be disciplined, you can't help him. Perhaps some kids do not know what it takes to be good. I think you have to sit them down and explain things to them. You have to spend a lot of time with kids that way. If you can't get them to make some sacrifices and have some discipline in their lives, you will have a hard time coaching them.

People say to me that we have a great graduation rate at Penn State. They comment on the fact that we make our kids go to class. They say a lot of typical things like that. This is only indicative of the kind of football player he will make. If we are going to win a national championship at Penn State—and that is the only thing we think about at Penn State—we must be realistic. If we want to win a national championship at Penn State we must be realistic. We can't win it with yo-yos. We can't win it with guys that come to play one game and do not come to play the next game. We can't get the job done if they can't get to practice willing to go all out to get the job done. If they can't get up to go to class, then that should say something about them. If they can't get the job done off the field, or if they can't get to practice to get certain things done, then we will not be able to trust them in a tough situation.

I am talking about being the best. I am talking about being the national champion. If you can be satisfied with 8-3, then that is fine. I am not talking about just keeping my job. I have always wanted to be the best. That is what I am talking about.

I think you must have a directive work ethic. I get involved with a lot of people at the university. I get involved with people in management. A lot of companies call on me to talk about decisions. I talk to a lot of executives. It amazes me how much complaining they do about things they cannot do anything about. We all have just so many hours in a day. There is just so much time in a day. You should direct your work ethic to that time. Concentrate on doing something that is going to make the situation better. Don't sit around and moan because your situation is lousy.

We do not have any signs up at Penn State. We do not put names on the back of our players' jerseys. We do not put anything on the helmets. Again, that is all a part of *Pride*, *Discipline*, and *Loyalty*. That is the team part of it. But there are only one or two signs that I have ever considered putting up in our locker room. One I saw in a school in New York. We always had to go see the films with the coaches down in the boiler rooms back in the early days. This one coach had this one big sign up. "D*on't complain about the kids, they are the only ones we have*." Now, you think about that. Hey, we are not in the pros. We can't trade them. We have to play with what we have. There is no sense complaining about it. The thing you want to do is to have a direct work ethic. Don't think things are going to be awful. *Think positive.*

It is so easy to get into a staff meeting and start griping about things. Don't do that. Be positive. Be confident in yourself. The one thing that I do a good job on, even when I did not know how to coach, and a lot of people think I still do not know how to coach, but I would work hard to prepare myself for the game. I really do. I have always felt that I would work harder, prepare myself better, and when I did everything to get things ready for a game, we were going to win that game. We were going to win it. I have always felt that my kids feel this way. I think the staff feels that way. I do not want them to leave a meeting unless they are confident with the game plan. You can't leave a coaching staff meeting where a couple of the coaches are unhappy with what the staff may have decided to do about the game plan. It is hard for them to go out and sell it to the kids. The kids will smell it. They will know if you are not honest with them and they will know you are not confident. You must start with the idea that you and the other coaches are going to be confident, and then the kids will be confident. If you lose, it is not going to be because you are not sure what to do, or you are a little uncertain if this is the right thing to do. You may have to give the other guys credit. You must believe in this to be successful. If you are confident, you can play as well as you can play.

How you treat your personnel is obviously important. It is important to treat them fairly if you are going to have *Pride, Discipline,* and *Loyalty.* There is only one thing that counts when you start evaluating people when it is all said and done. You ask them to make sacrifices and come in together, and you ask them to share values. You ask them to share the same values that the coaches have. We are all together. Then it all comes down to *performance.* Potential means nothing. Don't get trapped with the player that "looks" great. I have told this story over 150 times to emphasize this point. I believe in this story. As coaches we get so caught up with the great big kids. I played with a player who was 6'3" and 215 pounds, and boy, was he built. He was the greatest practice player you ever saw. My high school coach, who coached for 25 years, said this was the best player he had ever seen in his 25 years of coaching. But he really was not worth a damn in the games. I was a 145-pound guard and I could block him with ease. He could run, and he was a great athlete, but he was not a football player. There is only one thing that counts. That is performance. Look at the film and tell him if he doesn't do the job. I do not care how big he is. If he gets the job done, he is going to play.

I do not want you to think that we never disagree on our staff. We argue about this all of the time. There are a lot of gray areas in the things I am talking about. I think you have to keep some of these things in mind when you are working with personnel. First is consistency. Play the people that make the fewest mistakes. There are two things important in football: people who make big plays, and people who do not make big mistakes. I do not care how big the kids are.

Consistency is very important. Make sure your relationship is right. Try to be consistent in your attitude. This is tough. Try to be the same person tomorrow that you are today, regardless of what happens. Do not let family affairs and other personal problems influence you on Monday as opposed to who you are on Saturday. Try to be consistent in your relationships and attitudes toward your players. Try to be totally fair with your players. You must appear to be fair. You may not be fair, but you must appear to be fair. It is amazing how many times in a staff meeting I will say to the staff that so and so said to me that he does not think he is getting a fair shake. The assistants will reply that they have watched that player and they are aware of his talents. But that player still has a feeling that he is not getting a fair shake. "We must make sure it appears that we are fair." You have to do everything that you can to make sure that you appear to be fair.

I think we all have to give our best effort to make sure a kid feels he is getting a fair shake. I have always tried to get different assistant coaches to evaluate their players. I may have the defensive coaches evaluate the offensive players. I make some of the offensive people evaluate some of the defensive players. I may ask another coach how he feels about a player. We do a lot of this. I do not mean we do it every day. When I get concerned that we are overlooking someone, I will ask them to take a look at certain players. I have seen some coaches that want to go out and party the night before a game. I think coaches have to make some of the same type of sacrifices that players make. That is the same with a curfew. You had better be careful where you are at that time. Also, you must be careful about being physically ready to go every day at 7 or 8 a.m.

Let me talk about what I think is important as far as practice is concerned. As far as I am concerned, the best coach is the one who is best organized. You must sell your team on this. In order to play well, you must practice well. You must convince the team that you are going to practice well no matter what. If they are not going to practice well, tell them to get off the field. You may literally have to tell them to get the hell off the field in practice.

Every kid who has ever played for me has heard me say this a thousand times: "You either get better or you get worse." You never stay the same. You get better as a person or you get worse as a person. You do something every day to make yourself a better person. You go by and pick up a piece of paper and put it in the garbage can. That makes you a better person. The same is true in football. When you go out to the practice field, you are not the same player you were the day before. You are better or worse. That is life. If you go out and practice poorly, you start to go down. Make the effort to be a better football player. Do not just go out and practice. Think about the practice.

Your team does not need to practice every single day of the season. I do not think some of us really think through some of these things. We spend a lot of time talking about spending 15 minutes on this, 12 minutes on that, and eight minutes on that. We argue about this. Think about your practices. When you put a practice together, this is something you should remember. You can't have the same tempo. Kids get bored. Try to change the tempo. Change it up a little. Some of you may not have the staff to do this. Some of you have the numbers to change things up. Whatever you do, remember that kids get bored in a hurry. Don't just go out and bang, bang, bang. Change practice up a little. Do something to set a tempo for your team. You will get more out of practice. These are just basic teaching methods.

Let me talk about some things in general. Pay attention to details. I cannot remember ever walking off the practice field when I did not say something to one of the assistant coaches about something that happened in practice that day. It may be just some little thing that happened. The minute we say, "It is not going to happen in a game," that is when it happens. It's like a self-fulfilled prophecy. You have to pay attention to details.

I mentioned this about practice. Don't stay on one thing too long. Avoid a lot of verbal instructions on the field. This is the thing I see in most young coaches. They spend too much time talking on the field. Tell them once, and make them do it 1000 times. Teach in progression. A player must have a good stance. He can't come out of his stance until he has a good stance.

We do not want too many demonstrations by the coach. One year we had a terrific kicker at Penn State. He was an assistant coach. When we worked on punting he would let our regular punter kick one, and he would kick five. I do not want that kind of coach.

Keep up the morale of the kids you work with. Woody Hayes said to me one time, "I worry more about the worst player on my team or the squad." He went on to say this: "If I pay attention to the worst player on the team, and that player is a believer, and he hustles out there, and his friends know that I am interested in him, I will not have to worry about the rest of the team." None of us worries about the *cool cats* that we have, the stars. If you have kids that are not going to play and you spend time with them, then watch them. We have a sports camp at Penn State. We have 2300 to 2400 kids every year. It would be interesting if some of you would come up to watch the camp. We have some great athletes come to camp. One of the things I have been the most proud of is this: I am not that involved in the day-to-day operations. The best thing our coaches do is this. They pay as much attention to the kids who do not have a chance to be a football player. They work their butts off with all of the kids. They spend as much time with the average athletes as they do with the great athletes. The great athletes that come to our camp know this. When I sit down to recruit a player who has been to our camp, he knows the kind of people he is going to be with when he comes to Penn State. They know if they come to Penn State they will be treated like all of the other athletes. They know they will be in a disciplined program. When we say something, we mean it. I think you get my point.

Let me end this up with something that is not 25 years old. I would sum it up this way. Coaching for as long as I have, I am no different—and I am not saying that is good or bad—as far as my philosophy is concerned. I believe in certain things that I have shared with you today. There have been times when I have been challenged and people have told me I was "over the hill." There have been some times when I wondered about myself. I have wondered if some of the things I want to do were out of whack. I think you have to make some adjustments in dealing with kids. Some of the things we think are important, as far as rights and attitudes about social values, are outside the realm of the football program. I think you have to make some adjustments to those areas. In college football today kids have to be better than they have ever been. Kids today are better than they have ever been. I say that because of the pressures outside. Look at pro football and the big money. Look at recruiting today. All of these things have made kids different from what they were 25 to 30 years ago. So, when kids come to college now, they come with some baggage. I think most of them handle it very, very well. You can pick up the paper and find a couple of kids who do some stupid things. That is not the trend. Most of the kids work hard today. They work hard in the weight room. They are anxious for coaches to show them that this is the way to go. We have a tremendous spiritual revival going on college campuses today because kids are really searching for something. They have tried it the other way, and they do not like it. We have a tough responsibility. They do not want to be failures. You have to replace that with something. It may be with pride in an organization. The emotion and excitement that comes out of competition is great. Going out on the field on a Saturday, or whenever you play, and knowing you have worked with a group of people, and you held hands with them, and you suffered with them. The sound of the coaches yelling at you is part of the process. At Penn State the players are taught to love each other and to grow together because they all hate *Joe*. I do not care, as long as they grow together. They need it. We have a tough responsibility to our players.

Coaching is such a great challenge. People keep asking me when I am going to get out of coaching. Why would I want to get out? It is one of the greatest professions in the world. Every day is important. Every day is charming. Everything is exciting. When you stop wanting that, what do you do? Go out and work on my putting, and then go to a cocktail party at 5 o'clock? I do not want that, and I know you do not want that. I love the challenge of coaching. I hope I can do it 10 years from now. I do not know how long I can go but I will go until my health runs out or until I can't get the job done the way I think it should be done. I am getting a little too personal here.

Two years ago we had a wonderful woman who was honored as Distinguished Woman of the Year. She was an alumna of Penn State. She gave a very short speech; actually it was not a speech, it was just something she had put together. I asked her for a copy of it because it summed up pretty much where I have been most of my life. She called it *Anyway*.

Anyway

People are unreasonable, illogical, and self-centered.
Love Them Anyway
If you do good, people will accuse you of selfish, ulterior motives.
Do Good Anyway
If you are successful, you will not fault friends and true enemies.
Succeed Anyway
The deed you do today will be forgotten tomorrow.
Do Good Anyway
Honesty and frankness make us very vulnerable.
Be Honest and Frank Anyway
People favor underdogs but follow only top dogs.
Fight for Some Underdogs Anyway
What you spend years building may be destroyed overnight.
Build Anyway
People will need help but may attack you when you do help them.
Help People Anyway
Give the world the best of all and you still may get mistreated.
Give the World the Best You Can Anyway
Give it the best you guys have, *anyway*.

Chapter 14

FOOTBALL—A WAY OF LIFE

Eddie Robinson
Grambling University
1998

When you get my age you do not come in and draw up a lot of diagrams of X's and O's. I feel I would be remiss if I did not say some things about the game and give some advice to the young coaches.

When I started coaching the Single Wing was popular. Also, the Double Wing was in use. I started coaching in 1941. At the time I had Northwestern's Single-Wing playbook. It had the University of Michigan's techniques. I used Fritz Crisler techniques from Michigan with Northwestern's Single-Wing plays. So we ran the Single Wing for a long time after everyone else had gone to the T formation.

In the late 1950s Forest Evashevski was at Iowa. They won the Rose Bowl. They ran the Wing-T formation. They were so successful we decided to take a look at that offense. We looked at the Wing-T and went to it in 1959. From that time on I would go to clinics like this and take what I thought would work for us and adapt it to our Wing-T system.

I want to talk to you about the game of football. The thing I am most proud of concerns the relationship I had with my assistant coaches and players. When you talk about winning games, you know a man cannot win games by himself. He must have good assistant coaches and good players. If you don't have good assistants and good players you don't win.

I have been in this game 56 years. I have always wanted the best for our players. I was always concerned that they would get their education. I wanted them to be proud of the fact that when a player plays for us he would go on to graduate from school. I hoped he would not end up in trouble. I know we wanted to be able to run the off-tackle play, and throw the pass. Players come to me to talk about playing football. I tried to get them to make their own decisions because I had already made my decisions. This is how the players feel about you. You know what I am talking about. They are going to call you and ask you for advice about what they should do.

You are in the most rewarding profession in the world—the coaching profession. Alonzo Stagg said it best, "Coaching is the most rewarding profession in the world, and no man is too good to coach American youth."

We were in Washington at an awards ceremony a few years ago. Some of the recipients were from the NFL. As the winners came up to receive their awards, the young people would follow them up to the stage to get their autographs. Some of the players were hesitant in signing the autographs.

I am not trying to tell you what you should believe, but I believe we have to give football a great look. If these youngsters want autographs from you we should try to do it for them. I am just another football coach, but I wrote to our executive director and I told him we must take a look at the situation. We are always telling the young people we can't do this or that. I am not trying to tell anyone how to run his or her life, but we want people to love football. I want the parents to love football. I want the mother and daddy to love football. I want all of the other people in the school to know we outwork them. *We can do it*! I am just telling you to consider this. When this little kid comes to you with a piece of paper for an autograph consider what it means. If you can't, tell them when you can, and make it a point to do it then.

Recently I went to Canton, Ohio, to the NFL Hall of Fame induction ceremony because one of my former players was being inducted. Kids are smart about this today. They will come to your hotel room if you are out of town. I saw the kids lined up as we went to our hotel room. As the inductees came in they lined up immediately. I told my wife that I had to get her out of that crowd and up to the room. I told her I would have to come back down and sign autographs.

As I started up to the room with my wife they came to me for autographs. I told them my plans to take the wife to the room and then I would come back to see them. They replied, "It seems to me that we have heard that before." I said, "Perhaps you have and perhaps you haven't, but just let me get my wife up to the room."

I got my wife up to the room and I had nothing else to do but watch TV. So, I came back and I signed a lot of autographs. I cleaned the room of all autograph seekers.

Then on Saturday the former players who were inducted in the NFL Hall of Fame were signing autographs. I got an area and I started signing autographs. Someone asked me why I was signing autographs. I replied, "Because I am Eddie Robinson."

This is what I am trying to tell you about football. You must have a belief in yourself. I did it because that is the way Eddie Robinson wants to do it. When I went into football I did what I wanted to do after talking to all the other coaches. I talked to them about the passing game and all the other phases of football. But it was Eddie Robinson that was in what we did. These last few years have been difficult. Perhaps if I had kept Eddie Robinson out of it we may have looked a little better.

I am going to be talking about this point more and more as we go along. You have a good mind. You know about the game. You look at your practice. You have to believe in it.

We were in a game and it was third down and 16 yards to go from our own 20-yard line. We had a change to get a first down at the 36-yard line. I sent in the play and the coach in the press box called down and asked me what play I had called. I told him that I had called 17 Pass. He said, "Isn't that a dangerous play?" I told him damn right; it is dangerous to call the play anywhere on the field. But, you have to go with what you believe. You have to work hard and go with what you believe in.

With me, you have to pardon me because when you get old you forget a lot that makes up the game. But this experience with football has been a way of life for me. I wanted to coach since I was in the fourth grade. I knew what I wanted to do. I am saying this for some of the young coaches. We have to keep the young coaches coming in the profession. We have to feed our organization with young people. We must encourage the other young people.

I believe that Eddie Robinson has been lucky and blessed. I believe that God has blessed me. What happened to me did not happen to just anybody. It started out where I was born, in America. I will tell you if you don't know it, but this is the greatest country in the world. We get a lot of criticism about what is happening in America. But still it is the greatest country in the world. I tell my players that. I tell them about the opportunity they have in America. There is a lot of money in basketball and football. If you are willing to pay the price it is there for you. I can just come to you and tell you that we won a lot of games. We won some games but we won some people. We won over some guys that were not going to be good people. We got after them to get them to be better people.

A player came to my office to see me and talk. He told me he did not want to waste my time. I told him he was not wasting my time. "My time is your time." If he plays for me and he doesn't graduate he is a loser. He is a loser! I am like most of you, I want to win. But I think you must know where it stops and what you have to do to get them to do what is best for them. If it were not for the high school coaches in Louisiana and across the nation we would not have had the record that we have at Grambling. They put the football in the players' hands the first time. When they come to us, we put them into a position and tell them what we want them to do. I am saying this because we really do appreciate the high school coaches of America. I know all of the other college coaches in this room appreciate you. They have to. Without you and the coaches of Louisiana there would be no college coaching.

I do not know where Eddie Robinson would have been without people like you. I would probably be teaching math or science somewhere. If I were teaching science I would be trying to put someone on the moon. That is how football coaches think about the other areas. You send a well-trained athlete to us. You may say that I am pulling your leg. *No!* Not to people who put bread on my table. I want the players to come back to you as good people because that is how I got them.

What success we have had at Grambling, the high school coaches and the others in those high schools are responsible for. You are a part of it. I am talking for all the other college coaches. I know they have told you. I just want you to know how much we appreciate you. I wish we could come up with an award at the American Coaches Association national meeting. They should be smart enough to come up with something. You are a great breed of men. You can win it one year and lose it another year. Then you can come right back and do the job. President Clinton said, *"You make winners out of losers."* Some of the players who come to me have never won anything. They have come into our program and have turned out to be good people.

Our nation needs the leadership and the guidance that coaches are giving. I feel a person my age needs to say this so you can hear it so you can say that you know how important this is. We need you to call the players in the office and tell them that they have to pass their schoolwork. If you don't pass you don't play. If you tell him that he will believe it more then if his father tells him. If you call them in and talk to them about their potential it will do a world of good. I have used this technique before.

I have used Monday Night Football to motivate players. I tell them if I think they have potential to play at the next level. If they see that on Monday and can play on Saturday, you know they want to play in the pros. On draft day you know the college coaches have to stay at home or you have to let your wife know where you can be contacted because if they do not get drafted they are going to call you. "Coach I didn't get drafted. What can I do?" You can't tell him it is just one of those things. You can't do that. You have to come up with something for that player and tell him what he needs to do.

Recently I had a player contact me who had been trying to make it in the pros. He had tried out with three different teams and had not made it. I told him it was time he started thinking about doing something else. He called me and thanked me for talking with him. He told me he had talked with his father and that he was going into business with his father.

Football has been too good for me to walk away and not do what I can do for others. If I can help on a coaching clinic I will. John Burke and I were talking about that today when we went over to do an interview on the radio station. John was talking about the people who helped him in his career. The parents need you and your contribution with young kids today.

I had an experience with a young man that I want to relate to you. I was being the father figure for him. This young man was very outspoken. We were in our homecoming game. It was fourth down and the opponents were getting ready to punt the ball to us. He walked by the bench and made this statement to his teammates. "We are going to lose this game because our best return man is sitting on the bench." I heard that and I could not resist. I asked, "Who is it, who is it?" He said, "Mr. Neimiah Wilson!" I replied, "Who, you?" He said, "Yes sir, I am your best punt return man. Just give me a chance to show you."

We got the ball and ran three plays and kicked the ball away. I went to one of the other players and said, go down to the other end of the bench and tell Mr. Neimiah Wilson that he is to return the next punt. He was from Denver, and he played for Denver some years back.

They punted the ball to Neimiah Wilson and he went 79 yards for the touchdown. It was the only time in my life that I wanted to give the touchdown back to our opponents. Give it back! He took his time when he came back off the field. He walked right by me. He looked over at one of the players next to me and said, "Tell Mr. Robinson if he wants someone to run the punt back for a touchdown, I will be on the north end of the bench." I do not think I have ever recovered from that experience. I try not to make those mistakes. I do not want to dare a player in what he can do and what he can't do.

Our universities, and colleges, and our high schools really need you. You are an important person in your community. There are people all over town who would like to have the flair that you have with your players. If you could just let them walk your sideline and make substitutions in the game they would know what a great job you are doing. They want the respect that your kids are giving you.

We can see the same situations with other teachers. They say when they tell them something to do they will not do it. But when the coach tells them to do something they will do it. If they can't pass they can't play. That leads me to this story. It tells the academic side of the story.

This player was having trouble getting enough quality points to remain eligible. The coach asked the teacher to see if she could help the athlete with his lessons. He had an examination coming up the next week. The teacher told the athlete to come in to see her and she would help him with his lessons. Every day he went in to see her and they would sing this song over and over. Ole MacDonald Had A Farm: E-I-E-I-O. They sang that song over and over. They practiced and practiced: Ole MacDonald Had A Farm: E-I-E-I-O.

It came time for the examination. It was a one-question test. The question was this: Ole MacDonald Had A F_____? He looked at the question for a long time. He just could not figure it out. Finally, he leaned over to the guy sitting next to him and whispered. "What is the answer to number 1?" The guy next to him said, "Man, you sang it all last week. Ole MacDonald Had A F_____? That is FARM. Can you spell Farm?" The player replied; "Yes I can! E-I-E-I-O."

I really believe in football. I am not saying this because I am getting out of active coaching. You really enhance football. There is no other nation that can do football like we do. I have asked other countries to let us come over and coach their athletes. That would really be something. We could put together some good teams.

The people coaches deal with are America's most precious possession. If they don't cut the mustard, who is going to cut it? There is no one else to do it. Who is going to do it? They are the leaders of tomorrow. We have to get the players in the classroom and make sure they pass. They can take the job and do it.

Jack Kemp was at the meeting I attended in Washington. You could just see he was an impressive man. The way he talked and the way he maneuvered indicated that he had a lot of poise. They have to know what it is to deliver a blow and to never give up. This is the type of training we really need. We need that with our leaders of tomorrow. We can't send a pansy to do the job in the White House. Whatever we are and whatever we are going to be we need to make the young people of today stronger for tomorrow. That is how I see it. If our way of life is going to continue then we have to have strong people to go to the negotiations table.

Where football is concerned you must make a total commitment to win. I cannot remember a day that I walked off the football field that I did not give it everything I had. I wanted our players to be better people. I recall going to an All-Star Game in Chicago when I started coaching. All the way back on the train I wondered how I could ever get a player from Grambling to play in that game. I was really concerned about it. I told you at the beginning that I take a lot of pride in the fact that I have heard all of the great coaches in this game since 1941 speak. I have heard them all. I have notes on all of those lectures. I keep those notes. This is what I am saying. I knew what they said and I knew what it would take to be successful. Some of those great coaches have been very kind to us to help us in our program.

We have a great program at Grambling. We have played in New York every year since 1968 except one year. When the sponsors of the game could not sponsor us in 1977, George Steinbrenner sponsored the whole game.

The thing I am saying to you is this: We have to involve the people who can help us make this game of football important. You have an imagination of what you can do. You can bring new innovations to your area.

Since the time I was coming back from that All-Star Game in Chicago, we have played in Europe. We have what we call classics. That is when you are trying to make money because you are not making money by playing games on campus. We have a classic in New York, Dallas, Shreveport, and in New Orleans. We tried to have a game in New Orleans two or three years and lost our shirt. We went back and talked to the sponsors and told then we wanted to play only one school in New Orleans. Our two schools were only 200 miles away; Southern University and Grambling. When they announced the attendance for the first game it was 76,080. "Hell," I cried! I was so proud we could do this. We have sold out Yankee Stadium three years in a row with attendance of 56,000. We just have regular people. It is up to us to keep the game of football a great game. We have to keep it a great game.

A coach needs to have a commitment. You have to get a commitment from the players. That is a must. As a coach I believe you must have some knowledge about your offense. You must have a knowledge about your defense. In pro football they try to get coaches to run the right offense and defense. If they do not get the job done they fire that coach. In college, I have to know what my offensive and defensive staffs are doing. You must know what you are using. It is not because someone else beat you with something, but because you know what it takes to win. You have to study offense and defense. You have to read and study about the kicking game and special teams. What I am saying is that we must have some knowledge of what we are coaching. There is a lot to the game of football.

I want to tell you a little about how we ran the Wing-T Offense. In that formation you split the end and wingback and you have anything that anyone else has in their offense. You can do what you want to with it. People told me you cannot win all of the time. We have used a tight wing T to win most of our games.

If you do not know about the details of scoring from the 10-yard line going in, you are going to have problems trying to stop teams when you are on defense. Most of you are too young to remember when we had to look at film on a 16-millimeter projector. You would go to sleep and then you would wake up and the film would be beating the projector as it came off the reel up front. We don't do it like that now, but do you know what? I believe in borrowing films from other coaches, and borrowing film from the NFL has been a tremendous help in allowing me to coach what I wanted to coach. From the film we must be able to understand the strengths and weaknesses of our opponents on offense, defense, and the kicking game. You must have confidence in yourself and you must believe in yourself. You have to work hard enough to establish who is the leader. Even if others are doing the work you must be there to know what is happening.

Several years ago a coach came up to me and asked me this question. He said, "Coach Robinson, are you still using that same offense that we used when I was playing for you?" I said, yes we are and I will tell you why. We have not lost very many games in those last 10 years. What about you? He replied, "Well Coach, my quarterback got hurt, and then our best receiver hurt his arm." They are not going to write that up in the paper.

Legally, you must do whatever it takes to win. I would love for you to walk out of here and say that Coach Robinson did not talk about anything but having confidence in yourself to win. It is your thinking and how you see it. I believe if I were coaching the offensive or defensive line it may have made a difference in our team. I say that because I enjoy coaching. I tried to do a little of every kind of coaching possible. But I had the faith to believe in what we were using. Don't use an offense just because someone down the road is using it and having success. Don't do that. Do it because you know it and your coaches know it. This is what the game is all about.

I brought some information about the Wing-T. I am not trying to tell you what to do. I am talking about execution. The way to coach is to find out what makes an offense or defense work. Once you find out what makes it work you can stop it. It is like a car. If you know that car has to have gas or it will not start, then you need to get gas in it. If you don't, it will not start. Find out what makes an offense or defense work. Go to a place where teams run what you are working against and learn from them. If you must stop the isolation from the I formation, go visit teams that run the Iso and learn how they run it. Then you will know how to stop it.

Let me put this on you. We came up with a system for practice. I know you cannot do this in high school. We decided to quit going to the practice field on Monday. The reason is we had to do a lot of written reports and do a lot of other things. We decided to use that whole period to go over the offense and defense. We went over the entire scouting report. Then we could come on the field on Tuesday. Then we could work our game plan on Tuesday, Wednesday, and Thursday. If we played at home we would work out on Friday.

Chapter 15

KEYS TO THE WINNING EDGE

Sam Rutigliano
Liberty University
1992

If you will stay with me for the next hour or so, I promise you at least three points that will help you in coaching next year. First of all, the topic is very broad based. Every time I say something significant I will tell you to write it down. We need to teach the players that they need to *think picture*. Before we do that, let's talk about the problem we have in coaching.

This professor was teaching a class. He wrote the word *apathy* on the board. He asked the students what was the definition of the word apathy. There was no response. Finally, one of the students shrugged his shoulders and said, "Who cares?" In coaching, that is the biggest problem we have. Nobody cares. Basically, we are fighting a war on an island. There are 139,000 high school and college coaches in America. In the course of a normal coaching career, we have an opportunity to impact 20,000 young people as an educator and as a coach. I spent 18 years in the NFL with five different teams. I spent five years coaching in high school, and I am in my third job in college coaching. Of the 18 years in the NFL, I watched a mission. There are 1 million high school football players in America. Only 50,000 players go on to play beyond high school football. Of that 50,000 only one percent make it to the NFL. Out of the one percent that make it to the pro level, more than 75 percent of those players end up in divorce, more than 50 percent of them end up broke, and less than 30 percent end up with a college degree. I have watched the mission. Somewhere along the line, as we are on the island, *the process has failed*. I am not up here to talk a great deal about that issue.

I want to center my talk on a number of things. The first topic that I want to cover has been important in every single job that I have had. That is *communication*. This is an important point; write this down. *Think picture*. Give the players a horizontal and vertical picture of what you want them to do. Red Auerbach said the definition of overcoaching is "a coach that falls in love with the sound of his voice." Think about that for a second.

Make sure your team is focused. Let me give you a simple story to illustrate this point. This man owned a factory. One day all of the machinery in the factory stopped running. Something broke down and all of the machinery stopped working. The owner got on the telephone and called several repair companies to see if he could get them to come out and repair the machines. He was on the phone for one hour, but could not get anyone to come to repair the machines. A second hour passed and he became desperate. He could not find anyone that could repair the machines.

Over in a corner sat a small man with a hammer in his hand. He told the owner he could repair the machines and get them going again. The owner was amazed that the man would make such a statement. He told him to give it a try. The little man got a ladder and climbed up about 10 feet. He spotted a bolt up at 10 feet. He got out his hammer hit the bolt. The machines kicked back on as soon as he hit the bolt. The owner was delighted. He asked the little man how much he owed him. The reply was $1000. The owner said, "What? What do I owe you $1000 for?" The little man said, "You owe me $1 for hitting that bolt with the hammer, and $999 for hitting the *right bolt*. You see, that is what we must do as coaches. We must hit the right bolt. It is all relative. It does not matter what level you are playing on. Although I agree with everything Bill McCartney said—you never saw a jockey carry a horse across the finish line—you still must have the players.

Let's talk about some cellular points about communication. First, 75 percent of communication is nonverbal. It is not what I say; it is what you hear. As coaches we make mistakes because we make talk in words and phrases. *Think pictures*. Make sure the players see the pictures. If I am talking about a team function, I give them the story about the bolt. That becomes a picture in their mind and they can picture that scene in their minds. We can stress the importance in hitting the right bolt.

In 1980 we were sitting in the same division as the Pittsburgh Steelers. They had won the World Championship in 1978 and 1979. It was in preseason and we were sitting in a team meeting on the campus of

Kent State University. We were talking about goals and objectives for the upcoming year. Brian Sipe, our quarterback, was sitting on the front row. I walked up, and right in front of him I placed a 12-foot-long plank. I said, "Brian, if I asked you to walk across that 12-foot plank would you do it?" He replied, "Of course I would do it, Coach." Then I said, "Brian, suppose I take the 12-foot plank and place it between two 20-story buildings?" *That makes a difference*. The difference is this. The mind makes a difference. You have to *think pictures*. Don't fall in love with the sound of your voice.

The greatest experience that I had, which I felt put me above the other coaches in my profession in the NFL, was my experience as a high school teacher. The fact that I have been a high school teacher, where I had to go into a classroom and have an objective for my lesson each day, helped me as a coach in the NFL. In the classroom I had to have an objective for my lesson each day. I had to find a way to bring everyone into that objective and then finally summarize it and bring it together. As a teacher, I did not just sit up there and regurgitate information to my students. I had to make sure we had an objective and that everyone understood what we were trying to accomplish.

Let me give you two examples of what I am trying to get across to you. In 1983 we opened the season against the Minnesota Vikings. We were losing the game 27-21 in Cleveland late in the fourth quarter. The Vikings had the ball with a fourth down and 1 yard to go on their own 25-yard line. We had no timeouts left with one minute to go in the game. Bud Grant figured he could go for a first down because we had no timeouts. The Vikings went for it, and we stopped them for no gain. We got the ball back, but we did not have any timeouts left. Brian Sipe threw a pass to Dave Logan and we got the ball down to the 9-yard line. We had a first-and-goal, and the Vikings called timeout. Brian came over to the sideline and we talked the situation over. I said, "Brian, we are going to throw the ball into the end zone four downs. Don't force the ball. Don't take a sack." You want your quarterback to see the defense like it is in slow motion. When he gets refocused it looks like Times Square. You want your quarterback to have a clear picture. I went on to tell Brian, "If things get tight, throw the ball into some blonde's lap in the mezzanine, but *don't force the pass*. I will keep Mike Pruitt in on your blind side to protect you from the blitz." We went back out and ran the play. The Vikings ran the blitz and Mike Pruitt missed the rusher. Brian was cool enough to duck under the rusher and cause him to miss him. Now, Brian had to refocus. By now the defense looks like Time Square on New Year's Eve. *He forced the ball into the end zone, and the Vikings intercept the ball and we lose the game.*

I have always been taught that the players need us the most when we lose. I also took the advice my father gave me a long time ago. "When you get a chance to keep your mouth shut, take advantage of it." When I went to our locker room after the loss to the Vikings I was completely out of character. Now, I was a guy wearing a sombrero. I was the guy taking the heat over the loss. I was the guy that had to go to the press conference. I was the guy that had to go to dinner with the owner of the Browns that night. I was the guy; I was the guy; I was the guy. You could not believe I was the same coach at the press conference as I was the week before. Those press people have the serial number of the Unknown Soldier. They know all of the answers. The only exercise they get is jumping to conclusions. If you ever have a brain transplant, get it from a sportswriter because his brain has never been used. Hey, we are all horses' tails for five minutes a day. The secret is not to exceed five minutes a day, and I have just exceeded my limit.

The next day we went to our film meeting and it was the same thing with the team. I was the guy wearing the sombrero. The team could not believe it. The next day before the team meeting I was involved with something and was a minute late for the team meeting. I walked in and there were 45 players sitting there with sombreros on. They were saying to me, "Hey, Coach, we are in this game together. You told us we were in this thing together in our first team meeting. *We lose together, and we win together.*"

I have a 24-year-old daughter. When she was 16 years old she told me she was going to start dating. I said, "Fine, but there will be a curfew." She said, "Daddy, you have to be kidding me. You are going to put a curfew on me? You have to be an astronaut because you are living in outer space. A CURFEW!" I assured her we would have a curfew at 11:30 p.m. She said, "Daddy, everything just starts at 11:30 p.m." I said, "It is my way or it is over." I had a captive audience. I felt she would be home at 11:30 p.m. Right!

At 11:45 the first night she was still not home. I sat in the family room waiting for her. She came in before 12 and I could not wait to talk to her. She said, "Daddy, give me a break." I said, "I told you I play by the rules." I assured her if I could find out the rules I could pay the price because I learned to play by the rules. I told her, "If you want to continue to date, you had better be in here by 11:30 p.m." I figured this would get her home on time.

The next Saturday night she had another date. Midnight came and she was not home. About five minutes later I saw a car enter my driveway. I had a long driveway in Cleveland, so I went out to meet the car. I got right in the middle of the driveway and the car stopped. I go over to the driver's side and ask the driver to roll his window down. He did not know what I was going to do. I said, "Don't worry, she did not tell you the rules. I want to tell you my rules. If you want to date this girl again, don't bring her home after 11:30 p.m. again." He said, "I understand." My daughter jumped out of the car and yelled, "I hate you. When I go to school Monday, they will all be talking about me. I will never get another date. I will never speak to you again." Well, let me assure you, she and I have talked since that time. The fact is, she was learning to drive at the time, and I owned all of the cars at our home. That is called leverage.

The reason I am telling you this story is because she came to me recently and told me some things that I feel are important. She told me she did not agree with me on the dating principle. I said, "Look, I am just a parent. *There are no perfect scores. There are just batting averages.*" I went on to explain my story in detail. Pete Rose could have gone to the Hall of Fame. He got more hits than any player that ever played the game. Pete played 20 years and he batted .300, which means that he failed 70 percent of the time when he came up to bat. So, don't you see, "There are no perfect scores, just batting averages."

Here is the key, and you can write this down. She said, "Daddy, I knew you loved me because I had seen other friends whose parents did not love them. I know we have been involved in a lot of changes, but I knew you loved me." Just the other day she told her story to her present boyfriend. He is an offensive lineman at Liberty University and will graduate this year. If my father was alive today he would say this is the problem in our country today. *Our spinal column is lined with a wishbone instead of a backbone.*

I have been a coach in three Pro Bowls and two Senior Bowls. I was a coach in the NFL for 18 years, which is no big deal, except I had the opportunity to be around the best football players in the world. I have never been around a one that was worth a grain of salt that did not want to be disciplined. *Discipline does not mean punishment.* Discipline means *direction*. It comes from the word disciple. It means *follow a good leader*.

The second area I want to talk about is Philosophy. That really is a broad term. In the dictionary it states that philosophy "is a system of beliefs and guiding principles that are fully understood by everyone." What does this mean to a football coach? It means this. When you come right down to it, and you have decided what you want to do in football, but you have one player that questions what play you call, or questions what you do, then it means you must get rid of that person. You have to decide from a philosophical standpoint what you are going to do. So, when the bullets start to fly and things do not always work like you plan for them to work, you go back to your playbook and you go back to your philosophy, and that is the way you respond. You learn in football as a coach that there are a lot of right ways to do things. If you go to Japan and want to climb Mt. Fuji, you learn there are 12 different routes to get to the top. It does not matter which route you take, as long as you get to the top.

I want you to think about theses next three topics. First is offense. Offensively, you must do three things. You must gain a yard every single time in every situation you are in. I do not care if you are inside your 3-yard line or outside your 3-yard line. I do not care if it is third down or if it is fourth down. You must have a plan where you are guaranteed that you are going to make that 1 yard.

I can recall when I was a freshman at Tennessee. We would practice our goal-line offense. We would put the ball on the 2-yard line. They would put 50 players on defense. They would stack six or seven players in each gap. Our quarterback would get in the huddle and say POG. That was short for Protect Our Gaps. He would say, "No one offside, no penalties, and N.S.I.W." That was short for No Self-Inflicted Wounds. We are sure we are going to contain the jump line, and we are going to make sure we can gain that 1 yard.

Write this down because it is important. In times of crisis, *think players and not plays*." In times of crisis, think players and not plays. If we have a third down and 5 yards to go, I want to get the ball to Ozzie Newsome. I am going to get the ball to a man that I know wants the ball. I want the ball going to a player that I know will get the job done a high percentage of the time.

The third thing we want to do on offense is to hit the third-down critical pass play. I have elaborated on this. What system are you involved in? What player do you want to go to on the pass? What situation do you want to put that player in?

You must always punt the ball when you are planning on punting the ball. I never want to put myself in a situation where I take away my opportunity to punt the football.

Defensively, we have a few thoughts that are just as important. Without going into a lot of thoughts, I can remember Dick Nolan, who was the defensive coordinator for Tom Landry at Dallas, saying this about defense. "Number 1, *do as you are told and stay on your feet.*" It does not matter what system you use, as long as it is sound and you do as you are told and you stay on your feet. If you will do these two things, you can improve your defensive game immediately.

The third philosophical aspect is the kicking game. The kicking game is important because it avoids losing. If the kicking game is sound, it avoids losing. We came out on the practice field early for the kicking game at Cleveland. We had someone assigned to the players not involved in the kicking game to keep them involved. We did not want them on the field without someone coaching them. We did not want them fooling around.

Our kicking game preceded practice every day. Once the kicking game is over, we go into our warm-ups and then we go into our regular practice schedule. In terms of work place, the kicking game has to come out as the number 1 thing we do in football. We want them to think that way. If you emphasize this is a prioritized list then the players will believe that is the way it should be done.

The next area I want to discuss is *preparation*. People like to talk about the *motivation to win*. I have never been in a locker room when we were going to play against the great Steelers teams when I did not believe that we could beat them. That is really a misnomer. The important thing is to have the *will to win*. Luck is the residue of design. Luck is where preparation meets opportunity. Yes, Luck will grant you certain things, but preparation will grant you a great deal more.

Let me elaborate just a little about what Bill McCartney said about the off-season program. We have a strength coordinator at Liberty University who was at Alabama and Texas A&M before. I have been around a lot of strength coaches across the NFL, and I can tell you our man does the best job on strength of anyone I have been around. This is what he tells me. *Speed comes from developing the abdominal muscles and the ankles*. If you strengthen the abdominal muscles and the ankles, your players will gain speed. I have seen our strength coach take players that ran a 4.7 and get them down to a 4.5.

Recently he got an idea from the Rumanians. He has built a staircase of sand. We are going to run our players up staircases of sand. We plan to build a sand pit 15 to 20 yards long. We want the players to come off the sand pit and run on to an Astroturf strip and then run onto a grass field. All of you know how they train Arabian horses in water because of the resistance water gives them. The same principle is true with the sand. We are going into our off-season program geared to improve ever players' quickness and speed.

There are some things in terms of our budget we may have to do something different. When I first got to the Cleveland Browns in 1978, all we had was a Universal Gym. We only had a 70-yard practice field. The one thing that turned the program around in Cleveland was this. Our goal was to have more players living in Cleveland, working out in our preseason program than working out in the Dallas Cowboys program. At that time, Dallas was the program that everyone wanted to be like. Before it was over we had 60 players living in Cleveland year-round. You do not win games in September and October. You win games between December and September preparing during the off-season.

The important aspect about a program such as I have just mentioned is this. It is important to take each person as an individual. High school coaches do this better than college or pro coaches because you get kids before they develop a lot of bad habits. You get them at an early age and you can see them develop.

Let me get into the subject of a role model. Bill McCartney touched on this briefly. About five years ago I was working as a commentator for NBC. They asked me to go to New York to be on a TV program with Bob Trumpy. The subject to be discussed was "Random or Mandatory Drug Testing in the NFL," which I believe in. A counselor for the NBA was to discuss the flip side of the issue with me and Bob Trumpy running the show. I got to the studio about 4:30 p.m. for the 5 p.m. show. Our producer, Stu Black, said to me at 4:45 p.m., "The NBA counselor can't make the show, so we have a sub for him." I said, "Who is the sub?" He replied, "*F. Lee Bailey*, the attorney." For some of those that do not know it, F. Lee Bailey is one of the world's best attorneys.

For me to debate F. Lee Bailey would be like me playing basketball for the Detroit Pistons and Coach Chuck Daley saying to me in game seven of the NBA Championship against the Lakers, "Sam, you guard Kareem Abdul-Jabbar." This is a mismatch. There is no way I could guard Kareem. I told our producer that I could not debate F. Lee Bailey because he would embarrass me. I assured him I would not be able to get in one good point with him. Finally, about five minutes before the show was to start, I realized I would have to do the show against F. Lee Bailey.

F. Lee Bailey led off on the discussion. He went right to the First Amendment. He talked about the invasion of privacy. Then he made a statement that gave me an opening. He said, "I do not think professional athletes or college athletes have a responsibility as role models in this country." Now, I knew I had F. Lee Bailey where I wanted him.

I got my turn and this is what I said: "You go to Chicago and ask the kids there who the mayor is. You go to California and ask the kids who the governor is. You go to Boston and ask the kids there who the mayor is. I can assure you they will not know the mayors or governor." Now, let me assure you of this: "They will know who Michael Jordan is. They will know who Magic Johnson is. And they will know who Larry Bird is." *It is very important today for professional athletes to be role models for young kids.* The kids will not do everything they say, but they will do everything that they *do*. *"What you behold, is what you become."*

Coaches say that practice makes perfect. That is fine, but practice also makes permanent. We live in a society where we follow, follow, follow. We had 12 to 13 players at Cleveland that were cross addicts. They were alcoholics and drug addicts. They were only 23 to 25 years old. I could not believe the situation when I got there. This is what they told me. "Coach, it all started when we were in high school. It started with a six pack of beer on Friday night. The peer pressure was more important than self pull. As long as we could be accepted we went along with the group."

They were like caterpillars. Do you know what caterpillars do? They get in long lines and follow the lead caterpillar. No one ever gets out of line to see where the lead caterpillar is going. They never check to see if he knows what his final destination is. An entomologist proved this point. He took seven caterpillars and put them on the rim of a big flowerpot. Just inside the flowerpot was plenty of water and food. For seven days and seven nights the caterpillars followed the leader around the flowerpot. They all became thirsty and died after seven days. We do the same thing as caterpillars. We have had our problems on Wall Street, we have had our problems with the religious leaders, and we have had our problems with our politicians. The same types of problems continue to happen every day.

I can remember drafting Don Rogers in 1984. He was a free safety out of UCLA. I felt he would have had an impact on the NFL playing strong safety just as Ken Easley did. He was a Ronnie Lott-type player. When you draft a player number 1 in the draft, you expect that number 1 player to help you immediately. Don Rogers came to camp and we started making big plans for him. I told my coaches that I wanted to start Don. We started talking about him every night after practice. I wanted to know how he was picking up on what we were doing. Every night the coaches would tell me Don was picking up everything without any problems.

However, I did notice some other things off the field about Don Rogers. After a hard day of practice, eight or 10 of the guys would go out and find a "water hole" to have a beer or two after practice. We would check them off as they came back at night for our team meetings. Those same eight to 10 players would just make it back in time for our meetings. Don Rogers was a great player and he had it all. But Don wanted to be accepted by those other players he was associating with. It was obvious when we drafted Don he was clean. You do not draft a player number 1 without checking to make sure he is clean. Somewhere along the line he went astray. As great a player as he was, he was a caterpillar, and he got in the wrong line.

The same story can be told of Len Bias of the University of Maryland. He was the second player picked in the NBA draft. The night he signed a $1 million contract with Reebok, and the day before he was to sign his contract with the Boston Celtics, he overdosed and died on the campus of Maryland. Nine days later, Don Rogers did the same thing in Sacramento, California. The night before he was to be married, he overdosed on cocaine.

No one seems to learn those difficult lessons. It is difficult to follow a cue. The same thing is true with everyone in this room. You cannot tell me that everyone in your school, from top to bottom, is on the same page in terms of *discipline*. That is a joke. That is one of our problems. That coach knows the value of discipline and he may be in certain situations on an island by himself. He may very well be in that classroom where the kid translated *apathy* into "Who cares?" This is a major problem.

You can talk about the things the national champs did this year, or you can talk about the things Joe Gibbs and the Washington Redskins did this year. Today, I say to you that drugs and alcohol are far more of a crisis than any career-ending injury that any of your players may suffer.

We have a character crisis in our country. We have people who actually preach that there is no right and no wrong. They say as long as it makes you feel good then it is okay to do it. Well, *coaches don't build character. Families build character*. That is where character comes from. Coaches give players the opportunity to be in critical situations where they have to make decisions. They must make decisions and then those decisions become a part of them.

This past week I was in a town in Georgia. We were looking at a quarterback. We had the kid visit our campus at Liberty. I made a commitment to him on the assumption that he was going to visit one more college. He made that visit this past weekend, but that other school did not offer him a scholarship. His high school should have been right on top of that situation. As we neared the national signing date he should have sat that kid down and told him what his options were. He should have pointed out these facts. "School A has offered me a scholarship; School B, where I want to go, has not offered me a scholarship." The coach should have told the kid, "A bird in the hand is worth six in the bush."

On Monday I had to sit down with that kid's father and tell him we did not have a scholarship for his son. I had to tell him we had used up our limit of scholarships and that we could not take him. I feel high school coaches have a responsibility in these areas. They must make sure a kid does not lose that opportunity to gain a scholarship. Sure, it takes more time and effort, but what is the whole picture all about if it isn't about giving the kids an opportunity to better themselves.

When I went to college my father could not believe it. He did not believe that Tennessee was giving me a scholarship just to play football. I remember when I first started coaching in New York City, Dad came by to watch us practice and I asked him what he thought. He said, "Why don't you get a real job? You have been playing all of your life."

I am not going to spend a lot of time on this next subject. Drugs and alcohol are the biggest problems in this country today. People ask the question, *"What is the solution?"* It is like a young man standing on the banks of a river. While he is standing there two men come floating down the river yelling for help. This man standing on the banks cannot swim very well, but he jumps into the river and rescues the two men in the river. All of this time there is a second man standing on the riverbank watching the entire rescue. Finally, the rescuer looked over to the man watching and asked him why he had not helped him with the rescue. Before he could answer, three more men came floating down the river yelling, "Help." Again, the young man jumped into the river to rescue the drowning men. He pulled all three of them out of the river and saved their lives. He is exhausted. He can just make it out of the river. He is literally crawling back to the banks of the river. He crawled over to the guy watching the rescue and lit into him. "You have watched me save five people. I have almost drowned. Why haven't you helped me?" He replied, "I am not going to help you! I am going to go upstream and find out who is throwing those guys in the river." That is what coaches must do. We must find out the solution. You either become a part of the problem, or you become a part of the solution. We need to know who is throwing the guys into the river.

Statistics can point out anything you want. We have lies, darn lies, and statistics. Bear with me on this for just a few minutes. In 1987, of all of the kids that registered for the first grade in the United States, 55 percent of them come from a single-parent home. That is the battle you fight right now. We have the same problem in college. *Character comes from the family*. It comes from people that love you. We spend $6.8 million per hour on alcohol in this country. This year 150,000 people in the U.S. will die from alcohol, and the greatest number of that total will be related to auto accidents associated with alcohol. Another 350,000 will die because of cigarettes and tobacco. That is more then 1000 per day. Every 37 seconds there is a divorce it the United States. In the next 30 seconds, 90 abortions will occur in this country, and there will be 1300 new drug users. Of the 118 teenagers that will try alcohol, one eighth of them will become alcoholics. The average drinking age in the U.S. is 11 years old. Alcohol kills three times as many people as those who use drugs. Ninety-seven percent of drug dealers do not use drugs.

By the time a kid is 18 years old he will have seen 100,000 beer commercials. As the saying goes, "You Can Have It All." Yes, you can have it all. We have 18 million adults that are alcoholics and 4.5 million kids that are alcoholics. Some of you may not realize it, but the *drug of choice in the U.S. is beer*. The beer people make $42 billion per year just on college campuses in the U.S. That is correct: $42 billion. Every drug addict that I have ever come in contact with has told me that is where he or she got started on drugs. They start with beer in high school. In college they start on marijuana, and then when they can afford it, they go to the white stuff, and then they start snorting cocaine. But, they all start with a six-pack of beer.

As a Christian I can tell you right now, and I am going to the Bible and show you the answer is there. The Bible say, "Don't be filled with anyone else's spirits; be filled with the Spirit of God." I can tell you now, that *is* the only answer. It is the only answer, and that is the only way we are going to turn it around. Kids will do NOT what you say, but what you DO!

We have five percent of the world's population but we lead in the AIDS epidemic. We have five percent of the world's population but we consume 50 percent of all of the cocaine that is used in the world.

I know you have heard it all, and you have read about it, but we must make a stand in this world. That is why I went to Liberty University. Just listen to what we have to go through to recruit at Liberty University. We recruit on the 1-AA level. We are one step below the big schools. This is what is required of our recruits. No Drugs; No Alcohol; Random Drug Testing for players, coaches, and faculty. Most people will say you are abusing the First Amendment. *Come on*! Do you think the mothers of Don Rogers or Len Bias would have wanted me to have tested their sons for drugs? If you are on my team, how am I going to help you if I do not know you need help? It may not be the answer, but I will tell you what it will do. It will stop the bleeding.

You may have a lot of groups opposed to the testing but that is the only way we will stop the bleeding. People in professional sports are not going to demand drug testing. Do you know why? *They do not care*. The only thing they care about is the bottom line and how many people they can put in the stands. They are interested in the revenue. Why do you think they have the World Football League? They want the revenue from Europe and they want to hold down the players' salaries. We had a strike in 1982. They wanted 55 percent of the profit. When the United States Football League came into existence the average salary in the NFL was $65,000. After the USFL, the average jumped to $241,000 per player.

Let me get back to Liberty University: no drugs, no alcohol, no tobacco, and no coed dorms. We have a dress code, a curfew, and you have to go to church three times per week, and you have to go to chapel three times per week. You may say forget it. Obviously, this type of school must appeal to you before you would go there. The great thing about it is this. We recruit all across the country. Some college coaches look at 10 players to get one. I may look at 190 players that will tell me no way. Last week we finished our recruiting and we had a good year.

I can tell you today that people are fed up with all the things that are going on around us today. They are upset with all of the things we are allowing our kids to do today. We need to have a backbone, and not a wishbone, in our spinal columns. We need to stand for something or we will fall for anything. *This is the number 1 thing you need to do to build a winner*.

I am standing up here telling you the secret of the successful coaches such as Bill Walsh and Joe Gibbs. They go for the high-percentage passes first. That is their way of saying to establish the run first. It is not a bad theory. Spread the defense across the field and make them cover you from sideline to sideline. I got Ozzie Newsome to play tight end for us because we felt we could get the ball deep down the middle to him. There are no big plays designed in our system.

When most pro coaches get up to talk the first reaction of the high school coaches is this: "We can't do that in high school." They may be right. Regardless of the level you are coaching, you must have a system and you must have a basic philosophy. Your quarterback must be able to make choices, and he must be able to make decisions. You must have a basic plan to be successful.

The first thing Joe Gibbs does is to say he has to have four tight ends. He gives you a mirage of formations but all he runs is the Counter Trap, and the Lead play, and a play-action pass off those two plays. He will spread the wide receivers across the field and he will take his shots in the high-percentage short passing game with them. When the opportunity presents itself, by design and not physically, he goes for the *big play*. He shows a lot of patience and waits for the right situation. Systems do not win for you. You must have a philosophy.

Let me go into another phase with the time I have left. Let's talk about our staff. You may say that we can select a staff in college and that is true. When I was coaching in high school the basketball coach was my JV coach, and I was his JV coach, and we got along great. I know what you coaches go through today. I know it is difficult for you to bring your entire staff to this clinic. The way budgets are today, it is difficult to do that. Most staffs are counting on the head coach to tell them what to do. The big problem I had as a high school coach was the evaluation process. I was always talking to myself. In college and pro coaching we have people that tell us we should do it this way. This is where we can ask them why? When I was in high school I would get together with five or six other high school coaches and we would have our own clinic. We would take a topic every week and discuss it. We had clinics going on the entire year. Just as here, the best clinics are the ones you are having in the rooms, or in the lobby, or with another coach while you are having a meal. You are talking about things that will fit into your system. Again, it is not plays, it is player that is important as you make important decisions.

To me, when you select a staff, the number 1 thing is his confidence. Offensive linemen, the most important thing they must do is to occupy defensive linemen. It does not matter what aspect of offense you are taking about, he must occupy that defensive man. The remedial part for a defensive linemen is to make sure he can disengage and come off blocks and go to the ball. For receivers, it is not speed, but the ability to catch the ball. There are three reasons why you drop the football. First, is the lack of concentration. Second, is fear of getting hit. You get those receivers that can hear a cat sipping milk at 100 yards. They will not go inside. The third reason is fatigue. When a receiver is tired, he loses the balance in his legs. For running backs, without question, it is balance. You can see this in great backs like Barry Sanders. They have the ability to allude tacklers and to make yardage when the hole is not there.

When I look at a film of a high school back I look for his area of production. I want to know how many yards he gained on his own. I want to know how did he finish the run? How did he hit into the pile and how did he finish the run? As you go to the quarterback it is a tall order. When I first got the job at Cleveland and I saw Brian Sipe throw seven on seven he was not very impressive. He could not break a pane of glass at 20 yards. I had seen Terry Bradshaw and Kenny Anderson throw the ball, and I knew what they could do. However, Brian was the best when it came to things that counted. In 1980, 13 of our 16 games were decided in the final two minutes. I found out that Brian Sipe was the youngest catcher for a team that won the Little League World Series in Williamsport, Pennsylvania. Brian was from San Diego. I can remember in 1979, the week before we played Pittsburgh, we lost 33-30 in overtime. Brian's dad died that week. I can remember Brian's dad telling me earlier that Brian was a winner all of his life. I can never remember a time when it was a tight fit, when Brian came to the sideline where he did not know what we needed to do. We used to sit in the quarterback meetings and let Brian talk. I would tell the other coaches not to talk; just let Brian talk. Brian Sipe was a winner.

The staff is important at any level, but especially at the high school level. If I have a line coach working with the young players then he has to be an expert in that area. He must have confidence in doing his job. We must have common objectives.

Again, as a staff we must be focused. I had a dog named Ole Blue. Like all dogs he liked to chase rabbits. He chased the rabbit for one block. Then another dog joined the hunt. After 10 blocks, 10 other dogs joined the race. Eventually in the next 10 blocks those 10 dogs quit the hunt. The reason Ole Blue did not quit chasing the rabbit was because he was able to see the rabbit. None of the other ten dogs could see what Ole Blue was chasing. Ole Blue was focused. On common objectives, we all have to be focused on the same goal.

Have you ever watched geese when they fly south? They fly in V formations. The reason they fly in that formation is because they can fly 71 percent more efficiently. Every once in a while you will hear one of the geese "Honk" because he does not like the job one of the leaders is doing. If all of them are working together it will be a smooth ride. If they work in unison they fly with a 71 percent efficiency and they will get to where they want to go a lot faster. In our common objectives, we must make sure all on our staff are going in the same direction. We must always make sure we are horizontally and vertically on the same page. Yes, we can disagree, but don't be disagreeable. If you want to get your point across, that is fine. Get it across. I listen to what everyone has to say. I am not always able to take everyone's suggestion, but I do listen. In the final analysis, you make the decision and then you move forward on that decision. Everyone must be working together for one goal. The greatest defector of age is *ego*. You will never be able to hit the bull's eye if your eye gets in the way.

When I first got the head coaching job in Cleveland I got a lot of phone calls about assistants. I had been an assistant coach for 11 years for four different teams. I knew a lot of coaches. I got a lot of phone calls. If I had listened to all of the people that called me about hiring assistant coaches, I would have had to hold the first coaching staff meeting in a coliseum. I had a lot of friends, but I could only hire certain guys. Too many coaches want to be coordinators and not assistants. That is a problem today. We have too many titles. I hear people say, "It is my offense." It is not Joe Walton's offense. It is the Pittsburgh Steelers offense. When it becomes someone else's offense it gives a mixed message. To me it is like a quarterback that goes into the huddle and tells the line the cadence is on 1, and then he looks to the backs and tell them the count is on 2. They are not together. That is a mismatch. You get them working against each other. The same problem happens with stats today. Some players are more concerned about the stats than they are with winning the game.

The third thing is the individual is free. Who is in charge of your life? Don't take yourself too seriously. I always pray for strength before the game and at halftime. My prayers have always been answered. There are 800 million Chinese that do not care if we win or lose a football game. I want our players to know that winning and losing are not the most important things in my life. That is a great lesson in life. It has nothing to do with the way you play the game. In fact, most teams will play better with this attitude. They will be able to express their talent without that grapefruit in their esophagus.

As we won the 1980 division championship, I realized how important it was to the city of Cleveland. However, it was not the most important thing in my life. That was a great lesson for me. I never realized how much more I could do as a Christian as opposed to as just a coach. I did not realize how much I could really do as a Christian with the talent God gave me. Now, I also feel it was God's plan to get me fired in 1984.

When I first started working for NBC, the first game I did was in Pittsburgh. I did the Pittsburgh Steelers and Houston Oilers. I brought the papers from the Pittsburgh game and showed them to my wife. "You will not believe this. There is a coach at Pittsburgh by the name of Chuck Noll that has four championship rings and they are eating him alive. They have forgotten everything he has done for them." Tom Landry gave 29 years to the Dallas Cowboys. In one year he got fired, and went to the Hall of Fame. Does that tell you what this business is all about? I wrote Tom Landry a letter. This is what I told him. "Tom, you have a great opportunity as a role model to the coaches of this country because you are a winner. They are watching that spirit within you. That want to know if that spirit within you is for real."

Then I included a quote from Harry Truman. Write this down: *the way in which you endure that which you must endure, is more important than the crisis itself.* Don't worry about what other people are thinking. They are too busy thinking about themselves. They are not thinking about you.

The last point is Maturity. You have to pick the fruit from the tree. Red Auerbach will tell you it is important to chose quality people. Talent is important, but dependability is critical. In the final analysis, you want a kid who has a little less talent but is the kind of guy that is going to be with your program. The same is true of the assistant coaches. You will eventually win with people like that. I also think you will enjoy coaching more with people like that.

In closing, *be your own souls, learn to live. Men will thwart you, but take no heed. Men will hate you, but have no care. Just sing your song, dream your dream, hope your hope, and pray your prayer.* I have now given you our dream.

Chapter 16

DEVELOPING
A WINNING ATTITUDE

Bill Snyder
Kansas State University
1995

It is so easy to look at the X's and O's and think that is the answer to coaching. For me and the programs I've been involved with, that has not been the answer. Whatever you do, if you truly believe in it, you will get the job done. You have to get the people in your program to believe in it, also. That is why there are so many offenses and defenses across the country that are in successful programs. We have had some success offensively and defensively and I assure you, it is not the scheme that we have used. If football is important to you, you must establish some principles that are used to build your team. I hope you can take some of these thoughts away with you today and they become important to you.

To be successful you have to establish a foundation. That is what we are trying to do at Kansas State University. We have finished in the upper division four out of the last five years. When we went to Kansas State six years ago, it was termed as the school that had lost the most games of any program in the history of college football. Kansas State was the only football program in America that had lost more than 500 games. It had lost 30 straight ballgames. I had a chance to visit with some of the young people who had finished their eligibility there. They were good young people who wanted to win. What I found out is they were tamped down over an extended period of time. Our first class was a group of people who had not participated in a winning football game at the college level in their career. That was tremendously unfortunate and it had severely tamped down their lives.

201

Here are some things I share with our coaches and players.

1) **Be Around Great People.** That in itself is important, but at the same time it is important for your young people to find those people to be around. There are people in your town or community who have been successful. Those are the types of people I want our kids to know. Have people in your program that truly want to be in "Your Program." Our situation is a little different. For a guy to come to your high school, he probably doesn't have much of a choice. But for a youngster to come to Kansas State, we want to make sure he wants to be in that program. The same thing holds true with coaches. I can relate back to when I was a high school coach. I was not a very good high school coach. One of the main reasons was that I was half in and half out. After a period of time I realized it was important to be where you are. That meant as a football coach wherever I was, I needed to plant my roots and do the best job I could do. Whatever would come from that would come. I aspired to go to a higher level. I have seen too many coaches that were at one spot and trying to be somewhere else. If you do a great job at whatever you are doing, your time will come. Great opportunities will present themselves to you. If you are out looking for those opportunities instead of doing the job you have now, you are probably going to do a poor job of coaching.

2) **Expect a Great Deal out of Yourself.** I want to expect a great deal out of the coaches and players in our program. I can't do that unless I expect a great deal out of myself. If people know that, then it is easier for me to ask for a great deal from them. I have always shared with our players the fact that we would ask more of them then anyone in their lives. I wanted them to take that as a compliment. That meant we felt they were capable of so much more. So much of the game of football is attitude and motivation.

3) **Raise the Expectation Level of Your Players.** When you go to programs like the Kansas State program, to raise that expectation level is a very difficult process. They have no tradition and their attitude doesn't foster change.

To start to change the attitudes of people in your program, you have to start by:

4) **Giving Responsibility to Players and Coaches.** You have heard the statement about letting your coaches coach. I believe in that, but sometimes there is a little looseness in that. It is important for an

assistant coach to want responsibility. To do the best job he can, that assistant coach should strive to get more responsibility. We have graduate assistants in our program and I'm sure you at the high school level have a variety of walk-on coaches. I was a graduate assistant at the University of Southern California. I was a terrible graduate assistant because all I did was do what I was asked to do. I didn't try to seek out more responsibility. That happens so many times with young coaches. They don't understand how to be a viable member of the profession. I feel it is important for me to sit down with our graduate assistants and try to make them aware of trying to seek out more responsibility. I want them to go to the position coach and try to find ways that they can help.

As an assistant coach that is what I would try to do. I would go to the head coach and tell him my ideas that could help our program grow. I think it is important to hold people accountable for what they are doing. That goes for the coaches and players. That is hard in this day and age. We ask our players to hold themselves and each other accountable. Of course, that gets into leadership. I think as the head coach it is extremely important that you hold your coaches accountable for the responsibilities you have assigned them or the responsibility they have asked for. Maybe you can relate to this. I have had conversations with a variety of different coaches at a variety of different levels about coaching responsibilities.

What we are finding today is that it is a little harder to get younger coaches to provide the appropriate discipline. Sometimes the discipline is pushed up to the head football coach. It shouldn't be that way. I think it is important for coaches to provide appropriate discipline by being able to hold players accountable for things they are attempting to teach them. If your players are held accountable and have responsibility, seek responsibility, and react to responsibility then they are going to do the things you want them to do. We hold our players responsible for a lot of things. Above all however, we hold them responsible for their academic success. That doesn't mean we don't help them with all the support services, because we do. But I've also found out you can only guide those young guys around by the hand for just so long. To do them justice, you have to cut them loose and make them responsible for what happens to them eventually. They have to know how to be responsible for things that happen in their lives. That is a major concern of mine at the college level. We do so much for the college athlete today. I think the support services are good but sometimes I think we take away the opportunity for young people to hold themselves responsible for their actions.

I think it is the responsibility of our players to take care of their health. It is important for them to do the things that are right for them to be as strong, quick, fast, and healthy as they can be. If they are not healthy when you get them on Saturday afternoon or Friday night, than you have less of a chance to be successful. I think it is important to hold them responsible for their own effort. That is something they have complete control over. We talk about great effort in our program all the time. The height, weight, and size doesn't have anything to do with the effort put forth by the players. There is no excuse for any player to give you less effort than he is capable of.

5) **We Don't Want to Waste Time.** We talk about priorities all the time. That is something that can get away from us in this game of football. Trivia gets involved. We get overwhelmed with it sometimes. There is too much trivia today in college football for me. There is a paper world out there. There are too many things put down in the written word. We have notebooks that are four or five inches thick. I guarantee those youngsters are not reading everything in there. There are a lot things to teach in the game of football but I think you have to look at your stuff. You need to peal it down and get rid of the things that you don't need. I look around our program and try to find the things that are taking up our coaches' and players' time that are not instrumental in whether we win or lose. I believe a player or coach can succeed in anything he wants to do if he makes it important. If you put great emphasis on one area of your program, you will have success in it. If you get too many things and too much trivia, you can't spend enough time on the things that are really important. That cuts down on the number of successes you can have. To us it is important to be simple about things.

6) **Get People Involved in Your Program.** Involvement is extremely important. Sometimes we can get isolated. Our football complex is at the very edge of our campus. We don't have people milling around our complex very often. I don't think that is necessarily good. I'm going to do something about that. I think the more people you have on your side the less you have against you. There aren't too many people in this country that are neutral about football. They are either with you or against you. If you look around

your halls at school you will find there are people that really care about your program or they don't give a hoot about it.

I think it is important to go out and find the people that don't give a hoot about your program and get them to care about it. We do some things and I think you could do something similar at your high school. We have nine colleges at our university. I have an assistant coach assigned to each of those colleges. He has continual dialogue that goes on with the deans, associate deans, and faculty members in each of those colleges. I want to bring our program to them and for them to bring their program to us. It helps us in recruiting to understand about their college and it helps them to understand a little more about our program.

Our coaches call the parents of our players once a month, every month, 12 months out of the year. I know that is hard because our coaches are no different than anyone else. They work 18-hour days and do the job. But I see the rewards for doing that. I get calls and letters from our parents telling me how important that is to them. We don't call to report just the bad things that are going on. It is to keep the lines of communication open. We share things about our program and let them know that their young man is important to us as well as the parents' relationship to our program. I send a letter to our faculty members, parents, and supporters of our program that addresses our program and all aspects of it. I send a letter six or seven times a year. We have a great relationship at Kansas State with our faculty because we have let them know they are important to us. That is hard to do sometimes. It takes a lot of effort and hard work. It takes doing some things sometimes that you don't want to necessarily do at that given time. Nevertheless, we do it and it has paid off for us.

7) **Care About Your Players.** We want to have a genuine caring for our players and coaches that we work with. I know this is thrown around a lot. But I assure you, young people really understand whether you care about them. There is that misconception at the college level today about coaches proselytizing young guys in their programs. They come into your program, you have them for four years, they make a lot of money for your school, and then you push them back on the street. Some of them get their degrees and go into a career. Some are fortunate to be able to go into professional football. But there are many others that cannot survive without the degree or without someone really caring and helping them. Young people really know when you care. A lot of

guys give lip service to the fact that they care about their players. The important thing is that you don't talk the talk, you walk the walk. That doesn't mean you are not supposed to have discipline in your program. It is just the contrary. It means you have great discipline in your program, but at the same time you make young people feel important in it. The same thing is true with your staff. Every assistant coach has to feel he is an important part of what is going on in the program.

8) **Team Leadership.** Of all the things I have talked about there is nothing more important than this. That is going to come from within your team. We all have different ways to develop that. The seniors in your program have to provide leadership. We have player representatives within our team. We select the player representatives after the season for the next season. We select eight to 10 guys to represent the team. The next year when we find out who the true leaders are among that group, we select our captains. However, don't just expect that leadership will come from your team.

We have to do a job at teaching our kids how to lead. We have leadership meetings. We have many meetings but they are short. Our coaches will do it individually in their groups and we will do it collectively as a team. In these meetings we take one topic and talk about it. It may be "How to handle the media." It could be "How to help during the course of a practice to pick up a guy who is having a tough time." It might be "What is your role in the dormitory?" It could be a variety of things that we want these people to latch onto. They are short five-minute meetings. It doesn't go any longer. We get into the meeting and out of it that quickly. We are trying to make a point. Young guys will respond when you are brief and to the point. We select guys we think can be quality leaders and then give them some task to do within the team to make them good leaders. We may send him to see a freshman that is having a tough time and is not having too much fun. He probably is thinking about quitting and going home. We want that guy to tell him about how he felt and how he got over it. There are a variety of things we can ask that guy to do. I ask the position coaches to establish a list of tasks for that young man to perform to develop as a quality leader. I look them over and okay them and the position coach gets that guy aside and lets him know what we want him to do. He doesn't give him all the tasks at once but brings him along. Most young guys don't know how to do that naturally.

9) **Attitude.** There is nothing more important than this. That goes for not just your players but everyone around your program. When we went to Kansas State I met all the young guys who had finished their eligibility. There were 22 of them and I met with them for one hour. I didn't want them to name names of people they felt were problems. I just wanted to know how they felt at the present time. I wanted any suggestions to help me develop a better attitude in the program. What I found out was they had an attitude that wouldn't allow them to win. We developed a series of goals. We put it on a board in our locker room. It is part of our notebook. It is all over the place. It is called "Wildcats' 14 Goals for Success." There is nothing within these goals that has anything to do with conference championships, national championships, or any statistical goals for a football team. All the goals have to do with intrinsic values.

I'm going to touch on some of these goals. The first one is to *Improve Every Day*. The foundation of our football program is built upon improvement. I asked our football team to do this. I felt there were three areas of importance. Outside of their faith and family I felt it was important for them to be the best person, student, and football athlete that they could possibly be. I asked our players to do this. Every day of their life, find a way to be a little bit better person, student, and football player. If we can get 120 guys to do that, over the long haul we have a chance to be a darn good group of people, students, and football players. That is exactly the way our football team started. Every single football coach goes into the locker room after each practice, me included, and that is the first question we ask. "Did you get better today?" "How are you going to get better tomorrow?" It doesn't have to be in every area. It just takes one assignment, technique, or one area of improvement.

The next goal we use is *Toughness*. Toughness comes in a lot of different ways. Everyone always talks about physical and mental toughness. There is a word being thrown around these day that has to do with mental toughness. The word is "Focus." We talk about a breaking point with our players. A breaking point is that period of time where they lose focus. We ask our players to go on the practice field and give us 100 percent, be focused, and concentrate on what they are doing. We know that during the two to 2½ hours we are on the practice field that won't happen. After practice when our coaches are in the locker room talking to players, that is one of the things they want to know. They want to know how far into practice the guy got before he hit the breaking point. The next day we do the same thing. The goal is to complete a practice without the breaking point coming in. If that happens you will probably have a great player on your hands. You have to teach it and emphasize it. Self-discipline is part of not reaching that breaking point.

Enthusiasm has to be a part of every program. It applies to coaches and players. Just to say it does not get it done. Everybody has a different personality. Some people rant and rave and some are quiet. In both cases that is good. We can create enthusiasm. What I want our coaches to do every time we have a session is to have a plan to initiate enthusiasm before the session starts. When I have a coaches' meeting in the morning I want to have a reason for my coaches to be excited about being there in the morning. The same thing is true with football players. If that guy comes out of class having had a bad day he is not going to want to practice the way I want him to. If a guy can't get out of the locker room, you know he is not going to be enthusiastic about practice. We have a meeting as coaches before we go out to practice. Our coaches have an agenda for every single meeting they have with our players. I get a copy of that agenda. I want to know what is going to be covered by them and I want our coaches to be well prepared. Their agenda has three headings. One of those headings is for me because there are three or four things I want them to cover before they go on to the things they have pre- pared. One of the things on that agenda is enthusiasm.

The next thing is to Never Give Up. Expect more out of your players and yourself. Of that group I met the first year I came, I had a ques- tion from one of the players. I was an assistant at the University of Iowa before I came to Kansas State. We had played Kansas State that past year. He wanted to know the difference between the two teams. The game was close at halftime. I told him that both teams went to the locker rooms with a chance to win the football game. In the Iowa locker room we knew we were going to win the game. In the Kansas State locker room they knew who was going to win, too. Iowa came out and ran away with the game. That is part of the expectation level. This a tough age and society for young people to grow up in. Making decisions is a tough thing.

We have to keep things in perspective. We need as coaches to be very specific when we are talking to our players. They need to under- stand about never giving up. This thing that is going on in L.A. with O.J. Simpson is awful. I was at USC when he was playing there. None of us likes what's going on. Regardless of guilty or not guilty, none of us likes what happened there. Sometimes when it comes to human relationships, athletes who have been taught never to give up, never give up. Sometimes when you don't give up at a certain time you can create a tragedy in your life and the life of someone else. You see it in the papers all the time where a college athlete has done something wrong. It is important to stress in certain aspects of an athlete's life he has to give up.

When I coached at the high school level, it taught me a great deal about unity. Young kids of that age group really care about being together. But you better understand at the college level it is equally important. The last three years we have had 16 guys go into professional football. It is a new happening. They are back on our campus all the time and here is what they tell me. Every single one of them to the man tells me he would rather be at Kansas State than in the pros. They told me, "this is where it's at." The pro game is nothing but a business. Guys, they are just not together.

I know that unity and togetherness is important in our program. It has made a big difference. As we go back and relate to some of the things that have taken place at Kansas State during the last 100 years, the problem was that they weren't together. You have to coach that, also. You have to find ways to bring your guys together. Don't let your players sit on the fringe of your program. You know the story about one bad apple spoiling the whole barrel. You have to be selective about the people you have in your program, whether it is a coach or a player. We as coaches have to make the decision between potential and attitude. You know where I stand on that one. We want our players to come together better than any other football program in America.

Consistency and trust in a system is important. It is important for us to have mutual trust. You, as the coach, have to give the team reasons to trust you, because the perception of football across the country is not always one of trust. Clinics can give you a chance to be inconsistent in your approach. Coaches think there has to be something better. But that is not always the case. You may find some little things that you do that can be altered, but trust yourself. Six years ago when I came to Kansas State, I got the team together and showed them our offense and defense. That was it, and we were not going to change them. What we are going to do is give you a chance to get better every single day that you are on our campus at Kansas State University. If you are going to be here for five years, you will be doing the same thing every single day. If you can't get better doing the same thing every day, then you have a problem and don't need to be in our program. If I change from year to year our guys don't have a chance to get better.

Players get better through fundamentals. We all believe in fundamentals. Senior players are better than freshman ballplayers because they have spent four years doing the fundamentals over and over again. That's how you get better.

We talk to our players about individual goals. We approach goal setting in three steps. The first part is to establish the goals. Make sure they are important to you. How many times have we set goals and not followed through on them? Whatever the goal, you have to have a plan to help you achieve the goal. The one thing that young people don't understand is if they have a goal it is probably something that they have never done before. If we have never done it, how do we know the steps to go through to achieve that goal? You have to find people who have done it and find out how they did it. Establish a plan through some knowledge of people that have achieved those goals. The third thing is like the Nike commercial: *Just Do It*.

The next thing is humility. In today's society it is hard to corral the success of a successful program. I think this is something else you need to teach in your program. When you have success you are in front of the cameras and media all the time. We want our players to practice humility. There are a lot of good things that come to those who are humble. People are attracted to people who are humble. We want to distribute the credit to other people. We want to honor the team first.

Everyone is smart enough to come up with a plan to run an offense and defense. The thing that makes it work is repetition. Repetition leads to success. Our first year at Kansas State we were 1-10. It would have been easy for me to have told our coaches we were in the wrong offense and defense. Or I could have said that the things we were teaching were not working. That wasn't the case. I brought in an offense and defense and promised our players we were going to stick with it. That's what we did. We have never changed the structure or fundamentals of what we are doing and we have gotten better each year.

If you are a head football coach this probably hits home the quickest. Here is a quote: "If it is to be, it is up to me." I think it is important to provide responsibility to all people in your program. It is important to demand that it gets done, but if you are in charge of something, you better be prepared to do it yourself if all else fails. When you are dealing with people that can take place from time to time, particularly if you don't want it to.

You must have discipline in your program. I tell our guys that discipline and criticism are not personal. Too many times players will hear the tone of your voice and not hear what you have said. When that happens we have failed at being able to teach a young man. We have to get our players to understand and be tough enough to know that it is not a personal thing. That goes for coaches, also. Discipline does not mean we don't like the kid. Sometimes we don't take the time to let our players understand that.

Commitment is something I want to know from each of our players. I sit down and talk to all of our players. I want to get eye to eye and I want him to tell me how committed he is to our program. Before I do this I tell him what it means to me. I tell him how I want him to be committed. I tell him what it means to our program and then I ask him point blank how he feels. I also go into the fact that his answer doesn't make him a good guy or bad guy. The only thing that can make him a bad guy is if he lies. After you do that you have an idea of what you have to work with. I think too many times we talk to everyone collectively and we expect the same response. When you get eye to eye with a person, you'll know what kind of commitment you are going to get. Now you can do something about his commitment if it is not what you want.

If you are in the game of football you have to address problems daily. Kansas State is a unique university. I've been in that football office every day for almost six years and there hasn't been a day go by when there wasn't a problem jump up on my desk. Sometimes it is with players, coaches, or a lot of different areas. What I've always tried to believe in is this. Regardless of the issue at hand the problem can be solved. The second thing is to solve it as quickly as possible. If the problem involves two people and they care about solving the problem it will be solved. Don't let your problems pile up. That is what I tell our coaches. As soon as they know the problem, deal with it right then. That doesn't mean a particular decision has to be made on the spot. However, if you are thinking about a decision then you are addressing the problem right then.

I let players and coaches make decisions in our program. That doesn't mean they make all the decisions. They will not make a decision to run the ball on fourth down at midfield. But they make decisions that affect our program. Our players make our training rules. The players and coaches have to have an investment in the program. If they don't they are not going to be very good coaches and players.

The last thing I want to talk about is making decisions. This is probably the most complex time in the history of our society for young people. When I say young people I'm talking about the people that we are dealing with. That age group between 14 and 23 years of age is a special group. It is tough for young people to make decisions. I have been in the projects of New York, Miami, Los Angeles, and Chicago.

I have been in places where most people would dare not go. The sadness about it is there are young people who live in those areas. They walk out their front doors and the only thing that is visible to them is something bad. The dope pushers, rapists, muggers, and drive-by shootings are all there. That is all they see. There are no role models. They go to school and they find more of the same. That is unfortunate. But, we ask these young guys to make all the right decisions. We tell them not to get involved with all that kind of stuff, but that is all they see. These guys have to be able to make quality decisions for themselves. That is where you guys come in. You guys have heard it before, that you are the last chance the kids have. Well that is more true now than ever before. Coaches are the most important people in our society now because you have a chance to help young people make the right decisions for themselves.

You have people in your program that you will never have to worry about. But, you also have some guys in your program that are involved in the gangs and things like that. Those are the ones that need your help. I explain it to my players this way. I tell them they are going to make decisions every day of their lives for the rest of their lives. There is great peer pressure on the guys who are trying to make the right choices. Of the decisions they have to make every day, the biggest part of them are going to be insignificant. Some of the decisions are going to have a moderate impact on their lives. But, some of those decisions will have dramatic impacts on the rest of their lives. I ask them to take 10 seconds to think. That is not much time at all. Take 10 seconds, back up, and ask yourself a question. The question is, "If I do this thing that my peers want me to do, will it make me a better person, student, or football player?" If the answer is "Yes," do it with all the enthusiasm that you can muster. If the answer is "No," then why in the hell would you want to do it? *Don't do it*! They know what is right and what is wrong.

The problem is having a process where they can think and someone who will back them up and support their decision. That is you, their coach. You will have a great impact on the lives of the young people that you work with. Don't ever think you won't. That's why this is a special and great profession. That is one of the reasons I spoke to you about the things I touched on tonight. These are the guys that are going to be making a difference in our society at another level at another time. Our society cannot continue to go in the direction it is going now. The L.A. riot a couple years ago was not a black thing. It just happened to be in a black neighborhood. It was a youth thing. Those weren't 45-year-old guys running around burning and looting. Those were young people that didn't have a chance. Nobody gave them a chance and they didn't have anyone like you to help them.

Keep doing what you are doing. Keep helping young people because they will be in your seats doing something for young people they have a chance to work with.

Chapter 17

ALABAMA'S DEFENSIVE PHILOSOPHY

Gene Stallings
University of Alabama
1993

In order to win football games there are a few things that I believe are important. There are things that are important about winning football games. It does not make any difference if you are on the high school level or the college level or the professional level. I coached 18 years in pro football and I have been in college football 18 years. I never had the privilege of coaching high school football, but I know that there are basically three things that you must do. First, you must be able to run the football. Second, you must be able to stop the run. Third, you must be on the plus side in the Give Away-Take Away category. It does not matter what level you are on, these are the things you must do in order to win games.

We went into the national championship game with Miami and people were calling us a one-dimensional football team. They said we could not throw the football. Yet we beat Miami because we were able to run the ball for 275 yards. We held them to less than 50 yards rushing. We were in the *plus* in the Give Away-Take Away. It does matter what level you are on, you have to get ready to play a game or plan a season. You are not trying to entertain the fans. You are trying to win football games.

You must have a *philosophy* to win at football. It does not matter what level you are on. A philosophy says that this is an abstract statement on what I believe in. I get my staff together and I say to them: "What do I believe in defensively, offensively, and the kicking game?" Somewhere along the line I have to do what I believe in. I have a philosophy that says what I believe in. Then I have a method that says how I am going to do it. Then I have a quality control that I use to check to see if I do it or not. That is important. Philosophy is championship caliber. When you are sitting around making your goals, you are talking about your team that is coming up the following year. You must have a philosophy.

If someone would ask me what our philosophy was offensively last year, I would tell him this. Last year we were not a good offensive football team. People would ask me what I thought about our season coming up. I would tell them that I thought we were a year away. They wanted to know why I thought we were a year away. I told them we had a quarterback that had no experience at the quarterback position. We had a field-goal kicker that had never kicked a field goal in college football. We had a punter that had never punted in college football. Our backup quarterback had never played a down in college football. Our starting quarterback had played three games in college football. I told people that I thought we would struggle offensively. I thought we were going to be a good football team defensively.

We were going into the Miami game and the press was asking me all kinds of questions. The writers told me that Alabama was an underdog in the Sugar Bowl. I told them I did not think we were an underdog. They asked me why I did not think we were an underdog. I told them this. "I see our guys practice every day. *You are an underdog if you think you are an underdog.*" If you do not get anything else out of this talk, write this down: Y*ou are an underdog only if you think you are.* The press kept telling us we were an underdog by 7 to 8 and even 9 points. I told them I saw our players practice every day and I saw the intensity of the players.

We took 145 players to New Orleans. We had an 11 o'clock curfew for New Orleans. We were there for six days. We did not have one player that was late for a curfew or late for a practice. We did not have one player that was late for anything. To me that said that we went to New Orleans with the idea of winning the game. We are not an underdog. You win football games with players making plays. It does not matter what level you are on. You win with players making plays. You do not win with schemes.

I have been told over and over that we had a great defensive scheme against Miami in the Sugar Bowl. Hey, we have a good defensive scheme every week. You win football games with football players making plays. You do not win with schemes. If you think you win with schemes, then you are in the wrong business. Somewhere along the line you must be able to say I win football games because I am a technique coach. People ask me from time to time how to win football games. I win football games because I am a technique-oriented coach. You must play your techniques properly. I do not care if you play a 4-3 Defense or a 3-4 Defense. It makes no difference what offense or defense you play. The thing that is important is *how you play offense and defense*. You win football games with players making plays.

A philosophy is an abstract statement on what you believe. You ask me what my philosophy on offense is at the University of Alabama. My philosophy is this. When we get the ball I want to score; I want to kick to score; or I want to move the ball out far enough so when I do punt the ball the opponent will have 80 yards to drive for a touchdown. How do you do this? This falls under the area of method. Here is my method. Then I tell them about my method. Then I tell them how I make my method work. Then that falls under the area of quality control. It does matter what level you are on, you must have a method of what you believe in. I am not going to try to convince you that my method is better than your method. Chances are it is not. I am just telling you that you must have a method. I know that when you get the ball you have to score or you have to kick it to score or you have to move it out far enough so when you punt the ball they have to drive 80 yards to score. Then I know that you have to keep the ball seven plays or more 65 percent of the time. You may not know this, but I know this.

I never will forget the time I was in a staff meeting at Texas A&M. Elmer Smith was on my staff and we were talking about a particular way of doing something. Elmer kept saying something. I finally said, "Hey Elmer, wait a minute. What makes you think that will work? I have never heard of anyone doing it, and I have never seen anyone do it. What makes you think that this will work?" Elmer looked at me and said, "I will tell you how I know it will work. My 40 years of experience tells me that it will work." Somewhere along the line that is important to you, whatever you believe in. Elmer Smith believed in a particular thing because he has been doing it for 40 years. I said, "Elmer, that is good enough for me." We put it in at Texas A&M. What I am saying is that you must have a philosophy. Philosophy is championship caliber. Very few people ever meet their philosophy.

I could go around this room and ask you what your philosophy was on offense, defense, or the kicking game. You had better have one.

My philosophy on defense is this. I am trying to prevent the offense from moving the ball effectively. How do you do that? That falls under the area of method. How do you make sure your method works? That falls in the area of quality control.

Every Sunday after a game on Saturday I go into my office and look at the game charts. I have about 70 different items defensively that fall under the area of quality control. If we accomplish our goal it is colored blue; if we don't accomplish the goal it is colored in red. I can look at our quality control boards and I can tell you if we are playing defense correctly, offense correctly, or the kicking game correctly. I can tell just by looking at our quality control board.

What I am trying to say is that you must have a philosophy. When you get the ball on offense, what are you trying to do? When we get the ball I do not want to give it up. I do not care where we get it, I do not want to give up the ball unless we score. I do not want to give up the ball unless we kick it for a score. I do not want to give up the ball unless we move the ball down far enough so when I have to punt it, you will have 80 yards to go with it to get a touchdown. That is my philosophy of offense. That is championship caliber. If every time I get the ball and I score with it, or I kick it to score with it, or I move it out far enough so when I punt the ball you end up having 80 yards to go with it to score, what is going to happen? I am going to win the national championship. Very few people can do that.

What is your philosophy of defense? My philosophy of defense says that we are not going to allow you to move the ball effectively. That sounds good. How are you going to do that? That falls under the area of method. What am I going to use to check my method? That falls under the area of quality control. Then I check my quality control board that checks the method that checks my philosophy.

It doesn't make any difference what level you are on, if you are going to win football games, there are basically three things you must do. You must be able to run the football. This is true at all levels. If you can't stop the run you can't win. If you are not on the plus side in the Give-Away/Take-Away area you are going to lose the ballgame. The University of Alabama led the nation this past year in stopping the run. When it was all said and done, we gave up a little over 55 yards per game against the run. When it was all said and done, we were second in the SEC in running the football. We were a plus 18 in the Give-Away/Take-Away area. That says we got the ball 18 times more than we gave it away. Hey, now there is no question how we won football games.

I am going to talk about our defense in just a minute. Everyone keeps talking about our game with Miami. The reason we won the game against Miami is this. We had the ball 15 minutes more than they did. We ran the ball for 275 yards against Miami. They ran the ball for less than 50 yards. When the game was over we won. After a game it may not look good. The alumni may be asking why we are not entertaining them. Let me assure you our job is to win football games. You win football games by running the ball, stopping the run, and being on the plus side of the Give-Away/Take-Away area.

When the season was over we had played 13 games. There are only three college teams in history that ever won 13 games in a season. I do not know how they keep up with the stats, but after 11 games we were 11-0 and still had not won anything. In our conference, the SEC, we had to win our division and then we had to win our conference championship. The winner of the SEC championship game goes to the Sugar Bowl. We had won 11 games and Florida had won eight games. We had to play them to see who goes to the Sugar Bowl and who goes to the Citrus Bowl. We had won 11 games, Florida had won eight games, but we still had not won anything.

When I want my players to really pay attention I tell them to *run your antenna up on this*. Listen to what I am saying. After 11 games the University of Alabama of the SEC led every statistic defensively. The name of the game defensively is points. Say what you want to, it all boils down to how many points you give up. They can run up and down the field forever, but it all comes down to how many points you give up. We gave up a little over eight points per game. The second most important statistic is third-down effectiveness. If you want to know if you win games or lose games, and you do not know what statistic to look at, you look at how many points you give up and then you look at your third-down effectiveness, offensively and defensively. The opponents against the University of Alabama were a little over 22 percent effective on third down. That is suggesting that about 78 percent of the time we won the third-down effectiveness battle. That tells me they have to put their kicking team out on the field. That tells me offensively that we are going to be moving the football. We were an excellent third-down team. If I could just have one area where I really wanted to be good, I would want to be a good first-down defensive team and then I would want to be a good third-down defensive team.

Every time I walk into my office on Sunday I want to know about quality control. I want to know what percent of the time did we hold the opponent to less than 4 yards on first-and-10. It doesn't matter if it is a run or a pass. If the quality control is starting to get out of kilter I will check on it. "Our first-and-10 against the run is getting out of kilter. Our first-and-10 against the pass is getting out of kilter." Then we talk about it on Monday rather than waiting until the season is over. I want to be an excellent third-down team. This is a category that they do not keep in college football. They keep this in the pros. We were probably the best team in the nation on third down. That tells me we are getting the ball back to our offense and we are taking it away from their offense. What do you do on third down? I will cover that in a few minutes. The third down is the key, key, key! When I go into a season I know exactly what I am trying to accomplish. I know what I am trying to accomplish on a first-down situation and what I am trying to accomplish on second down. On third down I am trying to keep the ball offensively, and take it away from them defensively. Third down is an important area.

Going into the season this year I knew we were going to be a good team defensively. I told the press before the start of the season. They asked me why were we going to be good on defense. This is what I told them. "Because we have good football players." Listen to me on this. *You win football games with football players making plays*. You do not win football games with schemes. It does not matter what defense you are playing. When the game is on, your players have to make plays.

I tell our players this. They have heard me tell them this 10 jillion times. "You play 60 plays for the privilege to play on three or four plays that make the difference. If you do not make the play on those three or four plays that really make the difference, then you are not making a contribution to your team winning a game." You may not contribute to losing, but you are not contributing to the win. You have to get it across to your players that somewhere along the line they have to make a big play. When I am grading the film, I grade the players like this. I give them a plus or a minus, and I give him an RBI or an error. An RBI is something that contributes to winning games. Somewhere along the line defensively you have to cause a fumble or you have to recover a fumble. You have to force the quarterback to throw the ball before he is ready to throw it. You have to intercept a pass. You have to pressure the quarterback. You have to have a great coverage. You have to do something. Otherwise, you are not going to win. It is our business to win football games. How many times have I heard players say, "I just enjoy playing football"? Hey, the fun comes in winning the games.

You do not just play for the sake of playing. The fun is in winning. How do I win? I win by making plays.

You win with defense over offense. You entertain people offensively. You are looking at a coach that just coached the team that won the national championship. Do you know how many yards we threw for in the national championship game? It was the number 1 team playing the number 2 team for the national championship. We threw the ball for 18 yards. You can't get any worse than that. In order to have a good team *offensively*, you have to be able to throw the ball between 175 and 200 yards per game. You are not a good offensive team if you can't do that. We threw the ball for less than 20 yards against Miami. When the game was over we won the national championship. How did we do that? We ran the ball for 270 yards. We were in the plus Give-Away/Take-Away area. They ran the ball for less than 50 yards.

How may times have I heard people say that we were a dull offensive team? I have heard that 10 jillion times. Yet, when we had our awards ceremony the other day, do you know how many people were there? When we received our award for the national championship there were over 15,000 people at the ceremony. When you have a banquet you can expect 3,000 or 4,000 people. We had 15,000 at our awards banquet. We threw the ball for 18 yards in the Sugar Bowl and we can get 15,000 to come to our awards ceremony? The name of the game is to *win. How do you win football games*? I am going to repeat this over and over. You win football games by running the football, stopping the run, and you are in the plus on the Give-Away/Take-Away area.

After 11 games we led the nation in four categories defensively. We won 13 games. How do you keep up with statistics? The name of the game defensively is points. We gave up a little over eight points per game. We led the nation in total defense. We led the nation in run defense and pass defense. The four categories that are important on defense, we led the nation. Is there any question why the University of Alabama was playing in the national championship game?

Last night I was at a banquet in Birmingham, Alabama. They were honoring the quarterback of the University of Florida. He set 47 records at Florida throwing the football. Shane Matthews set 47 records at Florida. Our quarterback was only to throw the ball for 18 yards in the Sugar Bowl. We beat Florida and went on to play for the national championship. If I do not say anything else I want you to understand my philosophy.

You have to be able to stop the run. You have to be able to run the football. You have to be in the Plus on the Give-Away/Take-Away. We were plus 18 when the season was over. That is why we were in the championship game.

Let me talk about defense a little more. Everything starts on defense with the End Run Force. When you are talking about defense you have to be able to understand your End Run Force. When I present a defense to the squad I start with this. I may be different from some other coaches in college and the pros. I am involved in offense, defense, and the kicking game. We do not have what you call offensive coordinators or defensive coordinators. I have *coaches*. We have offensive and defensive coaches. I oversee the offense and I oversee the defense. I am not interested in a bunch of folks overseeing things.

You do not know a thing in the world about the coaches I have at Alabama, but they all fit into four categories. You can look at Mike DuBose, Bill Oliver, Mal Moore, whoever. First, the coaches at Alabama are good people. I am not the least interested in sitting around that table day after day, week after week, talking over offense or defense with someone that is going to be pouting. I tell my coaches all of the time that there is nothing wrong with disagreeing. I am not interested in you being disagreeable. This is a big difference. When you look at a coach at the University of Alabama you know he is a good person. Secondly, you know that our coaches can communicate with the players. In this day and time you had better be able to sit down with the players and talk with them one-on-one. Third, they are good teachers. I am not the least bit interested in hiring a coach that is not a good teacher. Now, we can't spend but 17 hours per week during the season. That is the big difference in college football. In the pros you have all the time you want to meet. In college ball you have a limited time to meet. This tells me when that coach goes into the room with his players he better be a good teacher. You ask me what I do and I will tell you that I am a *teacher*. I can go up to that board and talk to you about what we are doing offensively, and I can tell you what we are doing defensively. I can tell you what we are trying to do in the kicking game. I can do this because I am a teacher. The fourth thing about the coaches at Alabama is that they can coach on the field. If you want to be a college football coach, you had better be able to coach on the field. You have to be able to communicate and get the player to respond. It is the ability to perform.

I do not have a lot of slogans at Alabama. But I do have one and It goes like this: *Never confuse activity with accomplishments. Results are what count.* We live in a results-oriented community. It is 'what have I done?' that is what is important. I am not interested in a coach telling me how many hours he spent working. I am not interested in a player telling me how much time he spent working in the off-season program. I am interested in what you got done, brother. How do your players play? It is the ability to perform. Somewhere along the line we have to teach the player to make the play. He has to go out on the field and he has to perform. He has to make a play. We put him in a situation and he has to perform. It is his ability to make a good decision as opposed to a bad decision.

I have just finished a recruiting process. The players have to make a decision if they want to come to the University of Alabama or not. It is important for them to make the right decision. This is going to determine if they are going to be successful or not successful. It is the same for a defensive end. He has to make the right decision when he forces the quarterback to pitch. It has to be the right decision.

Everything on defense starts with the End Run Force. It does not matter if we are forcing with a linebacker, a strong safety, or with a cornerback. It has to start with a End Run Force.

Let me mention a few points about defensive football. It does not matter what level you are on. Defensive football is formation recognition and strategy situations. That is important. It is formation recognition and it is strategy situations. What are strategy situations? It is first-and-10; it is second-and-5 minus; and it is second and-6 to 9. That is a running situation. It is third-and-1; or it is third-and-2. That is a short-yardage situation. It is third-and-3 to 5; 6 to 9; 10 to 12; 14 to 17; and it is 17 plus. Those are strategy situations.

There is no substitute on defense for knowledge. If I put in a game plan on Monday, I do not expect the players to understand it that day. I really don't expect them to understand it on Tuesday. I am not really that concerned if they understand it on Wednesday. But by Thursday I want them to understand what I am talking about when I say it is a strategy situation and it is formation recognition. I will walk into the huddle and give them the situation. "It is a first-and-10, they are in the I formation. What are they going to do?" When you get ready to put in the game plan on defense you put into the plan a special or you call it a particular defense. For example, if I say I am going to play an Over with a 1 Call, when the offense comes up to the line we will play an Over with the front and play a 1 Call in the secondary. If we call a special, it says if the offense comes out in an I formation we will play a Rifle Force with a 1 in the secondary. If the offense comes out in a Red Set we are going to Box Force the play and play a 2 in the secondary. If they come out in a Brown, we are going to play a certain front, a certain force, and a certain secondary call. You may ask how can we do all of this? Because that is formation recognition and it is a strategy situation.

I am getting my football team ready to play and the offense comes to the line in an I formation. I know from the I formation in a run situation that 75 percent of the time they are going to do a certain thing. I know the wide receiver is going to run a deep route, a sideline route, or he is going to run an inside route. How do I know this? This is knowledge. Without knowledge as a defensive football player, when they break that huddle, without knowledge of a formation recognition in a strategy situation then I am just guessing. What I am saying is important. How many times do you break it down and it is a run situation, it is a first-and-10, it is a Brown formation, and every time in a Brown formation on first-and-10 the wing runs an inside route? Is that important to know? You bet it is. It is my job if I am the defensive coach that coaches the defensive backs to teach that cornerback that in that particular situation and that particular formation, that 90 percent of the time he is going to run a particular route. That falls under the area of what? *Knowledge!* There is no substitute for knowledge. I coached professional football for 18 years. The difference in a great football player and the average football player is knowledge. It is a third-and-3 to 5 and they are in a particular formation. The man that I am covering is going to run an inside or an outside route. Does that make a difference? You bet it does. Whose job is it to teach it to that player? It is the coach's job to teach it to that player.

We get ready for what a football team has done, not what it might do. There are 10 jillion things that they might do. Don't tell me what they might do. They might run a reverse, a halfback pass, a reverse pass. I can understand that. I want to know what do they do in that particular situation? I am telling you this is formation recognition and it is strategy situations. I can't coach the defense if I do not know this.

I am getting the football team ready to play. It is a first-and-10. It is an I formation. Every player we have knows what to do in a first-and-10 in that particular situation. That is what coaching is all about. It is a second-and-7 situation. They are in a Brown formation. Brown formation to me and a Brown formation to you may be two different things. To me it means they are going to go flow weak. The X is going to check. They are going to throw the ball to the weak side. I am going to have a defense that takes care of that. That does not say they are going to the weak side. They could go to the strong side. But I am going to stop what they do best in that situation. That is what defensive football is all about. I am going to make you beat me with something that you do not want to do. You have to understand this. I am going to say this over and over again because it is important.

I am a defensive football coach. If you can't score, you can't beat me. I want to know what you do, in what formation, in what situation. It is formation recognition and it is strategy situation. What is the strategy situation? What is the situation? It is a run situation or it is a pass situation. If you do not talk in these terms you are making a mistake. What is a run situation? It is a first-and-10; a second-and-6 to 9; second-and-5. That is a running situation. What is a pass situation? It is a third-and-3 to 5; it is third-and-6 to 9. What is a third-and-1? That is a short-yardage situation. Knowledge! I am telling you there is no substitute for knowledge. You can't just play a defense for the sake of playing it. What is a special? A special says if the offense comes out in an I formation we will play a 1 Coverage. If they come out in a Red situation we are going to play a 2 Coverage. If they come out in a Blue formation we are going to play a 3 coverage. If they come out in a Flip situation, we are going to play a particular coverage. If they go from a standard formation to Flip, or Flip to standard .... It just goes on and on.

To be a good team this is what you must be able to do. You must have the ability to handle the unusual formation and movement that comes off it. They come out and run a formation that we have not seen before and they have movement that comes off the formation. Our defense has to adjust to that situation. That determines if we can play the defense or not.

In order to be a good team on defense you have to be a good first-down team. You have to hold the offense to less than 4 yards on first down. You have to be a great third-down team. If it is third-and-6 and they make 7 yards then it is first-and-10 again. If it is third-and-6 and they only make 5 yards they have to punt the football. Your defensive team is off the field and the offense takes over. On defense we have to be able to recognize the unusual formation and I have to know the play that comes off that formation, and I have to know the movement that comes off that formation. That is coaching, men, I am telling you. If I am a defensive coach and I put my team out on the field, I have to be comfortable in all situations. That doesn't just happen. That is the difference in winning championships and not winning championships. It is the ability to perform, and the ability to recognize the unusual formation, and the movement that comes off it. Then all of a sudden it is your End Run Force.

At the University of Alabama we have three basic End Run Forces to the strong side. We say we will force the play with a strong safety. That says the strong safety is going to force the end run. Then we have a coverage in the secondary that goes along with that force that goes along with that front. I do not care what you call it. The strong safety forces the end run. Listen to me, men. You are not going to run the football. We force the ball with the strong safety and we force you to do something that you do not want to do.

In our terminology we call this a Rifle Force. When we call a Rifle it tells us the strong safety is forcing on the end run. Any time you have an end run three things must happen:

1. Someone has to force the end run.
2. Someone has to play pass defense.
3. Someone has to be responsible for the cutback.

That is the way you introduce defensive football. It is a Rifle Force. This tells us the strong safety is forcing, the cornerback is playing pass defense, and the linebacker is responsible for the cutback. You do not need two men forcing the play and no one to play the cutback. You do not need the strong safety forcing the play and the corner forcing it also. The cornerback plays pass defense. He can force and play pass at the same time.

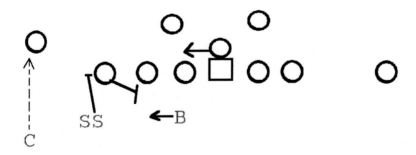

Our next call is the Pistol Force. Now we will force with the cornerback. The strong safety will play pass defense and the linebacker is responsible for the cutback.

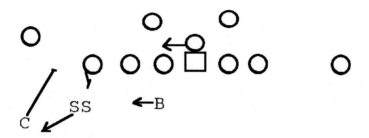

We call the Front Coverage, and then we call the Force. The next thing we call is a Box Force. That is when the linebacker is forcing. The strong safety is plugging the play, and the corner is playing pass defense.

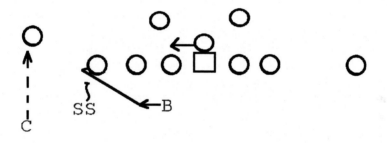

The next thing we try to do is to disguise our intentions. It looks like a Rifle Force but you are playing a Pistol Coverage. You can give them a Pistol Coverage but you are playing a Rifle Force. You give them a Box look and run something else. That quarterback is keying on someone. We give them one look and play another coverage. This falls under the area of disguising the coverage.

When you ask me my philosophy on defense this is what I say. My philosophy on defensive football is not to allow the offense to move the football effectively. That sounds simple. Everyone would like to have that. How do you do it? How do you keep them from moving the ball effectively? This falls under the area of method. How do you make sure your method works? That falls under the area of quality control. If I do not want them to move the ball effectively how do I stop them? That is what I do when I sit around during the off-season.

This is what we do when we have a staff meeting before spring practice and in the summer and before our fall practice. We talk about the philosophy of defensive football. We talk about everything. We settle on something. Whatever we settle on is what we go out and coach.

On defense, my philosophy is not to let the offense move the ball effectively. Now I break that down. I break it down into a run defense and a pass defense. Part of my pass defense is broken down into a pass rush or a pass coverage. Somewhere along the line you have to be fish or fowl. You have to run the quarterback or you have to play pass defense. You have to say I am going to blitz the quarterback. In order to blitz the quarterback you have to be able to play man-to-man in the secondary. If I asked everyone in this room if you knew anything about playing Man Defense most of you would say you don't know much about playing Man.

If I am coaching in high school or college I am going to make my players play man-to-man pass defense in the spring. I may not play it in the fall; I may be all zone in the fall. But, I am going to play man in the spring and early fall because I am going to make that player a better defensive player. Somewhere along the line he has to be a football player. When I talk about man-to-man defense, I am talking about one man being able to cover one player. I never ask a player in college except in the plus territory to play man-to-man defense. I ask him to play man-to-man inside and I ask him to play man-to-man outside. The plus territory to us is 18 yards in to the goal line. I ask him to play man-to-man because an inside route will beat you and an outside route will beat you. If we are out in the field and I am asking the player to play man-to-man, it tells him he is man-to-man inside or man-to-man outside.

There are a few things he must be able to do to play man-to-man. I ask him why does he backpedal? When I first started coaching at Texas A&M, backpedaling was not in my vocabulary. I did not want to hear anyone talking about backpedaling. When the ball was snapped we turned and ran backward. How many times have I told a player in college not to get beat deep on a pass play? If that happened, I was on the field as soon as he got to the hash mark letting him know that I was upset. In pro football if I have a player that gets beat deep and he comes off the field, I know he is concerned about what I am going to say to him. I say something like this to him. "Statistics tell me that you are going to get beat about three times on a deep pass before the year is over. Thank goodness one of those three has already gone." Now, I tell him a little different on Monday. When you lose your confidence as a defensive back and you lose confidence in playing man-to-man defense, we are in trouble.

I am going to teach the defensive backs to backpedal. So this is what I ask him. "Why do you backpedal?" You backpedal to gain a position on the receiver. You keep the shoulders parallel and you backpedal to gain a position. You do not have to tell him anymore than that. I backpedal to gain a position and it does not matter if it is inside or outside. Now I have gained a position on the man. If I tell him he is to play man-to-man inside, I do not want him to get beat inside and I don't want him to get beat deep. "If you get beat on the sideline, you will be close enough so you can make the tackle."

Most players in a Man Coverage want to intercept the football. I am not interested in the interception when I am playing Man. I am trying to shut you out. I am saying to you that you are not going to catch the football. *When you are playing man-to-man pass defense, the most important thing is concentration.* When the ball is snapped and I get into position on the man they could shoot off a cannon and I would never hear it because I am concentrating so strongly on the receiver. I do not feel anything, I do not hear anything, and all I do is see the receiver. Do you know how many players can do that? About 1 in 500. Not very many can do that. We do not look at the quarterback when we play Man Coverage. We concentrate on the receiver. If I ask you the key to playing Man Defense you should say *concentration*. We are not trying to make the interception; we are trying to shut the receiver out. When we play Zone we are trying to make the interception.

In pro football we have to be able to see things when I play Man Coverage. They react according to what the offense does after the snap of the ball. When the ball is snapped their assignment changes with the movement of the offense. They key the line as well as the receivers and backs.

Somewhere along the way I have to teach the players to see things on defense. The I formation tells me something. The Red formation tells me something. It is first-and-10 in an I formation. Is the wing going to go deep or run a sideline? That is my business as a coach. Why do I backpedal to take away the inside position? Because that is knowledge. That is my job as a coach. It is the knowledge the player has in a strategy situation. I can't say this enough times. You do not win games with schemes. You win football games with players making plays. As a coach it is my job to put the players in a situation where they can perform.

Somewhere along the line I have to let the players play. The worst thing I can do is to second guess my people calling the offense or defense. If you hire a coach you better put him in a position to let him work. If I want to call the defense, I will call it before they break the huddle. If I want to call an offensive play, I will call it before they break the huddle. If I want to send a play in, I will tell Mal Moore, our quarterback coach, to send the play in. I do not second guess what my coaches call by saying, "I knew that would not work." When you hurt the confidence of the coach, you also hurt the confidence of your players. You have to bring them together and let them know that the coach making the calls has the support of the head coach. I am involved in all phases of our program at Alabama. I do not care how anyone else does it.

This is how we work things at Alabama. When we put in an offensive game play, I put it into the squad. When we put in the defensive game play, I put it into the squad. When we talk about the kicking game, I introduce it to the squad. I introduce the offense and defense and the kicking game. Then all of a sudden Bill Oliver is coaching the defensive backs, Mike DuBose is coaching the front, Ellis Johnson is coaching the outside linebackers, and Jeff Rouse is working the inside linebackers. All of a sudden we are working as a *unit*.

The thing I am pleased about this past year is this. We struggled a little at the start of the year on offense. I never heard one defensive player fussing at the offense. I did not hear an offensive player fussing at the defense. All of a sudden we had a hard time covering kickoffs. We just were not a good team covering kickoffs. We worked on Tuesday on covering kickoffs. I did not hear anyone complaining about covering kickoffs. To me this tells me one thing. *We had an unselfish football team*.

When I was at Dallas I was big on setting goals. I am not going to get into goal setting, but I do want to tell you a few things that are important. When you set goals they must be obtainable and they must be measurable. Otherwise, they do not mean anything. If you have a team that only wins three games and sets its goal to win the state championship the next year, it does not make sense. If you win three games, you may try to win five games the next year. If I win five games, I may try to win eight games. If I win eight games, I may be talking about winning the championship. Goals must be obtainable and measurable. Also, if you can pyramid it down to the player, it does not mean anything. Goals come from what you did poorly the year before.

The year before, in 1991, we led the nation on points. However, we gave up too many big plays. I researched our films to see why we gave up too many big plays. The reason we gave up the big plays in 1991 was because we were a poor tackling team. We tackled at 76 percent effectiveness. We have to tackle at 89 percent effectiveness at Alabama. We had too many missed assignments.

I went into the 1992 season and I had one goal for our team. We wanted to reduce the big plays. How were we going to do it? We were determined to be a better tackling team and we were determined to reduce missed assignments. Every time I went into a meeting I was talking about tackling better and I was talking about missed assignments. We went from winning 11 games to winning 13 games.

I did the same thing with the offense. We say we want to keep the ball seven plays or more 65 percent of the time in order to score, kick it to score, or to move it up before we kick it so the defense will have to go 80 yards to score. We did not do this in 1991. We did it only 43 percent of the time. How come we only did this 43 percent of the time? We had way too many fumbles, and we had too many penalties. We were a poor offensive team on third down when it was 3 to 5 yards to go for the first down. Every time I went into an offensive meeting I told the team we had to reduce the fumbles; we have to reduce the penalties; we have to be a better team on third down on 3 to 5 yards to go. Every day in practice in the early part of the year we had a period on offense where we worked on third-and-3 to 5 yards to go. Why? Because that was a goal for the University of Alabama. Where did that goal come from? It came from what we did poorly the year before.

When the season is over you analyze your season. I do not care what it is, you did something poorly on offense and defense. That becomes my goal for the next year. Then you have a chance to make that goal. I am saying all of that to say this.

In 1977 we had 13 rookies make our team at Dallas. That is unheard of in pro ball. We sat around the table day after day trying to come up with a goal for the Dallas Cowboys in 1977. Do you know what we came up with? It was something that will apply to everyone in this room. The goal for the Dallas Cowboys in 1977 was this: *Have a genuine appreciation for the contribution that everyone makes*. That says for the offensive player to appreciate the defensive player; the defensive player to appreciate the offensive player. The coach to appreciate the player. The player to appreciate the coach. The player to really appreciate the trainer that keeps him on the field. To have a real appreciation for the man that takes care of the field so we are practicing on grass and not on just dirt. *A genuine appreciation for the contribution that everyone makes.* The last game we lost that year was in the Super Bowl. We had 13 rookies. We had an unselfish football team. Now we can practice for a purpose.

I just finished recruiting. Do you know what I told the high school players that came to visit with me in my office? I would tell him to listen to me. "Run your antenna up, son. If you don't want to come to Alabama, don't do it. Go somewhere else." We won the national championship at Alabama and I saw a common thread on that team. *Everyone on our team was there because he wanted to play at Alabama.* Everyone appreciates what each individual player does for our team. I could go out and tell the team that I want them to line up and run 20 100-yard sprints. No one would say a word. They would line up and run the sprints. This fall I would say we are going to run five 50-yard sprints and we would run five 50-yard sprints. Do you know why? When the players have an appreciation for what I am trying to do, and I have an appreciation for what that player is trying to do, the bottom line is that we are trying to win football games. You win football games with football players making plays. He has to be in a good frame of mind. You can't beat your players down and expect them to play. I do not mean that you do not work them. No one works harder than our players. Somewhere along the line they have to feel good about what we are trying to do. I try to get our team ready to play on Saturday. I am not interested in being ready to play on Thursday. If I put the game plan in and they understand it on Tuesday, then it is too simple. I want them ready to play on Saturday.

The game is settled between the players out in the arena. It is not settled by the media or the coaches. What some Miami player is saying down at Pat O'Brien's Restaurant has nothing to do with what the game is going to be like. The game is settled between the players making plays. That comes defensively from knowledge.

When we break the huddle, I could care less what we have called. I want to watch the point of attack. Bill Oliver calls our defense. He can call what he wants. I could care less. Why? Because we are not going to win with the call. Don't ever think you are smarter than the other coach. You win football games because your football players make plays. You put him into a position to make the big plays. He plays 55 to 60 plays for the privilege to make three or four plays that make the difference.

We are a coordinated defense at Alabama. That says that the End Run Force ties in with the front that ties in with the Pass Coverage. On the strong side we say it is a Rifle Force, a Pistol Force, or a Box Force. On the backside we say it is a Jet Force or a Fly Force. There is no question what we are doing. No one runs wide against Alabama. They do not do it because we have an End Run Force that is going to stop it. We are going to force the offense to run inside. Now the overs and unders and the fronts are going to stop them inside. If they can't run the ball wide, it is hard for them to beat you. If they run to the strong side we force the play with the strong safety, strong corner, or strong linebacker. If they run to the weak side, we force the play with the weak corner, weak linebacker, or the weak safety. That is where it starts. What happens if the play breaks down? Someone says he read the play wrong. We do not get worried about it. We correct the situation.

Real quickly, let me tell you a few things about third-down situation coverages. We play 4-0 Coverages. That says we may play with seven defensive backs, six defensive backs, or five defensive backs. What are the advantages of playing with a 4-0? We are playing with four linemen and seven defensive backs. What is the advantage? Advantages are:

1) You can double cover any receiver.

2) You can double one receiver and have post help.

3) You can disguise your intentions. I have seven defensive backs. I can double cover their two best receivers, with no post help. I can double cover their best receiver and have post help. I can disguise my intentions.

What are the disadvantages of playing a 4-0 or a Nickel Coverage?

1) You have no End Run Force. We have to have a Recognition Force. We recognize that we have no End Run Force. If the offense runs the ball to the outside someone has to recognize that we do not have End Run Force. They have to react to that. They know that is a weakness. There are no surprises. They make plays and they perform in crucial situations. It is my job as a coach to put the player in a position where they can make plays.

Every day in the United States we have 6000 new teenage alcoholics. Our job as coaches is to help our players. One out of nine students in the United States uses marijuana. It is our job as coaches to teach our kids what is right and what is not right. My job at Alabama is to graduate our players. It is not to make them pros. It is my job to graduate them. You ask me how many players graduate from Alabama and I will say everyone that wants to. It is my job to get it across to the players to graduate. There is nothing wrong with pro football because I made a living there for 18 years. As a high school coach, you have no greater responsibility than to see that your players qualify to go on to college. No matter how good the high school player is, the grades are very important. Somewhere along the line he has the main interest of the high school coach. I appreciate the coach that goes out in the arena and does everything and his players performs the way they should.

They interviewed 2000 teenage girls recently and they asked them this question. "If you could have any Daddy you want, who would you want?" Only 4 percent said they wanted the daddy that they already had. That tells us that 96 percent of those girls wanted someone else to be their daddy. Do you know why? Because we do not teach them the right things. Somewhere along the way we have to teach the young kids to stand tall, and to feel good about themselves, and to do right in their performance. Sir Isaac Newton said it best. *If it seems that I can see further than most people, it is because I have stood on the shoulders of a giant*. He said, "I have stood on the shoulders of a giant." Do you know what he is saying? He is saying, "I have surrounded myself with good people."

Now, when I put the player in the arena, he feels good about what he is doing. When the game is over there is hugging going on. The offense is proud of the defense, and the defense is proud of the offense. The players are proud of the coaches, and the coaches are proud of the players. That results in winning. The name of the game is winning.

It is my job to prepare my players so they can win. There is no substitute for knowledge. It is Formation Recognition. It is Strategy Situations. After the ball is snapped it is the ability to perform. That is what wins for you. There is nothing complicated about that. We have 11 players beating on *one heartbeat*. Pump! Pump! Pump! Every one of them is beating on the same heartbeat. We have 11 players on the same heartbeat. Line them up. It does not matter what the other team does. When the game is over you are going to win.

Chapter 18

COACHING IS MORE THAN X'S AND O'S

Grant Teaff
American Football Coaches Association
1994

Let me assure you I am always telling people that coaching is a lot more than just X's and O's. That terminology has always been a misnomer. I have been coaching for 36 years and I can never remember when I drew an X on the chalkboard in my career. We always say X's and O's. Now, they may draw X's and O's in basketball, but I have not used them in football. I have drawn a lot of T's, and upside down T's, circles, and squares, but not X's. The connotation is that coaching is much more than X's and O's. This means there is more to coaching than drawing plays or defensive alignments. That is what the X's and O's refer to; drawing plays and defensive alignments. We all love to draw plays and we love to draw out schemes and make use of all of the wonderful offensive formations and schemes that have come out in the last few years. Coaches have been doing that for more than 100 years. People have been dreaming up plays that will score. Every play is designed to score. They do not all score because every defense is designed to stop a play from scoring, or to keep the play to a 3-yard gain or less. Dreaming and scheming and the X's and O's are a big part of what coaches are all about.

I have been a coach for 36 years and I feel blessed in taking over the American Football Coaches Association in that I know where everyone is coming from. I have coached on every level except junior high. I have been very blessed in my coaching career. When I am asked to do something for coaches I do it. I became a head football coach in college when I was only 25 years old. I have been a head coach in college for 30 years. I had a lot of people that did a lot for me including the assistant coaches. We would develop concepts and ideas and they would loyally teach those concepts to the players. The players would believe in us and we were successful. We may not have had all of the right answers, but because of the points of loyalty, and because we cared about the players and they knew it, they would blindly do what we asked them to do. We were very successful most of the time. That is something you can never repay. I am referring to tremendous loyalty that is a part of team sports and is a part of our coaching profession.

A year ago in Atlanta at the AFCA meeting I gave a speech and at that time I issued a warning. Since that time everything that I said at that meeting has come true. Athletics across this country are in jeopardy. Everyone has to have training to coach. The colleges that train our coaches are under attack at this time. That is one of the reasons that I gave the AFCA a 10-year commitment. I think it will take every bit of that time to turn things around. This is true not only in athletics, but gender equity is also a big problem on both the college and high school level. It is going to be tough to make a turn back to the things that made this country great.

Again, I hesitate to talk about some of those problems because you are not here to hear gloom and doom. But I say it in a very positive light in a sense that I believe in doing something about those things that are negative and the things that are going to destroy the games that we love, football in particular. Eventually it could destroy our freedom in this country that we love so dearly. We are in bad shape, men. There are a lot of bad things going on out there. You know it and you see it. There is a decline in morals, effort, and attitude. There is a rise in racism in this country. It is very scary. Inner cities are crumbling. There is crime everywhere you look. There is a rise in teenage pregnancy. In the state of Texas more people die as a result of guns than die in auto accidents. That was announced today. In about three months that will be true for the entire nation. More people will die from gunshots than will die in auto accidents. You know how may people get killed in auto accidents? It is unbelievable. Every 40 seconds someone gets wounded or shot in the United States. We must address this serious problem.

One thing we can do as coaches is to make ourselves better and to do the best job we can where we are planted. Then we need to bloom where we are planted. It is essential that coaches and teachers take the lead in bringing education and athletics back to where it should be. Somehow we have to get the politicians to create those opportunities from a financial standpoint so young people can have the choice in participating in athletics. There have been a lot of studies on athletics. They found out that young women who are involved in athletics do not get pregnant as much as those that are not involved in athletics, on a percentage basis. They have something else that drives them. A high percentage of kids in athletics are not involved in drugs. Certainly, some athletes are into drugs. We do have some problems in this area. But athletics, and particularly football, are important to us as a nation and as coaches.

One thing I want to stress to you is this. As coaches, you are more than that. As we go beyond the X's and O's the first thing I would say to you is this. Not only are you a coach, but you are a teacher; interestingly enough, often the best teacher around. I have been asked to write a book, The concept of the book is going to be this: *Coaching is Teaching and Teaching Should Be Coaching*. The best teachers I ever had were my coaches. If you think about it, the best teachers that you know, when they are really motivated, are coaches. You have to be a teacher and you have to be a father in this profession. That is a part of the profession. I have been a father to many of my athletes. You have to be a psychologist. Many of us are not trained for this, so we have to study and understand what we are talking about. We need to be aware of what effect our action has on the people we are dealing with.

A coach has to be a motivator. A motivator is one that can inspire someone to better himself through his own talent and effort. We have to be role models. There are a lot of folks in our society that shun responsibility today. I saw where Charles Barkley said he did not want to be a role model for anyone. He makes about 40 jillion dollars and he is a role model, even if he doesn't admit it. Every coach at every level in this country is a role model. You are a role model to the young people that you work with and to the people in your community. The most recent study proved that the most influential people in any community are the coaches. That is true by far. Coaches are ahead of preachers, teachers, bankers, and university presidents. Coaches have the most influence, and we must recognize this and be role models.

A coach must be a disciplinarian. It starts with the coach. It is just like a teacher in a classroom. If you walk into a classroom and you do not have discipline, you are not going to get much accomplished.

You must establish discipline at the outset. As coaches, we must establish discipline.

Coaches must be more than just a coach. A coach must know the difference between motivation and psychology. There is a big difference. Motivation is important in everything we do. The most important motivation is self-motivation. This is true for yourself, your children, your family, and the young people you work with.

There are some component parts of self-motivation that I have taught as long as I can remember. I became self-motivated when I was 13 years old. That is when I decided that I wanted to be a coach. I set my goals to be a college head coach when I was 13 years old. I was too little and too slow, and I couldn't outrun an eight-day-old clock. I weighed 145 pounds until my senior year and then I got up to 150 pounds. I was extremely slow. It was then that I knew if I was going to meet my goals I would have to be highly self-motivated. It became incumbent upon me to teach my children and my students how to become self-motivated.

The first thing you must understand about self-motivation is the fact that everyone has what I call a *hot button*. The hot button is that entity within you that turns you on. It is what starts you moving into action. Every player that you coach has a hot button. The reason that you must use self-motivation is because they are the only ones that knows what that hot button is. You may hit that button so often, but you will drive yourself crazy trying to hit everyone's hot button at the same time. They do not all respond the same way. Therefore, if you are dependent on motivating the entire team based on your ability to find everyone's hot button, I can tell you they will not stay motivated very long. When you see a team that starts the season playing well and then they go down at the end of the season, you know they have not learned to be self-motivated. The coach cannot motivate a team week after week through articulation that may hit a lot of hot buttons. Not many coaches are going to be stupid enough to say something that ends up in the newspaper that you as a coach can use to motivate your team. If you want to be successful, you must be self-motivated and in turn, teach the basic principles of self-motivation to the individuals that you are working with. The hot button is essential.

The second thing you must understand is this. You must teach people to realize where they are. *At what level are you in terms of your own ability to be successful?* One of the techniques I have used is to set up a sheet or form for each player. I have them fill out the form two or three times a year.

We have the players make a list of what we call *Assets and Liabilities*. We have them write the things down that they believe are an asset to them, and then write down the things that they feel are a liability for them. It has nothing to do with finance. It has to do with what you feel are your assets and liabilities. It is amazing what individuals can find out about themselves if they will take this serious and think about it. The whole idea is to accentuate the positive and to eliminate the negative. Build on the good points you have and eliminate the bad points. If you are a hard worker, you should be aware of that. Don't let anyone outwork you. That is an asset. Eliminate things that keep you from being successful. "Well, it is hard for me to be at meetings on time." That is a liability. Come up with a *Time Plan* that will allow you to be where you are supposed to be on time. Every liability can be eliminated or improved and every asset can become better.

The second part of our player evaluation is to ask this question. "What are you committed to?" The first thing you have to do for most youngsters today is to explain what *committed* means. Unfortunately, they have not seen much commitment in their lifetimes. They may not see commitment at home. The only commitment they may see is on your staff or with teachers they have. Ask players what they are committed to and you will be surprised.

The next question we ask our players leads to goal setting. We ask them this. "How do you see yourself 10 years from today?" That makes you project yourself. We tell them to add 10 years to their lives and project what they think they will be doing. This will tell you a great deal about their goals and their expectations. This allows you to lead them into goal setting. This is essential to self-motivation. If you want to be a self-motivated person you must have goals and you must know where you are going. You must understand how goals work in your life. You must be broad-based in setting goals. You can't just set goals in one area of your life. You have to set goals in all areas of your life. You must be willing to set intermediate goals before you can set ultimate goals. You must work daily to make those intermediate goals become successful. Once you build on that success then you can start to set long-range goals. Too many people start out the season by saying we want to be state champions. That is fine, but it is not the normal time you would set that goal. You set that goal after you have gotten through two-a-day practices and you have acquired the work ethic it takes to get you where you want to go. If you have the talent then you can start talking about setting the goal to be state champions. There is an importance in the sequence of goal setting and the building of goal setting. It is important to write goals down.

One thing you can teach young people in self-motivation is account-ability. A lot of people in our society are not accountable. I call it T-C-B—taking care of business. It is important to take care of business on the field and off the field.

I have a commemorate ring that I gave every player, coach, and manager that worked with me my last year of coaching. It signified the 21 years from pride to excellence. It has a link on the top and a link on the bottom. On the side of the ring is T-C-B, a reminder to all of the guys that wear the ring that taking care of business is their responsibility. It is their responsibility and not mine. If you want to be a self-motivated individual that teaches self-motivation, you must be accountable and you have to teach it.

The last point I will make about self-motivation is that you must constantly build *a Positive Attitude*. You cannot expect your players to have a positive attitude if you or your coaching staff does not have a positive attitude. You have to work at this. It does not come easily. All you have to do is to watch TV and you know that we live in a country that thrives on negative attitudes. They talk about the negative side of the news. What you have to do is to teach the young people that you work with to develop a positive attitude. You must learn to eliminate negative thoughts and negative concepts that come into our computer. I learned a long time ago, in a very real way, that you better make yourself clear and explain yourself thoroughly. It is an exercise in eliminating the negatives from your life. Develop-ing a positive attitude can be done, but you must work at it. You have to look at things in a positive light and with a positive frame of mind. That can be hard to do at times. When you are teaching this concept they must understand that they must work on a positive attitude everyday.

Gary Austin was a great tailback for me at San Angelo State. He will remember this story. We were going to play Texas A&I University and they were the defending national champs at that time. We were discussing with the squad what we would do against the national champs. I started talking to the team about the only way we could win was to *believe we could win* and the only way we could win was to have a *positive attitude*. I made it a point to let them know we had to go into the game expecting to win.

So on Friday night I shared with them a group of words, or a saying that I had used to motivate me most of my life. Many people use these words today because I have shared them over the years. The way that I told my players that I used the words was that I used them every morning to set my attitude in a positive way to start each day. These are the words that I use.

I am only one — but I am one
I can't do everything
But I can do something
That which I can do
I ought to do
That which I ought to do
By god's grace I will do

I can say those words and I have a tingling up and down my body. I am like Pavlov's dogs. When I hear those words I am filled with positive thoughts. I have trained myself so those words fill me with positive thoughts. When I get up in the morning I use those words. We went on to beat Texas A&I that year. I had the words printed up on a blue background and they hung in our dressing room. I was going through some things in our dressing room recently and found that plastic that we used to display those words. A lot of people use those words today. It is amazing how positive those words are. In life itself, we are only one. There are no duplicates of us. We are created in the image of God, which is a revelation unto itself. "I am special. What I say is important. I can't do everything; but what can I do?" This zeros us in on the things we are capable of doing. A wide receiver can't play offensive tackle. "What can I do?" Realizing what I can do, I commit myself to do it. *That which I can do - I ought to do. That which I ought to do, by God's grace I will do*. A positive attitude has to be developed.

Those are the basics. Recognize that everyone has a hot button. Find your own hot button and teach your players to find their hot buttons. Use self-evaluations so players know where they are. Teach them how to set goals. That will make them very conscious of what they have to do on a daily basis. If you have goals on a daily basis you know what you have to do to be successful. You have to teach them accountability and to take care of business. You must teach your players to develop a positive attitude.

There are two reminders that I thought of in preparing what I would talk about today. It has to do with self-motivation and it has to do with being successful. One thought is of what we did back in the spring of 1979 to motivate our team. We had just come off a very tough year. We had a great team but ended up not doing as well as we were expected to do. I was on a one-year contract and I was told to fire three coaches. I asked them which three coaches I should fire? They told me any three I wanted to fire. I told them they could take their contract and keep it. I assured them we were going to do it our way and that I was going to keep the same staff that I had.

We were going into the 1979 season with all of this facing us. We had come off a great win against Texas at the end of the season. That game sort of turned things around for us. In fact, since 1979 only Texas A&M has won more games that we have in the Southwest Conference. That spring we had a great attitude. We had worked very hard and had set some very high and lofty goals. Before the team left for the summer I got this idea. I went down to the equipment room and got a roll of gold helmet tape and took a hole punch and punched a ton of gold dots. I put them in a little bottle and kept them in my pocket. I called all of the freshmen and invited them over to my house for some cookies. We visited and talked about the things we wanted to do for the next season. Before they were to leave we were all sitting around the floor and I told them I had a special announcement. I told them that each of them would be receiving a gold dot from me that night. In receiving the gold dot they would become a member of the *Secret Society of the gold dot*. I took one of the gold dots out of the bottle and placed it over the 6 on one of the player's watches. They did not understand what I was doing at first. I went around the room and put gold dots on each watch of the players. If they did not have a watch I put in on the inside of their billfold. The idea was that every time they looked at their watch they would see the gold dot. It would be a reminder to them of the goals that they had set, and the plans that they had made. When college kids go away in the summer, you have very little control over them. It was important that they keep their goals during the summer. I tied in the gold dot theme with the acronym G-O-L-D. It was spelled out! *G-O-L-D*.

This is what I told them. Every time you look at your watch you will see the gold dot and it will remind you of G-O-L-D. The G stands for your own personal Goals and your team Goals. The O stands for Oneness and the L stands for Loyalty. The D stands for Determination to do whatever it takes to get the job done. I went on to tell them that they could not tell others what the gold dot stood for. The other team members and the other coaches did not know what the gold dot stood for. The purpose of that was as they began to get questions about the gold dot it made it magnified in their own mind.

They would tell them that they could not tell them what it was for because it was a part of the Society of the Gold Dot.

The next night I added the sophomores, then I added the juniors, and finally we included the seniors. I still had not told the coaches what I was doing. They were going bananas. By the end of the week everyone on campus was asking about the gold dots. They would not tell what the gold dot stood for. Finally, in a staff meeting one of the coaches asked, "What in the world is going on with this gold dot business?" That is when I initiated them into the Secret Society of the Gold Dot. I had let it all build up for the entire week.

If you have ever been to a Baylor football game on the road or at home, from that day to this day, you should have seen our banner at the game. There is a green banner with a gold dot in the center of the banner. It goes on every trip with the team. It is at my house now, but will go in the Texas Hall of Fame in Waco soon. It hung in our dressing room where the players could see it. Over the years every freshman class at Baylor, up until 1992, has been initiated into the Secret Society of the Gold Dot. The idea was to come up with a way to remind them of the purpose and goals they had set.

I told you there were two links on the ring we gave to our players in 1992. They were chain links on the ring. I believe very strongly in the individual link being as strong as it can be to make the chain stronger. One day I went down to the hardware store and picked out a chain that had several links in it. Each link was about an inch wide and about two inches long. I asked the clerk if he had a bolt cutter that I could use to cut the chain with. He let me use his bolt cutter to cut the links apart. I got about 30 feet of the chain and took it with me. To get one full link from the chain you had to cut two off. I sat there and cut up the chain until I got about 30 links. The clerk asked me what I was going to do with all of those links. I told him that I was going to build a football team. He wanted to know if I knew what I was talking about, and I assured him that I did.

At the next meeting I started talking about the importance of the individual links of a chain to the overall strength of a chain. I made some illustrations and talked about how the chains are joined by the links. I stressed the fact that if there is one weak spot in the chain, the entire chain can be lost because of that one weak spot. I had them look at the links and then I had them feel the links. I told them that someone on this team would be the first guy to get one of these links. I told them they would have to be the strongest possible link to this team to get the first link. I told them I was going to give one link on offense and one link to a defensive player, publicly. For the rest of the team there will not be a public announcement on this. I may walk up to you and hand you a link. If I offer you a link, take it. You may be a starter or a walk-on. Until I give out all the links to this team, we can never be the team we need to be. If I do not give out all the links it means we still have weak links on our team.

We started out practice and got through our two-a-day sessions. Finally, I selected an offensive and defensive player, and at a team meeting I called each player up and gave them a link. I told them they could wear the link, put it in their pocket, or do whatever they wanted to do with it. It would always be a reminder that Coach Teaff believes you are the strongest possible link you could be based on your talent and your ability, and your ability to contribute to our team. The first player to get the link was J.J. Joe, a defensive back. The other players began to wait to see who would get the next link. It was about six days, just before our first ball game, before I gave any more links out. I gave out three links before that first game. After the game I studied the film. The players wanted to know who was going to get the next links. Finally, I gave out 10 links. Before that second game those 12 players had the links around their necks on a chain. They would not take the link off. It became a part of them. It became so valuable to them. The only meaning it had was that it came from me and it said to them that I believe they were the strongest link that they could be to our team. That team went on to be one of our great football teams. One of the reasons for this was because we have individuals on that team being conscious of the importance of the individual to the success of the total team. When you talk about links around our place, it has a very special meaning. Perhaps you can utilize that in some way. There are a lot of tie-ins you can make with this idea. A link is like a ring, it never ends. Those of you that have been in wedding ceremonies have heard the preacher say it is endless love. The link is a continuous circle and it goes around and around.

Let's talk about psychology. That is *Motivation*. That is how you get into self-motivation. Those are things that can help your team remember how to be motivated and the importance of motivation. Let's talk about the psychological aspects of it. I call this *Seizing the Moment*. There are times when something can be said or done that is a psychological ploy. If used properly this can be added to the overall motivation that you are using. When I was only 26 years old and coaching at McMurray College I used this form of motivation. I had not been fully developed in character and integrity at the time.

We were playing Arlington State coached by Cheena Gilstrap. He was one of the best coaches that ever came down the pike. They were tough and they were rough. We were playing Arlington State for our homecoming game. We were the McMurray Indians. We had a tepee village and we beat the toms-toms, and had mascots dressed like Indians. It was a very special time, but we had to play a tough team. We were the underdogs by about 30 points. We were not sure how our players would react to being such an underdog. We had a team meeting every Saturday morning at 10 o'clock. We met at our field house; our dressing rooms were at the other end of the field house. I was coming in for the meeting, and just before I got to the door of the field house I looked over and saw the schools pet dog, Ringer.

About two years before that, a big half-breed boxer dog showed up at one of our practices during our two-a-day sessions. Someone on our team took some black shoe polish and painted a ring around the dog's eye and called him Ringer. That came from the *Our Gang* comedy where they had a black dog with a white ring around his eye. They called the dog Ringer. So Ringer became the team dog. Ringer would go to class with the players. He had the run of the campus. You could go to chapel and he would come walking across the stage. He would always be at our pregame warm-ups. He would show his enthusiasm by barking as loud as possible. He would run through our drills and he was a part of our team. Everyone loved Ringer.

On this particular morning I was getting ready to go into the team meeting and I looked over and saw Ringer. I saw that Ringer was walking toward the door. He looked like John Wayne; he had his head over to one side and he was drooping. He had a big cut on his shoulder and his ears were bleeding. I looked at Ringer and could see that he had been out and probably had gotten into a dogfight. I reached down and picked ol' Ringer up. I picked him up into my arms. Suddenly I became inspired. I walked into the field house and kicked open the double doors to the meeting room. The players were waiting for me.

I walked into the room and there was a table off to the side. I walked over and put Ringer on the table. The players could see Ringer was bleeding and was hurt. Sometimes things just work out for you. Ol' Ringer rolled over and rolled his big eyes at the team. Everyone wanted to know what happened. "Men I want you to know that I found Ol' Ringer and he has been hurt. I want you to know what Arlington did to him last night."

We beat Arlington by three touchdowns that afternoon. After the game I went across the field to shake hands with Coach Gilstrap. He said, "That was a great game coach, but I never saw a team as mad as your team was. They were shaking their fists at me. I did not do a thing to them." I said, Cheena, "Do you remember the Gipper at Notre Dame?" He said, "Yea, but what does this have to do with our game?" I said, "Chalk this game up to Ringer!"

Years later I told this story in one of my books. Coach Gilstrap called me up later and told me now he knew what I meant when I said to chalk this game up to Ringer. Now, that is called at the spare of the moment, or seizing-the-moment-type of motivation. It will not last. It will not hold up and I am not proud of that type motivation.

Many of you have heard the story about the worm. I guess I will have to live with that story until I die. That story has been twisted and mangled through the years. Although I will continue to set the story straight, it was not motivation. I did not eat the worm; I did not swallow the worm. I simply put the worm in my mouth and chomped him a couple of times and then spit him out. My idea was very simple. That was during the 1978 season and we had been through a great deal. Psychologically, we had tried everything. Nothing worked. Sometimes not all things are successful, no matter how hard you try, no matter how well you are prepared, and no matter that you have a great positive attitude. Certain circumstances can put you on the downward spiral. We found ourselves in that situation in 1978. At the end of the season we were a quivering mass of jello. We had just lost to Rice and were headed home to play Texas. They were ninth in the nation and headed for a bowl game, and were favored over us by five touchdowns. There is a time when you have to set your jaw. I set my jaw. I said that our program was worth saving and the way we could save it was to beat the University of Texas. Then I told everyone how we were going to go about beating Texas.

The first thing we are going to do is to think and act like *winners*. The bad things that had been happening to us all year caused us to have expectations of losing. No matter how hard we played we figured some way in the fourth quarter we were going to lose it. We felt someone would fumble or throw an interception that would lead to our defeat. We were in a ploy of negative expectations. It happens. It is like the herd that is heading for the cliff. You had better find a way to turn things around or the team is going over the cliff. You must turn the herd or they are going down. We were at that point.

The first thing I said is that we must think and act like winners. I told the team it would be hard, but this is what we were going to do that week. "This week I want you to wear to class the best clothes you have." At that time we were 2-8, with the Texas game left to play. I told the players to greet everyone with this comment all week: *I am a winner, and we are going to beat Texas*. I warned them they would get some negative replies, but I did not want them to be offended. I told them when they got up in the morning and looked into the mirror and saw their image to say, *I am a winner, you are a winner, and we are going to beat Texas*. I told them to do that every day and every morning and they would start acting like a winner. We saw a great transition come about. It was interesting how something like this can affect you. If you think like a loser you become a loser. If you think like a winner you can expect to win. It takes more than just thinking about winning. We had other problems to solve. We switched quarterbacks. We made a few changes on defense. You could feel the confidence of our players begin to grow. But when you had the experience we had, there is one thing psychologically we had to remember. The team was fragile, individually and collectively. They were fragile in the sense if something bad happened, they could go down so fast psychologically it would make your head swim.

On Thursday this is what I stressed. I told them someone would have to rise to the occasion to do whatever it takes to win the game. It might be an interception on the 2-yard line. It may be running the ball in for the touchdown when there are five men hanging on you. You have to make the play. Someone must do whatever it takes to win the game *even though it may be painful or distasteful*. When I said distasteful I told them this story.

These two men were fishing on ice in Alaska. They had known each other all of their lives. They used the same type of fishing equipment. They drilled holes in the ice with the same equipment and used the same fishing tactics. One man caught all kind of fish and the other guy did not catch a single fish. Finally, after three days of not catching any fish, the guy looked at his friend and asked him how he was catching all of those fish, when he couldn't catch a single one. The guy told him, "You have to keep the worms warm." The players said they understood and let it go at that.

I was concerned about one other thing. We were very fragile and it did not take much to get us down mentally. I did not want to do anything that would push us over the cliff. Friday night I had a big lineman that was a senior and one that I respected a great deal. I asked him if I pulled off a psychological ploy would it help the team or would it knock them over the cliff. I told him what I wanted to do and he assured me it would help keep them relaxed and in a good frame of mind for the game. We knew Texas would come in relaxed and ready to play, and we wanted to be relaxed and ready to play as well.

That Saturday morning I was over on the west side of town looking for night crawler worms. I went to three stores but could not find any night crawlers. As I left the stores I could hear them talking about me. They thought I had lost my mind. They thought I was ready to go fishing and the kickoff was only three hours away. Finally I found a store that had night crawlers. I opened the box and saw that they were about the size of your little finger. They were perfect.

I went back to the office and I got one of the night crawlers out and washed him real goooooood. I put him in a little vial box and stuck him in my pocket. We go out to warm up and I met Fred Akers and we talked for a minute and then went on with our pregame. I looked at the little vial and saw the night crawler could not get any air and had died. I did not have time to go get another worm. The die was cast. We went back to the locker room for last-minute instructions. We went through all of the details before we got ready to take the field. I called them all together. I got them up tight, and I got up on a bench. This is what I told them.

Guys, it has been a great week of work. Everything has been super. You are acting like winners and we have a game plan that is outstanding. I am telling you it is going to be a great day for you. You have done everything we have asked you to do. However, there is not a thing the coaches can do now. It is your game. When you go out on the field, it is your game to win or lose. I have every confidence you will do what it takes to win. There is nothing any of our coaches can do. I do want you to know that there is something I want to do and I am willing to do. *While you are out on the field winning the game, I will be keeping the worms warm.* I got the worm out and raised him up and opened my mouth and dropped him in the corner of my mouth. I chomped down a couple of times. I looked at some of our players and I could see their eyes were just glazed over. I sent them out on the field. I took the little worm out of my mouth and threw him in the trashcan. The assistant coaches were in shock. One of them came over to me and said, "Coach, I am glad you did not call for volunteers."

We went out on the field and I could hear our players still talking about the worm. That is all they talked about the whole ballgame. They were having the best time of their lives. We beat Texas by 30 some points. It turned our program completely around. That is seizing the moment. That is the motivation at the moment. I can never use that tactic again. This allowed our players to go out and play the way they had been prepared to play. They were loose. When a bad thing happened they were laughing and just having a great time. The whole idea is that you must have a mental approach to every ballgame. As the coach, you must set that mentality. It has to do with psychology and not motivation. It is the psychological impact.

Jimmy Johnson of the Cowboys used this technique before the San Francisco game. He predicted the Cowboys would win the game. The media bit on his tactics. It was a psychological ploy. The 49ers bit on the ploy. It had a psychological impact on the game. That is what Jimmy Johnson wanted. Before the game everyone jumped on this ploy. I had never seen San Francisco come in and try to act like something they were not used to all year. Jerry Rice was ready to start a fight before the game started. He was not thinking about winning; he was thinking about what Jimmy Johnson wanted him to think about. That is psychological, not motivational.

If you are going to be a successful coach, or a successful father, husband, or businessman, you are the one that must create the climate in which others can prosper, grow, and develop. A simple climate is constructed on four basic entities.

The first is *Discipline*. You have heard me talk about discipline. I do not think you can be a success unless you have discipline. It all begins with you. If you are not a disciplined person, you can not expect those around you to be disciplined. If you demand discipline of your children and you are not a disciplined person, then you are a travesty of what you are trying to get across. Discipline is a foundation upon which you can build success. One of the problems we have in our country today is a lack of discipline. I hear teachers all over the country talk about the lack of discipline in their schools. That may come from the fact that they may not be getting support from the administration. But, I am going to tell you one thing, if I am in a classroom, I will have discipline in that room. They may not have discipline down the hall, but I am going to have discipline in my room. That is my responsibility. Let them know who is running the ship. It is important to be a disciplined person. I can tell you it works. I have seen some average football teams turn into great football teams because of discipline. I am talking about discipline on the field and off the field. It is essential.

The second climate is a *Work Ethic*, or what I refer to as *Effort*. I learned a long time ago this important lesson. I might have been slow and I may have been small, but if I gave a full effort on every play in every way, every day, I could be successful. No one is going to give more effort than I am going to give. If you teach your players to give the same effort off the field as they give on the field they will be successful in life. You must develop the *Concept of Total Effort*. If it is worth doing, it is worth doing right. I learned this when I was 5 years old from my father. I did something about halfway and he jerked me up and wore me out with a strap. He told me he was doing this to teach me a lesson. He said, "If it is worth doing, it is worth doing right with your full effort. If it is not worth doing, then don't do it." Rather than doing something halfway, just don't do it. It was a great lesson.

The third lesson is a climate of *Mental Control*, which will allow you to exercise to be error free. One of the reasons the Dallas Cowboys win is because they do not make mistakes. Normally, the Cowboys do not make mistakes. Once in a while one of them will make a mistake, but most of the time they do not make mistakes. Why? Because they work in a climate where it is important to be error free. If we can teach children to be error free in their judgment and their decision-making process, you have a chance to teach them to be successful.

The fourth is a climate of *Caring*. You have to care and it has to be important to you. The players must be important to you. You can't falsify or fake where you care or don't care. Your children and other children are extremely sensitive and they recognize in a New York minute a phony. I always got tickled in recruiting. Every player that every played for me can tell you that all I ever talked about was getting their degree. I would tell them the other things would fall into place. The important thing is to get that degree. I would tell them it was important to me to see that they got their degree and I let them know that I would do everything I could to see to it that they got that degree. I would get tickled when I went recruiting. This was way back before the NCAA had all of the academic rules. Other schools would come in to see a recruit and give them a big spiel about being the star of the team. One lady said, "Coach Teaff talked about education the whole time he was at my house. He just talked about caring about my son. He never talked about football at all." Other coaches would use that star spiel because they could appeal to the mothers and fathers and the kids. Later other coaches tried to emulate our approach. The thing that amazes me is that you can't do this unless the feeling is real. You can't falsify the idea that you care for someone or not. You have to make it important and they have to understand that there is some importance about what they are doing and therefore they must care about it. They must care about each other.

Love! In 1974 I was the Coach of the Year and spoke at the AFCA convention in Washington, D.C. I was the first football coach in the history of the game to say this: "It is okay for one man to tell another man that he loves him. It is okay for the coach to tell his team he loves them. Some teams you are going to love more than others, but you are going to tell them you love them. It is okay for you to go home from this clinic and tell your wife you love her. You must express care and love. It is okay to do that. As a matter of fact, it is essential to do that."

Youngsters are motivated by the fact that someone cares about them. A high percentage of the kids that you and I deal with are from homes where there is only one adult person in that home. Many of them do not get the proper love of a male in the proper way. It is important to express love and to create love. It is not a mamby pamby kind of love, it is a manly kind of love. It is a love because you love the same thing. You love the game of football. It is something you can love because it gives so much to so many. Everyone here today is here because of what the game of football allowed you to become as a person. It is okay to love the game of football. There is nothing wrong with that. Once you recognize the fact that you love the game, then you play the game the way it should be played. If you don't play the game the way it is suppose to be played, you are selling the game short. It is important to understand care and love in that climate. Kids will care if you care.

Let me move on to what I refer to the *10 Principles of Success*. If you have heard the "David Principles" you have heard these repeated. I am using these as chapter headings for a book I am doing for teachers. I am trying to give teachers an avenue of applying coaching motivation into their teaching skills. I just want to list these principles. If these principles are adhered to they will lead to success, not only in your life, but in the lives of those you teach these principles to.

1. ***OBEDIENCE***—To be a successful person you must be an obedient person. You have to obey the laws of God and you have to obey

the laws of man. In college recruiting we have to obey the laws of the NCAA. This is true even if we think the laws are silly and not worth the paper they are written on. They are laws and regulations and rules and it is important to abide by them. I have often wondered how anyone in coaching could buy a player to come to his school, and still go out and coach that young man. What do you say to a player when you want that same player to go by the rules of the game. How can you expect him to go by the rules when you have broken the rules to get him to come to your school. I never have been able to understand that. It is important to have obedience. Obedience allows success in our lives.

2. ***DEFINING A PURPOSE AND A CAUSE IS ESSENTIAL TO SUCCESS***—I have studied a lot of successful people. Every one of them that has had any success to any measure has always had a Cause and Purpose that they are living for, working for, and they are fighting for. That is why sometimes certain things you think are motivation are really just a purpose for playing the game or for winning the game. Before the Super Bowl this year the people were discussing why they were playing the game. Marv Levy said, "We are not interested if we win the game of not. We are interested in playing the game so well that we *can win* the game." He has taught his players this particular purpose. Jimmy Johnson has a goal. His goal is to *win the Super Bowl* for the second time. He wants to repeat as champs. That is fine, but each team is approaching the game in a different way and has a different purpose. It is essential for success in human life to have a cause and a purpose.

3. ***COMMITMENT***—An oral commitment is essential. One year I had a plan where I had the players sign off on a piece of wood that I had utilized to teach them a lesson. I asked them to make an oral commitment that they would abstain from any form of drugs or alcohol throughout the season, that they would be on time on the field and off the field, in the classroom, and to the meeting rooms, and that they make a commitment to give their full effort on every play in every way. If they did not want to make a true commitment I did not want them to sign the agreement. It took some players a long time to make that commitment. It is a tough thing to make a real commitment, but I think it is essential.

4. ***THE POWER OF BELIEVING***—Believe in god. Next to love, believing is the most powerful force the world has ever known. Love is the most powerful force, but next to love, is believing. It is believ-

ing in something greater than you that gives us a reason for living in this short life that we have on this earth. It is important to know there is something better down the road and that there is a power greater than you. I think it has a lot to do with our morals and values when we recognize and believe there is a God.

5. *TEACH OTHERS TO BELIEVE IN THEMSELVES*—The second part of this is to initiate the power within yourself to believe in yourself and to teach others to believe in themselves. That is called confidence. When I was growing up I had that trait but some people misread that into believing I was cocky. It was a simple matter. I believed in what I was doing and I had confidence that I was going to do it. That is essential to success.

6. *THE POWER OF BELIEVING IN OTHERS*—The third part of the power of believing is believing in *someone else*. In 1980 we were in the running for the conference championship again and we were undefeated. We were playing SMU at Waco. SMU had a good team. We were down 21-0 at the half. We came out in the third quarter; Jay Johnson was our quarterback. Most coaches believe the way you perform in the early stages of the third quarter will determine how you are going to play for the rest of the game. This is the way the tone is set for the second half. We received the kickoff from SMU and ran it back to the 18-yard line. On first down Jay sprinted to his left and threw back to his right. The wide receiver was cutting back on a slant over the middle. However, the cornerback from SMU, Simmons, was between Jay and the wide receiver. Jay hit the cornerback right in the chest with the football and no one was there to stop him and he just walked into the end zone. Now SMU was up 28-0 early in the third quarter. I know the horror that Jay felt. Now the opponents had scored and he had to come off the field.

I am sure he thought about going off on the other side of the field. He knew he had to come off on our side of the field. He came off down on the far end of the field at the 20-yard line. He came behind the bench as he came toward midfield. I finally got his attention and motioned for him to come over to see me. Just as Jay got about two feet from me he said, "Coach, am I going to get to go back in the ballgame?" I knew this was a good question. I reached over and put my hand on Jay's shoulder pad and pulled his jersey up tight and pulled him up close to my face so he could hear me. I said, "Of course you are going back in the game! *You are my quarterback*! *I believe in you*. Jay, you have the talent and ability to win this football game, and you are my quarterback." He said, "I am?" Jay went back into the game and we did pull the game out by winning 34-28. We went on to win the conference that year.

I have often wondered what would have happened to that team if I had put Jay on the bench where he probably deserved to be. However, instead of benching Jay I exhibited my belief in him and ignited in him that ability that he already had. He bounced back and became the all-conference quarterback and we won the SWC. The power you can invest in others through believing in them is very interesting. Try it with your own children. A lot of problems with children today are because no one believes in them. They hear so much negative. We need to utilize the power in believing in someone else.

7. *DON'T LISTEN TO THE NAY SAYERS*—The world is full of these people. It is so bad now in so many places. So many people think they know so much about the coaching business today. They see the pros and hear so much and read about football that they think they know all there is to know. It is important not to listen to the nay sayers and the negative fans.

8. *BE SELECTIVE*—Be very selective in the choices that you make. Everything you do is a choice. You think about this. I do not know how old we are when we start making our own choices, but it is early in age. We continue this until the day we die. The choices we make determine the outcome of our life. Where you go to school, who you marry, who you associate with, what you put in your mouth, what you drink, what you read, what you listen to, all of these choices affect who you become. You have to teach this to the young people that you work with. It is important that they make these choices correctly.

9. *THE POWER OF ACTION IS ESSENTIAL*—You can do all of the planning in the world and you can dream, but until you put wheels to those plans, you are not going to find success. You must have an *action* for everything that you do. I believe it is important to finish the jobs that you start. One of the worst things I can imagine is for a player to be within six hours of finishing his degree and leaving college to go play pro ball because he thinks he has the world by the tail. I hound those players until they get that degree. Ask some of my former players. I will do whatever it takes to help those former players to get that degree.

10. ***RECOGNIZE THAT DEFEAT COMES TO EVERYONE***—Sooner or later defeat is going to come. How you handle that defeat, how you bounce back from adversity, and how you arise to the occasion after you have been down is the key to ongoing success in life. One of the greatest things about the game that we love is that it teaches young people that there is defeat in life. You must bounce back from defeat. You can't linger on a loss. You must learn from a loss. That is the most important thing in life. Football teaches us this important trait. We must learn how to handle our defeats in life. If you want to be successful you must be able to handle defeat.

Let me move on to a story that everyone here has heard before. I tell the story over and over and it still moves me just in telling others this story. In 1979 we had a kid break his neck and become paralyzed. His name was Kyle Woods. Most of you know the story. He went the whole year in rehab. Our team ended up playing in the Peach Bowl in Atlanta. Kyle came to Atlanta for the game. The last time our players had seen Kyle he was paralyzed from his neck down and could not move anything except his eyes and mouth. He became a real inspiration to our team. The day before the game he came to Atlanta to be with us. The team had dedicated the game to him and they had hand towels with his number 23 on them. They were to wear them for the Peach Bowl. Our players told the media the day before the game they would beat Clemson even though we were a 10-point underdog. As a coach you do not like for your team to make those type statements, but they made the statement and they believed they would win.

The morning of the Peach Bowl I asked Kyle Woods to speak to our team. He hesitated to speak at first, because he did not think he could get through a speech to his fellow teammates. I was so glad that I was there to hear him speak in that magic moment. Here is a 19-yearold kid that is paralyzed from the neck down. His outlook for life and success was almost nil. Here he is at a game where his teammates are honoring him because he has been such an inspiration to them throughout the season. I asked Kyle to say something to the team.

He thanked them for the trip to come to Atlanta. We were in a beautiful hotel and he got to fly for the first time in his life. This is what he had to say to the team: "I know how tough it has been for you to get here as a team. I know about the two-a-day practice sessions and the heated Astroturf. I know the pain you went through when I got hurt in August. I know you lost to Alabama, and had to play in a conference game and overcome that defeat. I am proud of the team for being here. I know how you got here, but *I want you to know how I got here.*" You talk about hearing a pin drop. Every person in that room knew what Kyle had been through. He said there were two things that enabled him to be with the team.

"One, is my *faith*. God is real. Not once in this whole year has he forsaken me. He has been there with me as he promised me he would be. He has given me faith in myself and the belief and faith you guys have had in me has been an inspiration." He said, "The other thing is what my grandmother taught me. She was 87 and I was 10 years old. She took care of seven kids. That included my sisters and my cousins. She cooked for us and mended the cloths, and washed and did all of the things our mothers couldn't do because they were working. She walked on crutches. She had big knots on her hands. I now know she had arthritis, but I did not know when I was young. You could see the pain in her face with every step she took every day. She must have recognized that I was concerned about her one day because she asked me to come and sit with her beside her chair. I sat down on the floor and she began to tell me her story.

" 'Kyle, I can tell by the way you are looking at me that you are worried about me. I know that you think that I am in terrible pain, and I am. Every step I take, every meal I cook, every bed I make, I am in horrible pain. I am not going to lie to you. Kyle, I think it is important that you know how grandmother makes it through each and every day with the pain I am in.'" Kyle said he couldn't wait to hear what his grandmother had to say. "She looked down at me with those warm eyes and said, 'Kyle, it is simple. *I may give out, but I will never give up.*'" Kyle said, "That is it guys. We may have a weak physical body, but if you will not give up and you won't quit, you will not give out. You are not going to be defeated. Now, the clock may run out sometimes when the other team is ahead, but if you will not give up, you will never be defeated."

In the fourth quarter in the Peach Bowl we were down 10 points. During one timeout in that fourth quarter I saw our defensive team look over to Kyle on the sideline. They got their heads together and sure enough they got a turnover soon after that. Our offensive team went in and got into the huddle. Again, they looked over to Kyle. They scored on the very next play. We held on the next defensive series and got the ball back. We went down and scored again. We went on to win the game.

When the game was over Gary Bender had told the entire world (the game was on CBS-TV) what the impact Kyle had on our team. By the time we got back to Waco we had received hundreds of telegrams and phone calls from all over the world from people that were touched by the way Kyle had affected our team. If anyone had overcome defeat, it was not the Baylor team, *it was Kyle*. He learned as a 10-year-old kid that our physical bodies are weak and may give out, but our spirit is strong. As his grandmother said, "I may give out, but I will not give up."

To overcome defeat is an essential part of what we are and what we teach in the game itself. We need to utilize this in a powerful teaching manner and utilize this in our own lives. In your own communities you need to be diligent and articulate, and caring. You need to be the epitome of what a coach should be. You need to do this so when there are those in your community that might think they can do away with athletics. Let them look to you as a role model in your community. Let them see you as a product of the great game of football and other athletics.

About the Editor

Earl Browning, the editor of the By the Experts Series, is a native of Logan, West Virginia. He currently serves as president of Telecoach, Inc. — an organization that conducts football clinics and produces the Coach of the Year Football Manuals. A 1958 graduate of Marshall University, he earned his M.Ed. and Rank I from the University of Louisville. From 1958 to 1975, he coached football at various Louisville-area high schools. Among the honors he has been accorded are his appointments to the National Football Foundations and the College Hall of Fame Advisory Committee on moving the museum to South Bend, Indiana. He was named to the Greater Louisville Football Coaches Association Hall of Legends in 1998.

ADDITIONAL FOOTBALL
RESOURCES FROM COACHES CHOICE.

IN THE "BY THE EXPERTS" SERIES:

■ *COACHING THE DEFENSIVE LINE:*
BY THE EXPERTS—Earl Browning, Editor
1999 ▪ 6"x9" ▪ 184 pp
ISBN 1-58518-246-X ▪ $16.95

■ *COACHING THE OFFENSIVE LINE:*
BY THE EXPERTS—Earl Browning, Editor
1999 ▪ 6"x9" ▪ 176 pp
ISBN 1-58518-241-9 ▪ $16.95

■ *COACHING THE DEFENSIVE SECONDARY:*
BY THE EXPERTS—Earl Browning, Editor
2000 ▪ 6"x9" ▪ 184 pp
ISBN 1-58518-308-3 ▪ $16.95

■ *COACHING THE KICKING GAME:*
BY THE EXPERTS—Earl Browning, Editor
2000 ▪ 6"x9" ▪ 182 pp
ISBN 1-58518-307-5 ▪ $16.95

■ *THE 4-3 DEFENSE:*
BY THE EXPERTS—Earl Browning, Editor
1998 ▪ 6"x9" ▪ 216 pp
ISBN 1-58518-228-1 ▪ $16.95

TO PLACE YOUR ORDER:

Call TOLL FREE in U.S. (888)229-5745

Mail COACHES CHOICE
P.O. Box 1828
Monterey, CA 93942

Fax (831)393-1102

Online www.coacheschoiceweb.com